Sheffield Hallam University
Learning and Information Services
Adsetts Centre, City Campus
Sheffield S1 1WB

102 143 809 X

SHEFFIELD HALLAM UNIVERSITY
LEARNING CENTRE
WITHDRAWN FROM STOCK

This book is due for return on or before the last date shown below.

D1351067

SHEFFIELD HALLAM
LEARNING CE...
WITHDRAWN FROM STOCK

LEARNING AS A GENERATIVE ACTIVITY

During the past twenty-five years, researchers have made impressive advances in pinpointing effective learning strategies (i.e., activities the learner engages in during learning that are intended to improve learning). In *Learning as a Generative Activity: Eight Learning Strategies That Promote Understanding*, Logan Fiorella and Richard E. Mayer share eight evidence-based learning strategies that promote understanding: summarizing, mapping, drawing, imagining, self-testing, self-explaining, teaching, and enacting. Each chapter describes and exemplifies a learning strategy, examines the underlying cognitive theory, evaluates strategy effectiveness by analyzing the latest research, pinpoints boundary conditions, and explores practical implications and future directions. Each learning strategy targets generative learning, in which learners actively make sense of the material so they can apply their learning to new situations. This concise, accessible introduction to learning strategies is intended to benefit students, researchers, and practitioners in educational psychology, as well as general readers interested in the important twenty-first-century skill of regulating one's own learning.

Logan Fiorella is a Ph.D. candidate in psychology at the University of California, Santa Barbara (UCSB). His research focuses on identifying learning and instructional strategies that promote meaningful learning, particularly in the science, technology, engineering, and mathematics fields. He was awarded a Junior Scientist Fellowship from the American Psychological Association of Graduate Students as well as the Richard E. Mayer Award for Outstanding Research Contribution in Psychology from UCSB's Department of Psychological and Brain Sciences.

Richard E. Mayer is Professor of Psychology at the University of California, Santa Barbara. He served as president of Division 15 (Educational Psychology) of the American Psychological Association and as vice president of the American Educational Research Association for Division C (Learning and Instruction). He has received many awards, including the E. L. Thorndike Award for career achievement in educational psychology and the Sylvia Scribner Award for career research in learning and instruction. He has authored more than five hundred publications, including thirty books, among them *Applying the Science of Learning*, *Multimedia Learning*, *Learning and Instruction*, *e-Learning and the Science of Instruction* (with R. Clark), and *Computer Games for Learning*.

Learning as a Generative Activity

EIGHT LEARNING STRATEGIES THAT
PROMOTE UNDERSTANDING

Logan Fiorella

University of California, Santa Barbara

Richard E. Mayer

University of California, Santa Barbara

CAMBRIDGE
UNIVERSITY PRESS

32 Avenue of the Americas, New York, NY 10013-2473, USA

Cambridge University Press is part of the University of Cambridge.

It furthers the University's mission by disseminating knowledge in the pursuit of
education, learning, and research at the highest international levels of excellence.

www.cambridge.org
Information on this title: www.cambridge.org/9781107069916

© Logan Fiorella and Richard E. Mayer 2015

This publication is in copyright. Subject to statutory exception
and to the provisions of relevant collective licensing agreements,
no reproduction of any part may take place without the written
permission of Cambridge University Press.

First published 2015

Printed in the United States of America

A catalog record for this publication is available from the British Library.

ISBN 978-1-107-06991-6 Hardback

Cambridge University Press has no responsibility for the persistence or accuracy of URLs
for external or third-party Internet Web sites referred to in this publication and does not
guarantee that any content on such Web sites is, or will remain, accurate or appropriate.

CONTENTS

PREFACE

The ability to learn gives humans a tremendous advantage and enables our progress in developing as individuals and as a species. What does the research say about how to improve student learning? If you are interested in the answer to this question, this book is for you. During the past twenty-five years, researchers have made impressive advances in pinpointing effective learning strategies – that is, activities that the learner engages in during learning intended to improve learning. In *Learning as a Generative Activity: Eight Learning Strategies That Promote Understanding*, we share eight evidence-based learning strategies that improve learning, so you can get a better sense of what the research is telling us.

Learning as a Generative Activity: Eight Learning Strategies That Promote Understanding provides a concise and focused introduction to what we consider to be the eight most effective learning strategies for improving student learning. The unifying goal of the book is to take an evidence-based approach to "what works" in helping people learn. In particular, we focus on eight ways to foster *generative learning* – that is, helping learners to actively make sense of the material so they can build meaningful learning outcomes that allow them to transfer what they have learned to solving new problems. Each of the core chapters (a) describes and exemplifies an effective learning strategy, (b) considers the underlying cognitive theory, (c) summarizes the research base to assess the level of effectiveness, (d) notes the boundary conditions under which the strategy is most effective, (e) suggests practical implications, and (f) explores future directions. By using the same organization in each chapter and a friendly writing style, we intend to make the book accessible to a diverse array of readers.

WHY DID WE WRITE THIS BOOK?

Students of the twenty-first century need to learn how to come up with creative solutions to new problems, how to adapt to changing situations, how to integrate multiple sources of information, and how to make and understand arguments based on evidence. To do this, they need to learn in ways that promote understanding so they can create *transferable knowledge and skills* – that is, knowledge and skills that they can use to solve new problems they have not encountered before. The ability to transfer what you have learned to new situations is the primary outcome of generative learning. We wrote this book in order to explore how to promote generative learning.

WHAT DO WE MEAN BY "LEARNING AS A GENERATIVE ACTIVITY"?

What do we mean by learning? Learning is a change in what you know caused by your experience. Some theories view learning as strengthening a response for a given stimulus, such as learning to say "four" when the teacher says, "What is two plus two?" Some theories view learning as adding facts to memory for later retrieval, such as memorizing the definition of *learning* in the second sentence of this paragraph. These conceptions of learning may be useful for particular learning situations – such as response learning or rote memorizing, respectively. In this book, however, we focus on a third conception of learning as a process of sense making, in which you try to understand what is presented by actively selecting relevant pieces of the presented information, mentally organizing them, and integrating them with other knowledge you already have. Engaging in these three cognitive processes during learning (i.e., selecting, organizing, and integrating) is what we mean by generative learning.

This book is based on current research-based theories of how people learn, which can be called the *science of learning*. In particular, generative learning involves the learner engaging in appropriate cognitive processing during learning, including selecting relevant incoming material to attend to, organizing the material into a coherent cognitive structure in working memory, and integrating it with relevant prior knowledge activated from long-term memory. Learning is a generative activity when learners actively generate their own learning outcomes by interpreting what is presented to them rather than by simply receiving it as presented. According to generative theory, learning is a selective activity, a structure-building activity, and a knowledge-integration activity. Those kinds of processing can be influenced by the student's learning strategy – a study technique such as summarizing the material in one's own words – or the instructor's instructional method – a way of presenting the material, such as providing an advance organizer that summarizes background material before the lesson. In short, the outcome of learning depends both on the material presented to the learner and the learner's cognitive activity during learning. Effective teaching requires more than simply presenting the to-be-learned material to the learner; it also requires guiding the learner's cognitive processing of the material during learning. In this book, we focus on effective learning strategies for priming appropriate cognitive processing during learning.

WHY HAVE WE LIMITED THE BOOK TO "EIGHT LEARNING STRATEGIES THAT PROMOTE UNDERSTANDING"?

In reviewing the research base on what works in helping people learn, we were exhilarated to find many important discoveries to share. However, in the interest of giving you a concise introduction, we decided to limit this book to what we consider to be the eight most effective learning strategies. Our goal is to show you examples of what works, when it works, and how it works. Rather than trying to cover everything that we know at a superficial level, we instead go into some depth on eight important techniques that have strong evidence and high relevance for improving academic learning.

WHAT ARE THE MERITS OF TAKING AN EVIDENCE-BASED APPROACH?

There are plenty of books on the market that provide practical advice on how to study, but many are based on the wisdom of the author rather than on research evidence. Although expert advice can be helpful, we think an evidence-based approach such as taken in this book also can be helpful, especially in light of the advances being made in educational psychology research. Alternatively, you could try to navigate your way through massive research handbooks, with each chapter written by a different author, but in this book we have made your job a little easier by providing a concise and focused review of eight effective ways to help people learn. By looking at research evidence, you will have a surer sense of what works in helping people learn.

HOW IS THE BOOK ORGANIZED?

The book consists of an introductory chapter that spells out the rationale for studying how to improve student learning, defines and exemplifies learning strategies, and provides a theoretical framework for learning as a generative activity. Generative learning theory is based on the idea that effective learners engage in appropriate cognitive processing during learning, including selecting key information, mentally organizing it, and integrating it with relevant prior knowledge. The goal is to help learners produce meaningful learning outcomes that support problem-solving transfer – that is, being able to use what is learned to solve new problems. In each of the next eight chapters, we examine a generative learning strategy – summarizing the material in one's own words, translating the text into a spatial representation, creating a drawing that corresponds to the text, imagining illustrations that correspond to the presented text, taking practice tests on the material, explaining the material to oneself, teaching the material to others, and acting out the material. In each chapter, we provide a definition and concrete examples of the learning strategy, review the research literature to gauge the effectiveness of the strategy in promoting test performance, summarize the boundary conditions under which the strategy is most effective, and offer theoretical and practical implications as well as suggestions for future work. The final chapter summarizes the eight ways of helping people learn, compares them, and suggests additional techniques for priming generative learning in students.

WHO SHOULD READ THIS BOOK?

This book is intended for anyone who is interested in taking an evidence-based approach to improving how people learn, including learning in K–12 education, college education, and workplace training. The intended audience includes students in undergraduate or graduate courses in educational psychology and related fields, researchers interested in educational psychology and related fields, instructional designers tasked with developing instructional materials, educators interested in improving student achievement based on research evidence, and the general public. The book does not assume that you possess any prerequisite expertise in educational psychology.

HOW IS THIS BOOK DIFFERENT?

This book is not in competition with educational psychology textbooks but can be used to complement them by focusing specifically on effective learning strategies. The book is not in competition with comprehensive handbooks in educational psychology (such as *Handbook of Research on Learning and Instruction* by Richard Mayer and Patricia Alexander; *The APA Educational Psychology Handbook* by Karen Harris, Steve Graham, and Tim Urdan; or *The Handbook of Educational Psychology* by Patricia Alexander and Philip Winne), but can be used to complement them by providing a more focused and coherent review of research on learning strategies. The book has some similarity to *Visible Learning* by John Hattie or *The International Guide to Student Achievement* by John Hattie and Eric Anderman, but is much more focused, concise, and coherent in its review of what works in improving student learning with learning strategies. Overall, there is nothing quite like this little book on the market, which provides you with a concise review of the eight most effective learning strategies that have been shown to improve student achievement.

ACKNOWLEDGMENTS

We are grateful to our colleagues who have stimulated our interest in improving student learning, and we appreciate all those who have contributed to the research base reported in this book. In particular, we acknowledge the towering contribution of Merlin C. Wittrock, to whom we dedicate this book.

We appreciate the many useful comments from our colleagues who graciously reviewed chapters: Ken Kiewra, Claudia Leopold, Detlev Leutner, Scott Marley, Mark McDaniel, Alexander Renkl, and Rodney Roscoe.

Logan Fiorella wishes to thank his parents, Nick and Sharon, for their lifelong guidance and encouragement; and his fiancée Deborah Barany, for her enduring love and support.

Richard E. Mayer wishes to thank his wife, Beverly, for her unwavering support and for making life sweet; his children, Ken, Dave, and Sarah, and his grandchildren, Jacob, Avery, James, Emma, and Caleb, for bringing much joy; and his parents, James and Bernis, who are in his thoughts.

We also acknowledge David Repetto and the helpful staff at Cambridge University Press for all their assistance throughout this project. Preparation of this book was supported by a grant from the Office of Naval Research.

Logan Fiorella and Richard E. Mayer   Santa Barbara, California

ABOUT THE AUTHORS

Logan Fiorella is a doctoral candidate in psychology at the University of California, Santa Barbara (UCSB). His research interests are in identifying learning and instructional strategies that promote meaningful learning, with a focus on enhancing science education. He is a winner of the Junior Scientist Fellowship from the American Psychological Association of Graduate Students (APAGS) and Psi Chi, and the Basic Psychological Science Research Grant from APAGS. Recently, he received UCSB's Award for Outstanding Research Contribution in Psychology for his research investigating the cognitive mechanisms underlying learning by teaching.

Richard E. Mayer is Professor of Psychology at UCSB, where he has served since 1975. His research interests are in applying the science of learning to education, with a focus on multimedia learning. He served as president of Division 15 (Educational Psychology) of the American Psychological Association and vice president of the American Educational Research Association for Division C (Learning and Instruction). He is the winner of the Thorndike Award for career achievement in educational psychology, the Scribner Award for career research in learning and instruction, and the Distinguished Contribution of Applications of Psychology to Education and Training Award. He is ranked as the most productive educational psychologist in the world in *Contemporary Educational Psychology*. He has served as principal investigator (PI) or co-PI on more than thirty grants, including recent grants from the Institute of Education Sciences to investigate the effectiveness of features of an online tutoring system and from the Office of Naval Research to investigate how to improve the effectiveness of educational games. He is former editor of *Educational Psychologist* and former co-editor of *Instructional Science,* and he serves on the editorial boards of twelve journals mainly covering educational psychology. He is the author of more than five hundred publications, including thirty books, among them *Applying the Science of Learning, e-Learning and the Science of Instruction* (with R. Clark), *Multimedia Learning, Learning and Instruction, Computer Games for Learning, Handbook of Research on Learning and Instruction* (co-edited with P. Alexander), and *The Cambridge Handbook of Multimedia Learning* (editor).

1

Introduction to Learning as a Generative Activity

SUMMARY

This book is based on the idea that meaningful learning is a generative activity in which the learner actively seeks to make sense of the presented material. The study of generative learning has implications for the science of learning, the science of assessment, and the science of instruction. Concerning the science of learning, generative learning takes place when the learner engages in appropriate cognitive processing during learning, including attending to the relevant information (i.e., selecting), mentally organizing incoming information into a coherent cognitive structure (i.e., organizing), and integrating the cognitive structures with each other and with relevant prior knowledge activated from long-term memory (i.e., integrating). Concerning the science of assessment, generative learning is demonstrated when students who learn with generative learning strategies or generative instructional methods perform better on transfer tests than students who learn from standard instruction. Concerning the science of instruction, generative learning can be promoted through *instructional methods* aimed at designing instruction that primes appropriate cognitive processing during learning or through *learning strategies* aimed at teaching students how and when to engage in activities that require appropriate cognitive processing during learning. This book focuses on eight generative learning strategies that have been shown to improve student learning: summarizing, mapping, drawing, imagining, self-testing, self-explaining, teaching, and enacting. The concept of generative learning has roots in the work of Wittrock and others, continues as a dominant view of learning today, and shows promise of further development in the future.

GETTING STARTED

What Can You Do?

Suppose you sit down to read a book chapter, you attend a PowerPoint lecture, or you view an online multimedia presentation. You are proficient at reading and listening, so you can easily understand all the words. Yet, when you are finished with the lesson, you are not able to apply what you have learned to new situations or to use the material to solve problems. What could you have done to help you understand the material rather than simply to process every word?

This book is concerned with exploring what the research evidence has to say about answering this seemingly simple question. Our proposed solution is that you could engage in *generative learning strategies* during learning – activities that are intended to prime appropriate cognitive processing during learning (such as paying attention to the relevant information, mentally organizing it, and integrating it with your relevant prior knowledge).

For example, you could try to summarize the material in your own words (perhaps by taking summary notes), you could create a spatial summary of the material as a matrix or network, you could make a drawing that depicts the main ideas in the text, or you could just imagine a drawing. These are all ways of translating the lesson into another form of representation.

Alternatively, you could give yourself a practice test on the material (such as trying to answer some questions), you could explain the material aloud to yourself during learning, you could explain the material to someone else, or you could use concrete objects to act out the material in the lesson. These are all ways of elaborating on the material.

Exploring each of these eight kinds of generative learning strategies is the primary goal of this book.

Try This

Let's begin with a brief assessment of your view of learning. Most people have an implicit theory of learning, because we all have spent so much time in school. Please place a check mark next to each item that corresponds with your conception of how learning works.

— Learning works by engaging in hands-on activity, so it is better for you to learn by doing rather than by being told.
— Learning works by building associations, so you should practice giving the right response over and over.
— Learning works by adding information to your memory, so you should work hard to find and memorize new material.
— Learning occurs when you try to make sense of material you encounter, so you should strive to relate new information with your prior knowledge.
— Learning is a social activity, so it is better for you to learn with others in a group than to learn alone.

If you checked the fourth item, your view of learning corresponds to the conception of generative learning proposed in this book – which simply shows you have the good common sense to agree with us. As you will see in this book, the learner's cognitive processing during learning is a major contributor to what is learned.

If you are like most people, you made some other check marks. The first item is appealing, but according to the generative learning view, it focuses too much on behavioral activity and not enough on cognitive activity. Doing things does not necessarily cause learning, but thinking about what you are doing does cause learning. Thus, the first item should be modified to say, "Learning works by engaging in appropriate cognitive activity during learning."

The second item also seems appealing and is consistent with the first theory of learning to emerge in psychology and education more than a century ago – which can be called *associative learning*. However, according to the generative learning view, learning by forming associations applies to a narrow band of learning situations – such as learning to give the right response for a given stimulus. Associative learning is not wrong, but it is just too limited. It does not deal with learning by understanding, which allows people to take what they have learned and apply it in new situations.

The third item may sound familiar because it seems consistent with some common educational practices such as asking students to attend hours of lectures or read hundreds of textbook pages. What is wrong with this item, however, is that humans do not work like computers. We do not simply take in what was presented and put it into our memory. Instead, we interpret it, we reorganize it, and we relate to what we already know, thereby changing what is presented from information (which is objective) into knowledge (which is personal).

Finally, the last item is consistent with an emerging vision of learning based on the idea that generative learning occurs best within group contexts – that is, when you can interact with others during the learning process. However, research on group learning tends to show that all group interactions are not equally helpful in promoting meaningful learning. Thus, generative learning theory – indicated by the fourth item – can be expanded to include social activities that promote appropriate cognitive processing during learning and to exclude social activities that do not. Overall, the point of this little exercise is to help you understand how the generative learning view is different from what might seem like some common-sense views of learning.

Turning Passive Learning Situations into Active Learning Situations

Suppose that you are about to read a textbook chapter on the history of the U.S. postal service, attend a PowerPoint lecture on how a virus causes a cold, or view an online narrated animation explaining how lightning storms develop. Each of these activities – reading a book, attending a lecture, or viewing an online presentation – seems like a passive experience destined to foster suboptimal learning.

You might be surprised to learn that there are effective techniques that can be used to turn such seemingly passive learning situations into active learning experiences that produce meaningful learning. This book presents eight ways to help people learn based on a generative theory of learning – the idea that meaningful learning occurs when people engage in generative processing during learning. In particular, each of the techniques seeks to encourage learners to relate the represented material to what they already know, or reorganize the presented material into a coherent structure, or distinguish what is important from what is not. In this chapter, we describe what we mean by generative learning; explain how generative learning contributes to the science of learning, the science of assessment, and the science of instruction; and end with a brief review of the history of scholarship on generative learning.

WHAT IS GENERATIVE LEARNING?

Learning is a generative activity. This statement embodies a vision of learning in which learners actively try to make sense of the instructional material presented to them. They accomplish this goal by actively engaging in generative processing during learning, including paying attention to the relevant aspects of incoming material (which we call *selecting*), organizing it into a coherent cognitive structure in working memory (which we call *organizing*), and integrating cognitive structures with relevant prior knowledge activated from long-term memory (which we call *integrating*).

As you can see, the learner's cognitive processing plays a central role in generative learning. Learning is not simply a process of adding information to memory, as in a computer. Instead, learning depends both on what is presented and on the learner's cognitive processing during learning.

Similarly, the learner's prior knowledge plays a central role in generative learning. Prior knowledge includes schemas, categories, models, and principles that can help guide what the learner selects for further processing, how the learner organizes it, and how the learner links it with other structurally similar knowledge. Thus, learning depends both on what the instructor presents and what the learner brings to the learning situation. This is why two learners can be exposed to the same learning scenario – such as attending the same lecture or viewing the same online presentation – and come away with quite different learning outcomes.

As summarized in Table 1.1, not all forms of learning are *generative learning* – that is, learning by understanding, which results in meaningful learning outcomes. Another common form of learning is *rote learning* – that is, learning by memorizing, which results in rote learning outcomes. Finally, there is also *associative learning* – that is, learning by strengthening associations, which results in rapid responses to well-learned stimuli. Although there are other forms of learning, in this book, we focus on

TABLE 1.1. *Three kinds of learning situations*

Learning situation	What happens	What is enabled
Generative learning	Making sense of information	Solving new problems
Rote learning	Memorizing information	Remembering what was presented
Associative learning	Building associations	Giving a response for a stimulus

generative learning. In particular, we focus on ways to promote generative learning because we are interested in helping students transfer what they have learned to new situations.

Our rationale for focusing on generative learning is that the twenty-first century needs problem solvers and sense makers (Pellegrino & Hilton, 2012). The need for rote learning and associative learning is somewhat reduced because we now have access to databases that can store vast amounts of information or give answers to simple questions. The world needs people who can select, interpret, and use information to solve new problems they have not encountered before. In short, today's focus on twenty-first-century skills such as creative problem solving, critical thinking, adaptability, complex communication, and constructing evidence-based arguments can be seen as a call for generative learning that helps people develop "transferable knowledge and skills" (Pellegrino & Hilton, 2012, p. 69).

IMPLICATIONS OF GENERATIVE LEARNING FOR THE SCIENCE OF LEARNING

The science of learning is the scientific study of how people learn (Mayer, 2011). This section examines the cognitive processes, memory stores, and knowledge representations involved in generative learning, as well as the motivational and metacognitive processes that support them.

Cognitive Processes in Generative Learning

How does learning work? The basic premise of generative learning theories is that learning occurs when learners apply appropriate cognitive processes to incoming information. Figure 1.1 summarizes the *SOI model of generative learning,* which focuses on three cognitive processes indicated by arrows – selecting, organizing, and integrating. As indicated by the arrow from *instruction* to *sensory memory,* instruction from the outside world enters your cognitive system through your eyes and ears (or other senses) and is briefly held in your sensory memory for a fraction of a second. If you pay attention to some of this fleeting information in sensory memory, you transfer the attended material to working memory for further processing (as indicated by the *selecting* arrow). In working memory, you can mentally reorganize the selected material into coherent mental representations (as indicated by the *organizing* arrow). You can also activate relevant prior knowledge from long-term memory and integrate it with incoming material in working memory (as indicated by the *integrating* arrow).

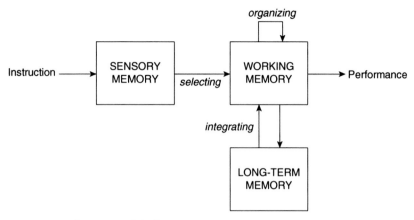

FIGURE 1.1. The SOI Model of Generative Learning.

TABLE 1.2. *Three cognitive processes in generative learning*

Cognitive process	Description	Arrow in SOI Model
Selecting	Attending to relevant material	Arrow from sensory memory to working memory
Organizing	Mentally organizing incoming material into a coherent cognitive structure	Arrow from working memory back to working memory
Integrating	Connecting cognitive structures with each other and with relevant material activated from long-term memory	Arrow from long-tem memory to working memory

The knowledge you build in working memory can be stored in long-term memory for future use (as indicated by the arrow from *working memory* to *long-term memory*) and can be used to solve problems you encounter in the outside world (as indicated by the arrow from *working memory* to *performance*).

An important instructional implication of the SOI model is that the instructor's job is not only to present information but also to make sure his or her students engage in appropriate processing during learning – including selecting, organizing, and integrating. Similarly, the learner's job is not to memorize the information exactly as it is presented but to engage in appropriate cognitive processing during learning. Table 1.2 summarizes the three cognitive processes in the SOI model of generative learning, which has been continuously adapted to the study of learning strategies over the past thirty

TABLE 1.3. *Three memory stores in generative learning*

Memory store	Description	Capacity	Duration
Sensory memory	Holds visual images and sounds of what was presented	High	Very short
Working memory	Allows pictures and words to be held and manipulated	Limited	Short
Long-term memory	Acts as permanent storehouse of knowledge	High	Long

years (Kiewra, 2005; Mayer, 1988, 1994, 1996, 2011; Peper & Mayer, 1986; Shrager & Mayer, 1989; Weinstein & Mayer, 1985).

Memory Stores in Generative Learning

The SOI model of generative learning shown in Figure 1.1 contains three memory stores, indicated by the boxes. *Sensory memory* holds sensory copies of the visual images you saw and the sounds you heard (and other input from other senses) for a fraction of a second, so it has high capacity for a very short duration. In *working memory*, pieces of information can be consciously held and manipulated, but the capacity of working memory is quite limited so you can actively process only a few pieces of information at any one time (and without active processing, information is lost within about twenty seconds). *Long-term memory* is your permanent storehouse of knowledge, so it has high capacity and long duration.

According to the SOI model shown in Figure 1.1, working memory is a sort of bottleneck in your cognitive system because it has limited processing capacity (i.e., only a few elements can be actively processed at one time), whereas sensory memory and long-term memory on either side of it each have large capacities. An important instructional implication of this bottleneck is that rapidly presenting a lot of information to a learner is likely to overload the learner's working memory and result in much of the information being lost. The three memory stores in the SOI model of generative learning are summarized in Table 1.3.

Knowledge Representations in Generative Learning

In addition to understanding the boxes and arrows in Figure 1.1, it is worthwhile to consider the kinds of external and internal representations involved in generative learning. For example, consider what happens when

TABLE 1.4. *External and internal representations in generative learning*

Representation	Type	Location
Printed words, spoken words, graphics	External	Instruction
Visual images and sounds	Internal	Sensory memory
Spatial and verbal representations	Internal	Working memory
Knowledge	Internal	Long-term memory

you attend a narrated slideshow lecture. We begin with the instructional presentation involving *spoken words, printed words, and graphics*, which become *visual images and auditory sounds* in your sensory memory, *spatial and verbal representations* that can be manipulated in working memory, and *semantic knowledge* stored in long-term memory. The conversion of presented information (i.e., the external representation) into constructed knowledge (i.e., the internal representation) is what happens when learners engage in generative learning. Three important steps in the development of knowledge in working memory are to select the pieces of information for further processing, to build internal connections among them so they form a coherent representation, and to build external connections with other representations in a systematic way. Table 1.4 lists the progression of representations in generative learning.

Metacognition and Motivation in Generative Learning

Generative learning requires that learners apply appropriate cognitive processes during learning, but how do learners know which processes to apply and when to apply them? How do you know which information to select, what kind of organization to build, and which aspect of prior knowledge to activate? Monitoring and controlling your cognitive processes during a cognitive task (such as learning from a lecture or from a book) is called *metacognition*. Thus, an important task of generative learning theories is to understand the workings of metacognitive strategies – that is, strategies for monitoring and controlling cognitive processes.

Even if you are skilled in using the cognitive processes of selecting, organizing, and integrating, and even if you possess the metacognitive strategies for orchestrating them, you may still not engage in generative learning because you just don't want to. What causes people to initiate and maintain generative processing at a high level during learning? *Motivation* is defined a cognitive state that initiates, energizes, and maintains goal-directed behavior. In short, motivation drives the cognitive system, so it is crucial to incorporate motivational mechanisms into generative learning theory. In particular, the learning strategies suggested in this book are intended to motivate learners to engage in productive cognitive processing during learning.

We refer to metacognition and motivation as the *Mighty M's* because they power the SOI model of generative learning shown in Figure 1.1. Without the motivation to make sense of a lesson, generative learning would not be initiated. Without the metacognitive skills to control cognitive processing during learning, attempts at generative learning would not be effective.

IMPLICATIONS OF GENERATIVE THEORY FOR THE SCIENCE OF ASSESSMENT

The science of assessment is the scientific study of how to determine what people know (Anderson et al., 2001; Mayer, 2011; Pellegrino, Chudowsky, & Glaser, 2001). In this section, we describe two kinds of test items and three kinds of learning outcomes.

Two Kinds of Test Items

Table 1.5 summarizes two kinds of test items that can be used to assess what students have learned, based on the classic distinction between *retention* and *transfer*. Retention is the ability to recall or recognize what was presented. Thus, retention items are used when the goal is to assess how much of the presented material can be remembered. Transfer is the ability to apply what was learned to solve new problems. Thus, transfer items are used when the goal is to assess how well someone understands the presented material.

If we asked you to define *retention*, you could simply reproduce the second sentence of the preceding paragraph, which is an example of a retention

TABLE 1.5. *Two kinds of test items*

Item	Target	Description	Example
Retention	Remembering	Ability to recall or recognize what was presented	What is the definition of retention?
Transfer	Understanding	Ability to apply what was presented to solve new problems	Create a transfer item for this lesson.

item. If we asked you to create a transfer item for the foregoing paragraph, you would have to use what you learned to create a novel solution, which is an example of a transfer item. Retention and transfer are qualitatively different kinds of assessments – retention items focus on how much you remember material whereas transfer items focus on how well you understand material.

In updating Bloom's taxonomy of educational objectives (Bloom et al., 1956), Anderson and colleagues (2001) identified five kinds of transfer items:

> *understand* – constructing meaning from lessons, such as paraphrasing, summarizing, explaining, or exemplifying the presented material
> *apply* – carrying out a procedure in a familiar or unfamiliar situation
> *analyze* – breaking material into parts and determining how they relate to one another, such as distinguishing relevant from irrelevant material or attributing the author's point of view
> *evaluate* – making judgments based on criteria, such as detecting errors in a product or solution process
> *create* – putting elements together to form a coherent structure, such as inventing a new solution or generating alternative hypotheses

In contrast, they identified only one kind of retention item (called *remember*), involving the ability to recognize (e.g., "Which of the following is the definition of *retention*?") or recall what was presented (e.g., "What is the definition of *retention*?"). As you can see, devising ways to assess how well someone understands the presented material continues to be a major task in the field of generative learning.

Three Kinds of Learning Outcomes

Table 1.6 summarizes three kinds of learning outcomes based on the learner's pattern of performance in retention and transfer tests. No learning has occurred if someone performs poorly in both retention and transfer.

TABLE 1.6. *Three kinds of learning outcomes*

Outcome	Retention	Transfer	Description of knowledge
No learning	No	No	No knowledge
Rote learning	Yes	No	Fragmented knowledge
Generative learning	Yes	Yes	Integrated knowledge

Rote learning is indicated when someone performs well on retention but poorly on transfer, that is, the learner can remember the material but can't use it to solve new problems. Generative learning is indicated when someone performs well on retention and transfer, that is, the learner can both remember and use what he or she has learned to solve new problems. As you can see, transfer items distinguish rote learning outcomes from generative learning outcomes. In short, we can infer that people have engaged in generative learning when they perform well on transfer items. For this reason, we focus mainly on measures of transfer in our summaries of research on generative learning strategies reported in the following chapters of this book.

IMPLICATIONS OF GENERATIVE THEORY FOR THE SCIENCE OF INSTRUCTION

Two Ways to Improve Learning

The science of instruction is the scientific study of how to help people learn (Mayer, 2008, 2011). Table 1.7 summarizes two approaches to helping people learn – *instructional methods*, which focus on changing the instruction presented to learners in ways to prime the cognitive processes of selecting, organizing, and integrating; and *learning strategies*, which focus on changing the learner by equipping the learner with activities that can be applied to processing incoming instructional presentations. In short, *instructional methods* are techniques for presenting lessons (such as adding a graphic organizer) and are intended to prime appropriate cognitive processing during learning. *Learning strategies* are activities that the learner

TABLE 1.7. *Two approaches to improving learning*

Approach	Description	Focus
Instructional methods	Design instruction in ways that prime appropriate cognitive processing during learning (selecting, organizing, and integrating)	Change the instruction
Learning strategies	Teach students how and when to engage in appropriate cognitive processing during learning (selecting, organizing, and integrating)	Change the learner

engages in during learning (such as summarizing) and are intended to activate appropriate cognitive processing during learning. In this book, we focus on learning strategies (also called study strategies) for promoting understanding.

Three Goals of Instruction

Table 1.8 summarizes examples of learning strategies that support three instructional goals:

fostering selecting – helping students attend to the relevant material

fostering organizing – helping students mentally organize the relevant material into a coherent cognitive structure

fostering integrating – helping students activate relevant prior knowledge and connect it with incoming material

For example, suppose students are attending a slideshow lecture, viewing an online narrated animation, or reading a textbook section. What are some learning strategies that could guide the cognitive processes of selecting, organizing, and integrating? The learning strategy column lists three examples. To guide the cognitive process of selecting, students can engage in the learning strategy of summarizing the presented material, which helps them distinguish between important and unimportant material. To guide the cognitive process of organizing, students can engage in the learning strategy of mapping, which involves drawing a spatial arrangement of the key information as a structure, such as a matrix, hierarchy, or flow chart, or even just an outline. To guide the cognitive process of integrating, students can engage in the learning strategy of self-explaining, in which they use their prior knowledge to elaborate on aspects of the lesson that need to be explained.

TABLE 1.8. *Examples of learning strategies to support three goals of instruction*

Goal	Learning strategy
Foster selecting	Teach students how to distinguish between important and unimportant information (e.g., by summarizing)
Foster organizing	Teach students how to organize information within a coherent structure (e.g., by mapping)
Foster integrating	Teach students how to relate incoming information with relevant prior knowledge (e.g., by self-explaining)

TABLE 1.9. *Eight generative learning strategies*

Name	Description
Summarizing	You create a written or oral summary of the material in the lesson
Mapping	You create a spatial representation of the key ideas in the lesson
Drawing	You create a drawing that depicts the key material in the lesson
Imagining	You imagine a drawing that depicts the key material in the lesson
Self-testing	You give yourself a practice test on the material in the lesson
Self-explaining	You create a written or oral explanation of portions of the lesson that you identify as confusing
Teaching	You explain the material in the lesson to others
Enacting	You act out the material in the lesson

Eight Generative Learning Strategies

Table 1.9 summarizes eight generative learning strategies that have been shown to be effective in promoting generative processing under certain conditions, based on rigorous research evidence: summarizing, mapping, drawing, imagining, self-testing, self-explaining, teaching, and enacting. Chapters 2 through 9 review the research for each of these learning strategies, respectively. We call these generative learning strategies because they are learner activities that are intended to cause learners to engage in the cognitive processes of selecting, organizing, and integrating during learning.

The learning strategy research reviewed in this book takes a value-added approach in which we compare performance on a test of learning outcome (such as a transfer test) of a group that receives standard instruction (the control group) and a group that receives the same instruction but is also asked to engage in a specific activity during learning (the strategy group). We include only studies that meet the standards of scientific rigor for experimental research (Mayer, 2011):

> *random assignment* – participants are placed in the control group and strategy group based on chance
> *experimental control* – the control and strategy group are identical except for one instructional feature (i.e., the learning strategy used by the strategy group)
> *appropriate measures* – the researchers report the mean, standard deviation, and sample size for the control group and the strategy group on a measure of learning outcome such as a transfer test

In particular, we compute effect size (d) by subtracting the mean score of the control from the mean score of the strategy group and dividing by the pooled standard deviation. We focus on instructional methods that produce median effect sizes greater than $d = 0.4$, which is the level that is considered educationally important (Hattie, 2011).

WHAT IS THE PAST AND FUTURE OF GENERATIVE LEARNING?

Where Did Generative Learning Come From?

The theory of generative learning has its roots in Bartlett's (1932) vision of learning as an act of construction in which new experience is integrated with existing schemas, Piaget's (1926) vision of cognitive development as a process of assimilating incoming experience to existing schemas and of accommodating existing schemas, and the Gestalt psychologists' (Katona, 1940; Wertheimer, 1959) distinction between learning by memorizing and learning by understanding.

In the modern era, Wittrock (1974, 1978, 1989, 1991, 1992; Mayer & Wittrock, 1996, 2006; Mayer, 2010) relentlessly showed how the concept of generative learning could be applied to educational theory and practice. Wittrock (1974) showed how learning depends both on what is presented and what the learner already knows: "People tend to generate ... meanings that are consistent with their prior knowledge" (p. 88). In particular, he showed that learning happens when people build connections between the presented material and their prior knowledge: "Learning with understanding ... is a process of generating ... associations between stimuli and stored information" (p. 89).

Wittrock's vision of generative learning was based on the idea that learning from text depends both on what is presented and on the learner's cognitive processes during learning: "reading comprehension is facilitated when, during encoding, learners use their memories of events and experiences to construct meanings for the text" (Doctorow, Wittrock, & Marks, 1978, p. 109). Generative learning involves the cognitive processes of integrating existing knowledge with new material and mentally reorganizing the new material: "reading comprehension occurs when readers build relationships (1) between the text and their knowledge and experience, and (2) among the different parts of the text" (Linden & Wittrock, 1981, p. 45).

Wittrock and colleagues tested the educational implications of generative learning theory by showing that students learn better when they are asked to generate summaries (Doctorow, Wittrock, & Marks, 1978), to generate analogies (Wittrock & Alesandrini, 1990), or to use a combination of generative learning strategies (Kourilsky & Wittrock, 1992; Linden & Wittrock, 1981).

As noted in Mayer (2010, p. 48), Wittrock's (1989, pp. 348–9) articulation of generative theory maps directly onto the SOI model of generative learning summarized in Figure 1.1 (with our annotations in brackets):

> The mind, or the brain, is not a passive consumer of information.... Our minds are much more than blank slates that passively learn and record incoming information. The stored memories and information-processing strategies of our cognitive systems interact with the sensory information received from the environment [This is an initial step in *integrating*.], selectively attend to this information [This is what we call *selecting*.], relate it to memory [This is what we call *integrating*.], and actively construct meaning from it [This is the outcome of selecting, organizing, and integrating.].... Generation is more than the fitting of information into slots or schemata.... Generation is an active construction of relations among parts of the text [This is what we call *organizing*.] and between the text and knowledge and experience [This is what we call *integrating*.].... People retrieve information from long-term memory and use their information-processing strategies to generate meaning from the incoming information [We call this *integrating*.], to organize it [We call this *organizing*.], to code it [This is part of *integrating*.], and to store it in long-term memory [We call this *encoding*.].

In a succinct summary, Wittrock (1992, p. 532) focused on "generative learning processes ... to selectively attend to events [corresponding to what we call *selecting*] ... and generating relations both among concepts [corresponding to what we call *organizing*] and between experience or prior learning and new information [corresponding to what we call *integrating*]." Consistent with the vision of generative learning presented in this book, Wittrock (1974, p. 89) was interested in measuring the effects of generative learning "by long-term memory plus transfer to conceptually related problems." We gratefully acknowledge Wittrock's contributions to the conception of learning presented in this chapter as a foundation for this book, as well as earlier formulations (Mayer, 1984, 2009).

Where Is Generative Learning Going?

The future will require people who can adapt to new situations, synthesize multiple sources of information, and come up with creative solutions, so they need to learn in ways that produce transferable knowledge and skills (Pellegrino & Hilton, 2012). This is the task of generative learning. As we continue to see growth in the research base on effective generative learning strategies and effective generative instructional methods, the future looks bright for applying the science of learning to education (Mayer, 2011).

The concept of generative learning has had important impacts on research on the teaching of learning strategies (Mayer & Wittrock, 2006; Weinstein & Mayer, 1985) in the past, and it shows signs of accelerating impact in the future by pinpointing "what works" (Dunlosky et al., 2013). The concept of generative learning has also had important impacts on research on the design of learning environments, including computer-based multimedia learning environments that are expected to dominate in the future (Clark & Mayer, 2011; Mayer, 2009, 2014; O'Neil, 2005). In the future, educators can apply this base of evidence-based methods and strategies more systematically to improving K-12 learning, college learning, and adult training.

REFERENCES

Anderson, L. W., Krathwohl, D. R., Airasian, P. W., Cruikshank, K. A., Mayer, R. E., Pintrich, P. R., Raths, J., & Wittrock, M. C. (2001). *A Taxonomy of Learning for Teaching: A Revision of Bloom's Taxonomy of Educational Objectives*. New York, NY: Longman.

Bartlett, F. C. (1932). *Remembering*. Cambridge, UK: Cambridge University Press.

Bloom, B. S., Engelhart, M. D., Furst, E. J., Hill, W. H., & Krathwohl, D. R. (1956). *Taxonomy of Educational Objectives: The Classification of Educational Goals. Handbook I: Cognitive Domain*. New York: David McKay.

Clark, R. C., & Mayer, R. E. (2011). *e-Learning and the Science of Instruction*. San Francisco: Pfeiffer.

Doctorow, M, Wittrock, M. C., & Marks, C. (1978). Generative processes in reading comprehension. *Journal of Educational Psychology, 70,* 109–18.

Dunlosky, J., Rawson, K. A., Marsh, E. J., Nathan, M. J., & Willingham, D. T. (2013). Improving students' learning with effective learning techniques: promising directions from cognitive and educational psychology. *Psychological Science in the Public Interest, 14,* 4–58.

Hattie, J. (2011). *Visible learning*. New York, NY: Routledge.

Katona, G. (1940). *Organizing and Memorizing*. New York, NY: Columbia University Press.

Kiewra, K. A. (2005). *Learn How to Study and SOAR to Success*. Upper Saddle River, NJ: Pearson Prentice Hall.

Kourilsky, M., & Wittrock, M. C. (1992). Generative teaching: an enhancement strategy for learning economics in cooperative groups. *American Educational Research Journal, 29,* 861–76.

Linden, M., & Wittrock, M. C. (1981). The teaching of reading comprehension according to the model of generative learning. *Reading Research Quarterly, 17,* 44–57.

Mayer, R. E. (1984). Aids to prose comprehension. *Educational Psychologist*, 19, 30–42.

(1988). Learning strategies: an overview. In C. Weinstein, E. Goetz, & P. Alexander (Eds.), *Learning and Study Strategies* (pp. 11–22). Orlando, FL: Academic Press.

(1994). Study habits and strategies. In T. Husen & T. N. Postlethwaite (Eds.), *International Encyclopedia of Education* (2nd ed.; pp. 5829–31). Oxford, England: Pergamon Press.

(1996). Learning strategies for making sense out of expository text: the SOI model for guiding three cognitive processes in knowledge construction. *Educational Psychology Review*, 8, 357–71.

(2008). *Learning and Instruction* (2nd ed.). Upper Saddle River, NJ: Pearson.

(2009). *Multimedia Learning* (2nd ed.). New York, NY: Cambridge University Press.

(2010). Merlin C. Wittrock's enduring contributions to the science of learning. *Educational Psychologist*, 45, 46–50.

(2011). *Applying the Science of Learning*. Upper Saddle River, NJ: Pearson.

(Ed.). (2014). *The Cambridge Handbook of Multimedia Learning* (2nd ed.). New York, NY: Cambridge University Press.

Mayer, R. E., & Wittrock, M. C. (1996). Problem solving and transfer. In D. Berliner & R. Calfee (Eds.), *Handbook of Educational Psychology* (pp. 45–61). New York, NY: Macmillan.

(2006). Problem solving. In P. Alexander, P. Winne, & G. Phye (Eds.), *Handbook of Educational Psychology* (pp. 287–303). Mahwah, NJ: Erlbaum.

O'Neil, H. F. (Ed.). (2005). *What Works in Distance Learning: Guidelines*. Greenwich, CT: Information Age.

Pellegrino, J. W., Chudowsky, N., & Glaser, R. (Eds.). (2001). *Knowing What Students Know*. Washington, DC: National Academy Press.

Pellegrino, J. W., & Hilton, M. L. (2012). *Education for Life and Work: Developing Transferable Knowledge and Skills in the 21st Century*. Washington, DC: National Academies Press.

Peper, R., & Mayer, R. E. (1986). Generative effects of note-taking during science lectures. *Journal of Educational Psychology*, 78, 34–8.

Piaget, J. (1926). *The Language and Thought of the Child*. London: Kegan, Paul, Trench, Trubner, and Company.

Shrager, L., & Mayer, R. E. (1989). Notetaking fosters generative learning strategies in novices. *Journal of Educational Psychology*, 81, 263–4.

Weinstein, C. E., & Mayer, R. E. (1985). The teaching of learning strategies. In M. C. Wittrock (Ed.), *Handbook of Research on Teaching* (3rd ed.; pp. 315–27), New York, NY: Macmillan.

Wertheimer, M. (1959). *Productive Thinking*. New York, NY: Harper & Row.

Wittrock, M. C. (1974). Learning as a generative process. *Educational Psychologist*, 11, 87–95.

(1978). The cognitive movement instruction. *Educational Psychologist*, 13, 15–29.

(1989). Generative processes of comprehension. *Educational Psychologist*, 24, 345–76.

(1991). Educational psychology, literacy, and reading comprehension. *Educational Psychologist*, 26, 109–16.

(1992). Generative processes of the brain. *Educational Psychologist*, 27, 531–41.

Wittrock, M. C., & Alesandrini, K. (1990). Generation of summaries and analogies and analytic and holistic abilities. *American Educational Research Journal*, 27(3), 489–502.

2

Learning by Summarizing

SUMMARY

Summarizing involves restating the main ideas of a lesson in one's own words. For example, a student may read a chapter in a history textbook and write a one-sentence summary stating the main idea after each paragraph. The theoretical rationale for summarizing is that it encourages learners to select the most relevant material from a lesson, organize it into a concise representation, and integrate it with their existing knowledge by using their own words. In twenty-six out of thirty experimental comparisons, students who were asked to generate summaries during learning performed better than a control group that was not asked to generate summaries on a subsequent test of the material, yielding a median effect size of $d = 0.50$. Regarding boundary conditions, summarizing may be most effective when students are provided with pretraining in how to summarize and when lessons do not involve complex spatial relations. Regarding applications, summarizing can be used as a form of note taking when learning from text or from lecture-based instruction.

BOX 1. *Overview of Learning by Summarizing*

Definition	Learners restate the main ideas of a lesson in their own words.
Example	Students are asked to read a history lesson and to write a summary sentence stating the main idea in their own words after each paragraph.
Theoretical rationale	Summarizing involves selecting the main ideas from the lesson, organizing them into a more concise cognitive representation, and integrating them with prior knowledge by restating the material in one's own words.
Empirical rationale	The summarization effect is upheld in twenty-six of thirty tests, yielding a median effect size of $d = 0.50$.
Boundary conditions	The summarization effect may be strongest when students receive instruction in how to summarize effectively and when the content of the lesson does not contain complex spatial relations (such as physics or chemistry concepts).
Applications	Summarizing can be applied as a note-taking strategy for learning from text passages and from lecture-based instruction, and for topics within the social sciences and humanities, as well as narratives.

CHAPTER OUTLINE

1. Example of Summarizing as a Learning Strategy
2. What Is Learning by Summarizing?
3. How Does Summarizing Foster Learning?
4. What Is the Evidence for Summarizing?
5. What Are the Boundary Conditions for Summarizing?
6. How Can We Apply Summarizing?
7. Conclusion

EXAMPLE OF SUMMARIZING AS A LEARNING STRATEGY

Please read the following passage and write a summary sentence stating the main idea in your own words:

> To be assured her brothers would be prepared, she had prepared a message in advance. Since specific officials examined all of the slaves' mail, Harriet's message was addressed to a man named Jacob Johnson, who secretly assisted the Underground Railroad, and who was one of the relatively free black men in Maryland. However, even Jacob's mail might be searched, so Harriet had to be cautious. Her message stated: "Inform my brothers to always be devoted to prayer, and when the sturdy aged fleet of vigor glides along to be prepared to unite aboard."

Write your one-sentence summary here:

Now, as a test of your understanding of the story, without referring back to the passage or your summary, please circle the letter corresponding to your answer for the following question:

> Harriet's code which told her brothers to "be prepared to unite aboard," meant:
>
> a. To beware of specific officials
> b. To get ready to escape
> c. To visit her parents
> d. To contact Jacob

You have just engaged in a learning strategy called *summarizing*. If you are like most students in a study by Doctorow, Wittrock, and Marks (1978, p. 111), you were better able to answer comprehension questions like the preceding one if you had been asked to generate a summary during learning than if you had been asked to reread the paragraph. In this chapter, we examine the idea that generating a summary during learning can be an effective way to promote generative learning.

WHAT IS LEARNING BY SUMMARIZING?

Summarizing occurs when learners restate the main ideas of a lesson in their own words. Summarizing is often used as a strategy to help learners comprehend text-based materials, such as a passage in a textbook. It can also be used for lessons in which words are presented orally (such as in a lecture) or for lessons in which both words and pictures are presented (such as a slideshow, narrated animation, or printed text with illustrations). The unit to be summarized can range from short (e.g., each slide in a slideshow, each segment of a narrated animation, or each paragraph in a chapter) to long (e.g., an entire slideshow, narrated animation, or chapter), and the summaries that students generate can range in length from a sentence or a heading to a paragraph. Although there are many forms of summarizing, the defining feature of a summary is that it is a shorter statement of the main points of a lesson.

As noted by Pressley and colleagues (1989, p. 5), summarizing refers to a "family of strategies" that can be used by students and teachers in several different ways. In this chapter, we focus on learning by generating *verbal* summaries, such as by stating the main ideas of a lesson as headings, sentences, or paragraphs. Summaries can also be represented spatially, such as by drawing a picture or by creating a knowledge map of the material. We discuss research related to learning by mapping in Chapter 3 and learning by drawing in Chapter 4. In this chapter, we focus on the effects of generating summaries *during* learning (i.e., when the learner has access to the learning materials) rather than after learning (i.e., when the learner no longer has access to the learning materials). Activities that occur after learning are testing events, which themselves can provide important learning benefits. We discuss research related to the benefits of self-testing in Chapter 6. Finally, summarizing has often been used as an assessment of reading comprehension; however, we focus on how the act of summarizing while studying can serve as a learning tool. In the remainder of this chapter, we present the theoretical and empirical rationale for learning by summarizing, followed by a discussion of boundary conditions and applications to educational practice.

HOW DOES SUMMARIZING FOSTER LEARNING?

Early research on text processing has indicated that learner-generated summaries represent reliable indicators of the types of cognitive processes that occur during reading (Brown & Day, 1983; Brown, Smiley, & Lawton, 1978).

In fact, according to W. Kintsch and van Dijk's (1978) model of text processing, comprehension largely depends on the learner's ability to engage in summarizing processes. For example, readers must be able to mentally delete irrelevant or redundant information, substitute fine details for more general statements, and finally, construct the general meaning, or "gist," of the material (E. Kintsch, 1990; W. Kintsch & van Dijk, 1978). Therefore, when learners generate summaries, they are more likely to engage in these essential cognitive processes and consequently are more likely to construct deeper meaning from the text. In short, the purpose of learner-generated summaries is to promote the cognitive processing necessary for achieving meaningful learning.

Similarly, according to the generative theory of learning (Wittrock, 1974, 1989), summarizing is an effective learning strategy because it forces learners to engage in generative processing – that is, learners are required to extract the main ideas from a lesson, make associations between related ideas, and make associations between the newly acquired information and knowledge already stored in memory. Therefore, the model of generative learning predicts that learning will be enhanced to the extent that learner-generated summaries tap into each of these processes. In other words, students will learn more deeply if they are able to effectively select main ideas, organize them, and then restate them in their own words. On the other hand, students unable to perform these tasks are not expected to benefit from employing summarization strategies. For example, younger students have much more difficulty identifying main ideas in text passages than older students (Brown, Smiley, & Lawton, 1978; Brown & Campione, 1979; Brown & Day, 1983; Brown & Smiley, 1978; Garner, 1982). Further, students who simply copy main ideas verbatim from a lesson understand less than those able to restate the main ideas in their own words (e.g., Brown & Day, 1983). In short, the theoretical goal is that learners use summarizing as a means to promote generative processing but they may need guidance.

According to the cognitive theory of multimedia learning (Mayer, 2009, 2014), summarizing serves to prime the cognitive processes of selecting, organizing, and integrating, as shown in Table 2.1. Selecting involves choosing which elements of information are most important to include in the summary. Organizing involves constructing a concise representation of the selected material by relating the elements of information to each other. Integrating involves using prior knowledge to put the summary into the learner's own words. Thus, the cognitive benefits of summarizing depend on learners constructing a concise representation of the key points from a lesson that makes use of their existing knowledge.

TABLE 2.1. *Three cognitive processes activated by summarizing*

Cognitive process	How summarizing primes the process
Selecting	Learners choose which pieces of information are most important for inclusion in the summary.
Organizing	Learners relate the pieces of information to each other within a coherent summary.
Integrating	By having to use their own words, learners relate the material to relevant prior knowledge.

WHAT IS THE EVIDENCE FOR SUMMARIZING?

Table 2.2 presents the effect sizes of thirty experimental comparisons testing the effects of learning by summarizing. These experiments directly compared the learning outcomes of students who were asked to generate summaries as they learned (the summarizing group) against students who studied the same material using more passive strategies such normal studying or rereading (the control group). Studies that did not measure learning outcomes, examined more general note-taking strategies, did not include a control group, or did not include sufficient statistics to calculate effect size were not included in this analysis. The analysis reveals positive effects of summarizing for twenty-six of thirty tests, yielding a median effect size of $d = 0.50$. Overall, there appears to be evidence for the benefits of generating summaries during learning, although its effects may depend on the prior knowledge of the learners and the nature of the learning materials.

Core Evidence for Learning by Summarizing

In a classic experiment by Doctorow, Wittrock, and Marks (1978), low- and high-ability sixth graders were given a narrative text and either asked to read the passage normally or to write one-sentence summaries in a blank space above each paragraph. The results showed that those who wrote summaries for each paragraph understood the story much better than those who read the story normally, as indicated by performance on a subsequent comprehension test. Further, this effect was even larger for low-ability readers ($d = 1.58$) than for high-ability readers ($d = 0.99$), suggesting that instructions to generate paragraph summaries may be especially helpful to students who otherwise have difficulty selecting main ideas from text.

TABLE 2.2. *Effect sizes for learning by summarizing*

Citation	Population	Subject	Outcome	Effect size
Doctorow, Wittrock, & Marks (1978), low-ability students	Middle school	Narrative text	Comprehension	1.58
Doctorow, Wittrock, & Marks (1978), high-ability students	Middle school	Narrative text	Comprehension	0.99
Bretzing & Kulhary (1979), immediate test	High school	Imaginary African tribe	Comprehension	0.50
Bretzing & Kulhary (1979), delayed test	High school	Imaginary African tribe	Comprehension	0.46
Alesandrini (1981)	College	Electrochemistry	Comprehension	0.23
Annis (1985), low-ability students	College	History	Comprehension	0.40
Annis (1985), high-ability students	College	History	Comprehension	0.30
Annis (1985), low-ability students	College	History	Transfer	-0.85
Annis (1985), high-ability students	College	History	Transfer	-1.58
Spurlin et al. (1988), frequent summaries	College	Plate tectonics	Recall	0.21
Spurlin et al. (1988), infrequent summaries	College	Plate tectonics	Recall	0.86
Wittrock & Alesandrini (1990)	College	Marine life	Recall	0.87
Hooper, Sales, & Rysavy (1994)	College	Marine life	Recall	0.26
Foos (1995), one summary	College	Blue shark	Recall	0.42
Foos (1995), two summaries	College	Blue shark	Recall	0.08

Study	Level	Subject	Measure	Effect size
Leopold & Leutner (2012)	High school	Chemistry	Comprehension	−0.40
Leopold & Leutner (2012)	High school	Chemistry	Transfer	−0.39
Bean & Steenwyk (1984), rule-governed training	Middle school	Prose passages	Comprehension	1.27
Bean & Steenwyk (1984), intuitive training	Middle school	Prose passage	Comprehension	0.71
King, Biggs, & Lipsky (1984)	College	History	Recall	1.97
King, Biggs, & Lipsky (1984)	College	History	Comprehension	1.22
Taylor & Beach (1984)	Middle school	Social studies	Recall	0.82
Taylor & Beach (1984)	Middle school	Social studies	Comprehension	1.09
Taylor & Beach (1984)	Middle school	Social studies	Transfer	0.72
Rinehart, Stahl, & Erickson (1986), major information	Middle school	Social studies	Recall	0.62
Rinehart, Stahl, & Erickson (1986), minor information	Middle school	Social studies	Recall	0.35
King (1992), immediate test	College	Social studies (lecture)	Comprehension	1.37
King (1992), delayed test	College	Social studies (lecture)	Comprehension	0.48
Cordero-Ponce (2000), immediate test	College	Foreign language	Recall	0.77
Cordero-Ponce (2000), delayed test	College	Foreign language	Recall	0.41
MEDIAN				0.50

In a study by Bretzing and Kulhavy (1979), high school students read a passage describing an imaginary African tribe; some students were asked to write a short summary of each page of text (the summarizing group), whereas others did not receive instructions to summarize (the control group). After reading the text, students took immediate and delayed comprehension tests based on the passage. Results indicated that the summarizing group significantly outperformed the control group on both tests (immediate: $d = 0.50$; delayed: $d = 0.46$). The summarizing group also outperformed a group asked to take verbatim notes of the passage and performed similarly to a group asked to paraphrase the passage.

In a study by Alesandrini (1981), college students read a lesson about the electrochemistry of a battery with instructions either to generate summaries after the presentation of each concept (the summarizing group) or to read about each concept twice (the control group). In addition, some students received more specific summarizing instructions to focus on how each concept relates to the overall workings of a battery (the holistic group) or to focus on specific attributes and characteristics of each battery component (the analytic group). The results indicated that the summarizing group (who received generic summary instructions) did not significantly outperform the control group on a subsequent comprehension test ($d = 0.15$). Students also did not significantly benefit from specific instructions to generate holistic ($d = 0.35$) or analytic ($d = 0.19$) summaries. Overall, the average effect size across the three summary groups was $d = 0.23$. One explanation for this finding is that generating summaries is not as effective when learning from text that describes complex spatial relations. Instead, drawing a picture to represent the text may be more appropriate. Indeed, other students in the study by Alesandrini who were given instructions to generate drawings (either general instructions or instructions to generate holistic or analytic drawings) generally performed better than those who generated verbal summaries.

In a study by Annis (1985), college students read a text-based history lesson either normally (the control group) or while generating paragraph summaries (the summarizing group). One week later, both groups were given a test on the material, which contained items targeting each of the levels of Bloom's taxonomy (i.e., knowledge, comprehension, application, analysis, synthesis, and evaluation). Results indicated that generating paragraph summaries was most effective at the application level (low-ability students: $d = 0.72$; high-ability students: $d = 0.61$) and generally effective across the knowledge, comprehension, and application levels, which we combined to form a single measure of comprehension (average $d = 0.40$ for low-ability students; average d = 0.30 for high-ability students). However, generating paragraph summaries was highly ineffective at the higher levels of synthesis and evaluation (average d = -0.85 for low-ability students; average d = -1.58 for high-ability students). Overall, this study suggests that while summarizing appears to benefit general understanding of a text, it may not be sufficient to prime deep creative thinking.

In a study by Spurlin and colleagues (1988), college students studied a geology text on plate tectonics with instructions to summarize four times at different points throughout the passage (the frequent summary group) or to summarize two times throughout the passage (the infrequent summary group), or they received no instructions to summarize. On a subsequent delayed recall test, infrequent summarizers significantly outperformed the control group (d = 0.86); however, frequent summarizers did not significantly outperform the control group (d = 0.21). One possible explanation for this finding is that students expend more effort when they are asked to summarize relatively infrequently as opposed to frequently.

Wittrock and Alesandrini (1990) tested whether the effects of generating paragraph summaries hold when students in the control condition are asked to reread each paragraph (rather than read the material only once). In the experiment, college students were given instructions to read a text about marine life and generate paragraph summaries (the summarizing group) or read and reread the text (the control group). Results indicated that the summarizing group outperformed the control group on a subsequent completion test (d = 0.87), which only required learners to recall information presented in the text. Thus, one limitation of this study is that it did not include a measure of deep learning, such as comprehension or transfer.

Hooper, Sales, and Rysavy (1994) attempted to replicate the findings of Wittrock and Alesandrini (1990). However, the summarizing group did not significantly outperform the control group on the final completion test (d = 0.26). Closer examination of the data indicated that students struggled to generate accurate summaries during learning. This suggests that some students may need explicit instruction in how to generate quality summaries.

In a study by Foos (1995), college students read a text passage about blue sharks with instructions to write one summary or two summaries (i.e., one for each half of the text) of the passage, or without instructions to summarize (the control group). All groups then completed a recall test of the material consisting of multiple-choice and fill-in-the-blank questions. Results indicated that students who generated one summary significantly outperformed the control group (d = 0.42); however, students who generated two summaries did not significantly outperform the control group (d = 0.08). This study provides support for the idea that students may benefit from less frequent summarizing, possibly because students invest more effort to generate one summary than to generate multiple summaries.

Recent research by Leopold and colleagues (Leopold & Leutner, 2012; Leopold, Sumfleth, & Leutner, 2013) further demonstrates the limitations identified by Alesandrini (1981) of generating verbal summaries when learning from science texts that describe spatial relations. In one experiment by Leopold and Leutner (2012), high school students studied a science text about water molecules with instructions to generate paragraph summaries (the summarizing group) or no instructions to use a learning strategy (the control group). Results indicated the summarizing group performed significantly worse on subsequent comprehension (d = –0.40) and transfer (d = –0.39) tests than the control group. A follow-up study by Leopold, Sumfleth, and Leutner (2013) found similar negative effects of generating summaries on science understanding.

Importantly, in both studies by Leopold and colleagues, generating pictorial summaries (i.e., drawings) was more effective than generating verbal summaries or not generating a summary. This suggests that when learning material that contains complex spatial relations (such as components of water molecules), it may be more appropriate for students to generate a spatial representation of the material, such as by drawing a picture. The effects of learning by drawing are discussed more fully in Chapter 4.

Summarization Training

As mentioned previously, the effects of summarizing as a learning strategy depend on whether learners are able to generate quality summaries (also see Bednall & Kehoe, 2011; Garner, 1982). For some learners, explicit summarization training may be necessary. Although some studies have focused on the effects of summarization training on the quality of learners' summaries (e.g., Friend, 2001; Hare & Borchart, 1984), in this section we focus on whether summarization training improves students' ability to recall and comprehend new materials.

In a study by Bean and Steenwyk (1984), middle school students were provided with extensive training on how to use one of two summarization strategies. Some students were trained on how to use a rule-governed approach, whereas others were trained on how to use a more intuitive approach. The rule-governed training consisted of instruction and practice exercises using six rules for summarizing text: (1) delete unnecessary material, (2) delete redundant material, (3) compose a word to replace a list of items, (4) compose a word to replace the individual parts of an action, (5) select a topic sentence, and (6) invent a topic sentence if one is not available. On the other hand, those trained to use the more intuitive approach received instruction and completed practice exercises on how to create summaries of sentences and paragraphs. Students began by composing summaries of individual sentences and progressed until they could create summaries of entire paragraphs. A control group received the same amount of practice as the two training groups but was not provided with explicit instruction on how to summarize; instead, these students were simply told to write summaries by finding the mains ideas of the lesson. The results indicated that both the rule-governed and intuitive summarization training groups performed better than the control group on a subsequent standardized test of paragraph comprehension, yielding effect sizes of $d = 1.27$ and $d = 0.71$, respectively. This study suggests that explicitly training students how to summarize a text can produce large gains in comprehension.

King, Biggs, and Lipsky (1984) trained college students how to use a rule-based summarization approach similar to that of Bean and Steenwyk (1984). The training consisted of whole-class instruction and practice in using each of the six summarization rules, followed by small-group activities, during which students had the opportunity to compare the summaries they generated to those generated by their peers. A control group completed the same practice exercises and group activities using their normal note-taking strategies, but without any direct training in how to use the summarization rules. All students then read a text-based history lesson and either applied the summarizing strategies they learned or took notes normally. Results indicated that students who were given direct instruction on how to summarize performed much better than the control group on two measures of recall (average $d = 1.97$) and an essay test targeting comprehension ($d = 1.22$).

In a study by Taylor and Beach (1984), middle school students received seven weeks of training and practice generating hierarchical summaries of social studies texts (the summarizing group). Hierarchical summaries, similar to outlines, contain numbered headings and subheadings intended to organize the main ideas and supporting details from a text. Other students did not receive strategy instruction (the control group). During the eighth week, both groups read either a familiar or unfamiliar passage while applying their respective training. The summarizing group generated a hierarchical summary of the passage, whereas the control group reread the passage. Then both groups completed a recall test and a short-answer comprehension test on the passage, and one week later, they completed a writing post-test in which they were asked to write an opinion essay about their favorite season. Results indicated that the summarizing group outperformed the control group on the recall test (d = 0.82) and the comprehension test (d = 1.09). Further, students receiving summarization training were able to transfer their acquired skills to producing better-quality essays than students in the control group (d = 0.72).

The study by Taylor and Beach (1984) provides strong support that students who are trained on how to generate summaries learn better than those who receive no special strategy instruction. However, it is important to note that a third group was also included in the study that received seven weeks of conventional instruction involving reading and answering practice questions on the same social studies texts (the conventional group). Comparison between the summarizing group and conventional group indicates much more modest benefits of summarization training. In particular, the summarizing group significantly outperformed the conventional group on recall of the unfamiliar passage; however, there were no other differences between the two groups on the recall, short-answer, and writing tests.

In a study by Rinehart, Stahl, and Erickson (1986), sixth grade students received five sessions of training on how to generate summaries based on rules similar to those identified by Bean and Steenwyk (1984). The training followed five primary principles of direct instruction: (1) providing explicit explanation, (2) modeling, (3) practicing with feedback, (4) breaking down complex skills, and (5) using scripted lessons. A control group received normal reading instruction, which involved completing readings and worksheets from basal readers. On a subsequent test that involved reading and recalling a chapter from a social studies textbook, students who received summarization training were significantly better able to recall major information (d = 0.62), but not minor information (d = 0.35), compared to the control group. Thus, summarizing instruction helps learners recall the main ideas from a text but may not be effective in helping learners recall minor details from a text.

Does summarization training help students comprehend material from lectures? In a study by King (1992), college students were provided direct explanations, cognitive modeling, and scaffolded practice on how to "generate summaries of the lectures by linking ideas from the lecture together and using only their own words" (p. 310). The instructor also explained the benefits of summarizing as a learning strategy, including its usefulness for effective self-regulation and for enhanced encoding and recall of material. A control condition did not receive strategy instruction but took notes normally during the practice exercises. During testing, both conditions took notes while watching a videotaped social studies lecture. The training condition summarized their notes afterward, whereas the control condition only reviewed their notes. The results showed that students who were trained to summarize their notes performed better on both immediate ($d = 1.37$) and delayed ($d = 0.48$) comprehension tests than those who only reviewed their notes.

In a study by Cordero-Ponce (2000), college students learning a foreign language were trained in how to summarize French texts. Training was provided during two hour-long sessions presented on consecutive days, and consisted of direct instruction on summarization rules that progressed from how to summarize simple English texts to how to summarize French texts. A control group did not receive summarization training. On subsequent immediate and delayed post-tests, both groups were asked to read French passages and recall them in English. Results indicated that students who received summarization training performed significantly better than the control group on both the immediate tests ($d = 0.77$), but the effects did not reach statistical significance for the delayed ($d = 0.41$) tests. However, this may have been due to the study having a relatively small sample size.

Overall, the preliminary findings reviewed in this section suggest that pretraining in summarization techniques can be helpful.

WHAT ARE THE BOUNDARY CONDITIONS FOR SUMMARIZING?

Research on learning by summarizing provides important boundary conditions for its utility as a generative learning strategy. For example, summarizing appears to be most effective for relatively short expository texts (such as a passage about an historical event). Summarizing may not be effective when the material involves information that is highly spatial in nature, such as science concepts related to physics or chemistry. There is also some evidence that summarizing material relatively infrequently (such as one time after reading a short passage) may be more effective than generating frequent summaries (such as generating summaries four different times while reading a short passage). However, there is some evidence that frequent summarizing is effective, particularly when the summaries are short (such as generating one-sentence paragraph summaries).

One potential drawback of summarizing is that learners may need explicit training in how to generate quality summaries. Some learners may not be able to identify main ideas from a text successfully and restate them concisely by connecting the ideas with their existing knowledge. Instead, they may simply resort to copying notes verbatim from a lesson, which does not involve generative processing and does not result in deep learning. Summarization training programs can be effective; however, they can also be time consuming, and it is at this point unclear how training in summarizing compares to other forms of instruction aimed at enhancing reading comprehension.

HOW CAN WE APPLY SUMMARIZING?

Summarizing can be applied to learning from short text–based lessons that do not contain highly spatial content. For example, summaries may be more appropriate for learning from narrative or historical texts rather than scientific texts. Summarizing can also be applied as a note-taking strategy for learning from lecture-based instruction or from narrated animations; however, much less research has been conducted on the effects of summarizing lessons that are not text-based.

Although summarizing is a relatively simple learning strategy to implement, students across grade levels would likely benefit from first receiving direct instruction in basic techniques of summarizing. Students may need practice in identifying relevant elements of information from a lesson, fitting related elements together into a coherent structure, and articulating the material concisely in their own words. Once students have developed this set of competencies, teachers can easily integrate summarizing within classroom instruction, and students can employ summarizing within their repertoire of study strategies.

This chapter focused on the effects of summarizing while learners have access to the learning materials. Other studies have considered the effects of not allowing learners to refer back to the materials while summarizing (e.g., Coleman, Brown, & Rivkin, 1997; Dyer, Riley, & Yekovich, 1979; Ross & Di Vesta, 1976; Stein & Kirby, 1992). This relies not only on the ability effectively summarize but on the ability to retrieve the material from memory. The existing research does not provide a clear answer as to which approach is more effective (Dunlosky et al., 2013), but the effects likely depend on how well learners initially process the material and how well learners are able to generate quality summaries that involve using their own words. As is discussed in Chapter 6 on the effects of learning by self-testing, if learners are not able to retrieve material from memory successfully, it is important that they receive some form of corrective feedback. Thus, in the case of summarizing when the learning materials are not present, students may benefit from being able to refer back to the material after generating their summary.

CONCLUSION

Overall, the literature provides support for generating summaries when a few key conditions are met. First, learners must possess the requisite prior knowledge to effectively select main ideas, make connections among them, and restate them in their own words. Research has shown that young children are often unable to select main ideas from a text; however, even college students can have difficulty constructing quality summaries. In these situations, more direct summarization training may help overcome these deficits.

Summarizing in words may be most beneficial for content areas that are not inherently spatial in nature, such as areas within the social sciences and humanities, as well as narratives. Subjects that are more spatial in nature, such as chemistry, may not be best represented in the form of a verbal summary, but rather a spatial representation (such as a drawing) may be more appropriate. In short, the effectiveness of generating summaries appears to depend largely on learners' prior knowledge and the subject area of the lesson to be learned.

REFERENCES

Alesandrini, K. L. (1981). Pictorial-verbal and analytic-holistic learning strategies in science learning. *Journal of Educational Psychology*, 73(3), 358–68.
Annis, L. F. (1985). Student-generated paragraph summaries and the information-processing theory of prose learning. *Journal of Experimental Education*, 54(1), 4–10.
Bednall, T. C., & Kehoe, E. J. (2011). Effects of self-regulatory instructional aids on self-directed study. *Instructional Science*, 39, 205–226.
Bean, T. W., & Steenwyk, F. L. (1984). The effect of three forms of summarization instruction on sixth graders' summary writing and comprehension. *Journal of Reading Behavior*, 16(4), 297–306.
Bretzing, B. H., & Kulhavy, R. W. (1979). Notetaking and depth of processing. *Contemporary Educational Psychology*, 4, 145–53.
Brown, A. L., & Campione, J. C. (1979). The effects of knowledge and experience on the formation of retrieval plans for studying from texts. In M. M. Gruneberg, P. E. Morris, & R. N., Sykes (Eds.), *Practical Aspects of Memory* (pp. 378–84). London: Academic Press.
Brown, A. L. & Day, J. D. (1983). Macrorules for summarizing texts: the development of expertise. *Journal of Verbal Learning and Verbal Behavior*, 22(1), 1–14.
Brown, A. L. & Smiley, S. S. (1978). The development of strategies for studying texts. *Child Development*, 49(4), 1076–88.
Brown, A. L., Smiley, S. S., & Lawton, S. Q. C. (1978). The effects of experience on the selection of suitable retrieval cues for studying texts. *Child Development*, 49(3), 829–35.

Coleman, E. B., Brown, A. L., & Rivkin, I. D. (1997). The effect of instructional explanations on learning from scientific texts. *Journal of the Learning Sciences*, 6(4), 347–65.

Cordero-Ponce, W. L. (2000). Summarization instruction: effects on foreign language comprehension and summarization of expository texts. *Reading Research and Instruction*, 39(4), 329–50.

Doctorow, M., Wittrock, M. C., & Marks, C. (1978). Generative processes in reading comprehension. *Journal of Educational Psychology*, 70(2), 109–18.

Dunlosky, J., Rawson, K. A., March, E. J., Nathan, M. J., & Willingham, D. T. (2013). Improving students' learning with effective learning techniques: promising directions from cognitive and educational psychology. *Psychological Science in the Public Interest*, 14, 5–58.

Dyer, J. W., Riley, J., & Yekovich, F. R. (1979). An analysis of three study skills: notetaking, summarizing, and rereading. *Journal of Educational Research*, 73(1), 3–7.

Foos, P. W. (1995). The effect of variations in text summarization opportunities on test performance. *Journal of Experimental Education*, 63(2), 89–95.

Friend, R. (2001). Effects of strategy instruction on summary writing of college students. *Contemporary Educational Psychology*, 26, 3–24.

Garner, R. (1982). Efficient text summarization: costs and benefits. *Journal of Educational Research*, 75(5), 275–9.

Hare, V. C., & Borchart, K. M. (1984). Direct instruction of summarization skills. *Reading Research Quarterly*, 20, 62–78.

Hooper, S., Sales, G., & Rysavy, S. D. M. (1994). Generating summaries and analogies alone and in pairs. *Contemporary Educational Psychology*, 19, 53–62.

King, A. (1992). Comparison of self-questioning, summarizing, and notetaking-review as strategies for learning from lectures. *American Educational Research Journal*, 29(2), 303–23.

King, J. R., Biggs, S., & Lipsky, S. (1984). Students' self-questioning and summarizing as reading study strategies. *Journal of Reading Behavior*, 16(3), 205–18.

Kintsch, E. (1990). Macroprocesses and microprocesses in the development of summarization skill. *Cognition and Instruction*, 7(3), 161–95.

Kintsch, W., & van Dijk, T. A. (1978). Toward a model of text comprehension. *Psychological Review*, 85(5), 363–94.

Leopold, C., & Leutner, D. (2012). Science text comprehension: drawing, main idea selection, and summarizing as learning strategies. *Learning and Instruction*, 22, 16–26.

Leopold, C., Sumfleth, E., & Leutner, D. (2013). Learning with summaries: effects of representation mode and type of learning activity on comprehension and transfer. *Learning and Instruction*, 27, 40–9.

Mayer, R. E. (2009). *Multimedia Learning* (2nd ed.). New York, NY: Cambridge University Press.

(2014). Cognitive theory of multimedia learning. In R. E. Mayer (Ed.), *The Cambridge Handbook of Multimedia Learning* (2nd ed.; pp. 43–71). New York, NY: Cambridge University Press.

Pressley, M., Johnson, C. J., Symons, S., McGoldrick, J. A., & Kurita, J. A. (1989). Strategies that improve children's memory and comprehension of text. *Elementary School Journal*, 90, 3–32.

Rinehart, S. D., Stahl, S. A., & Erickson, L. G. (1986). Some effects of summarization training on reading and studying. *Reading Research Quarterly*, 21(4), 422–38.

Spurlin, J. E., Dansereau, D. F., O'Donnell, A., & Brooks, L. W. (1988). Text processing: effects of summarization frequency on text recall. *Journal of Experimental Education*, 56(4), 199–202.

Stein, B. L., & Kirby, J. R. (1992). The effects of text absent and text present conditions on summarization and recall of text. *Journal of Literacy Research*, 24(2), 217–32.

Ross, S. M., & Di Vesta, F. J. (1976). Oral summary as a review strategy for enhancing recall of textual material. *Journal of Educational Psychology*, 68(6), 689–95.

Taylor, B. M., & Beach, R. W. (1984). The effects of text structure instruction on middle-grade students' comprehension and production of expository text. *Reading Research Quarterly*, 19(2), 134–46.

Wittrock, M. C. (1974). Learning as a generative process. *Educational Psychologist*, 11(2), 87–95.

(1989). Generative processes of comprehension. *Educational Psychologist*, 24(4), 345–76.

Wittrock, M. C., & Alesandrini, K. (1990). Generation of summaries and analogies and analytic and holistic abilities. *American Educational Research Journal*, 27(3), 489–502.

3

Learning by Mapping

SUMMARY

Learning by mapping occurs when learners are asked to convert a text lesson into a spatial arrangement of words such as a concept map, knowledge map, or matrix graphic organizer. A concept map is a spatial array consisting of nodes (typically ovals or rectangles) containing words representing key concepts, and lines that connect the nodes and represent key relationships (typically with words describing the relationship written along the lines). A knowledge map is a special kind of concept map in which the kinds of relationships are limited to correspond to basic types of prose structures such as hierarchy (with "part of" or "type of" links), chain (with "leads to" links), and cluster (such as "characteristic of" or "evidence for" links). A graphic organizer is a specific kind of concept map that corresponds to a specific rhetorical structure such as compare and contrast, which is represented as a matrix with the to-be-compared elements listed across the top as columns and the dimensions on which they are compared listed along the left side as rows. The theoretical rationale for mapping is that students are encouraged to mentally select the key elements and organize them into a coherent structure. The empirical rationale for mapping is that superior test performance was found when students were asked to engage in concept mapping ($d = 0.62$ with positive effects in twenty-three out of twenty-five comparisons), knowledge mapping ($d = 0.43$ with positive effects in five of six comparisons), and graphic organizer mapping ($d = 1.07$ with positive effects in eight of eight comparisons) as compared to students who took conventional notes or read the material without mapping. Regarding boundary conditions, the effects of mapping are stronger for lower-performing students ($d = 0.45$ based on four comparisons) rather than higher-performing students ($d = 0.08$ based on four comparisons). There is also some evidence that younger learners benefit more when mapping is supported with more guidance during learning. In terms of practical applications, mapping can be used as an effective learning strategy, particularly for less able learners, but effective mapping strategies require extensive training, depend on the learner's willingness to do extra work, and presuppose that the instructional material has a clear underlying structure.

BOX 1. *Overview of Learning by Mapping*

Definition	Learners create a spatial map containing key words and relations among them.
Example	Learners read a passage about first aid for wounds as they create a map showing the key concepts in ovals and the relations among them as labeled lines (such as "part of," "type of," or "leads to"). Learners are asked to read a lesson on steamboats as they fill in a matrix that compares eastern-style steamboats and western-style steamboats along several dimensions.
Theoretical rationale	Asking learners to create spatial maps showing key concepts and relations among them encourages learners to identify key words in the text for nodes (i.e., engage in the cognitive process of selecting) and spatially arrange the words in their map (i.e., engage in the cognitive process of organizing).
Empirical rationale	The mapping effect is upheld in twenty-three out of twenty-five tests involving concept maps yielding a median effect size of $d = 0.62$, five out of six tests involving knowledge maps yielding a median effect size of $d = 0.43$, and eight out of eight tests involving matrix graphic organizers yielding a median effect size of $d = 1.07$.
Boundary conditions	The mapping effect is strongest when learners are low in experience or ability ($d = 0.45$ based on four comparisons) rather than high ($d = -0.08$ based on four comparisons). Younger learners may benefit from guidance during learning such as providing partially completed maps.
Applications	Mapping can be an effective learning strategy especially for less able learners, but the material must have a coherent structure and the students may need extensive training before learning and guidance during learning.

CHAPTER OUTLINE

1. Example of Mapping as a Learning Strategy
2. What Is Learning by Mapping?
3. How Does Mapping Foster Learning?
4. What Is the Evidence for Mapping?
5. What Are the Boundary Conditions for Mapping?
6. How Can We Apply Mapping?
7. Conclusion

EXAMPLE OF LEARNING BY MAPPING

Mapping involves creating a spatial arrangement of words that are presented linearly, such as in a paragraph. For example, consider the following information:

There are three cognitive processes required for meaningful learning: selecting, in which the learner attends to the important information; organizing, in which the learner mentally arranges the selected material into a coherent structure; and integrating, in which the learner connects the incoming information with relevant prior knowledge activated from long-term memory. Selecting is represented by the arrow from sensory memory to working memory. Organizing is represented by the arrow from working memory back to working memory. Integrating is represented by the arrow from long-term memory to working memory.

You could convert the text into a concept map by creating nodes (which represent the key concepts) and lines between them (which represent the relations), such as shown in Figure 3.1.

As you can see, the key concepts are in boxes and the relations are represented as labeled lines. When the links between nodes in a concept map are limited to a small predefined set such as "part of," "type of," "characteristic of," and "leads to," it can be called a knowledge map.

Alternatively, you could create a graphic organizer by laying out a matrix in which the three types of cognitive processing are listed as rows on the left side and the "description" and "represented by" are listed in columns to the right, as shown in Table 3.1.

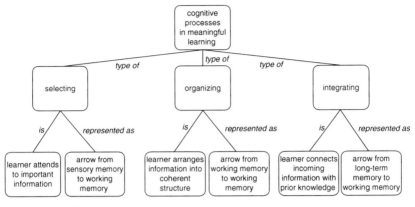

FIGURE 3.1. Concept Map.

TABLE 3.1. *Three cognitive processes in meaningful learning*

Name	Description	Represented by
Selecting	Attend to important information	Arrow from sensory memory to working memory
Organizing	Arrange information into a coherent structure	Arrow from working memory to working memory
Integrating	Connect information with relevant prior knowledge	Arrow from long-term memory to working memory

Now that you know a little bit about how to engage in the learning strategy of mapping, please read the following paragraph, and as you read try to draw a concept map consisting of nodes and lines connecting them:

Mapping (sometimes called a spatial learning strategy) is a kind of learning strategy in which the learner converts printed or spoken text into a spatial arrangement of words consisting of key words (represented as nodes) and relations between them (represented as lines). Three kinds of mapping are concept mapping, knowledge mapping, and graphic organizer mapping. In concept mapping, the nodes are key words and the lines are either labeled or not. Knowledge mapping is a special kind of concept mapping in which there are only a limited number of types of lines such as "type of," "part of," "characteristic of," and "leads to." Graphic organizer mapping is an even more restricted form of mapping in which the elements fit within a structure such as a matrix.

Draw your concept map in the space below. First make a list of the nodes and then figure out where to place them and how to label the lines connecting them.

Make your concept map here:

Now, without looking back at the paragraph or your concept map, please write a summary of the material you just read.

Write your summary here:

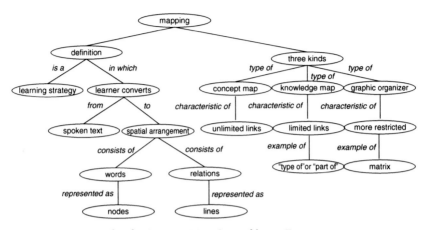

FIGURE 3.2. Example of a Concept Map Created by an Expert.

Did your concept map look anything like the one in Figure 3.2? Although this concept map was created by an expert, there may be many ways to create a concept map for the presented material; sometimes students may need some guidance – such as being given a list of the main concepts (i.e., the nodes), a list of the relationships (i.e., the lines), or even a partially completed map.

Does creating a concept map help you learn the material? That is the question we address in this chapter. In particular, we are interested in the learning outcomes (e.g., retention or transfer test performance) of students who read while creating a concept map versus those who read without creating a concept map.

Let's try one more example. Please read the following paragraph (in Figure 3.3) about steamboats. As you read, please fill in the diagram on the right to compare the eastern-style and western-style steamboats: in the box in the middle column of each row, put the characteristic that is being compared; in the box on the left column, put the description of that characteristic for eastern-style steamboats; and in the box on the right column, put the description of that characteristic for western-style steamboats.

Now, without looking back at the paragraph or your diagram, please write a summary of all the important material you can remember about the steamboat paragraph in the box that follows Figure 3.3.

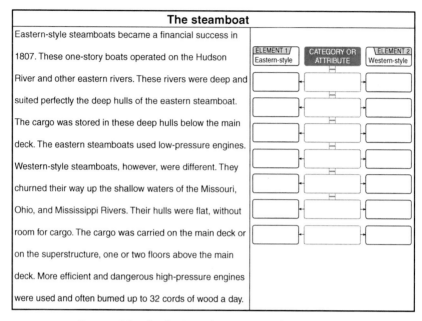

The steamboat

Eastern-style steamboats became a financial success in 1807. These one-story boats operated on the Hudson River and other eastern rivers. These rivers were deep and suited perfectly the deep hulls of the eastern steamboat. The cargo was stored in these deep hulls below the main deck. The eastern steamboats used low-pressure engines. Western-style steamboats, however, were different. They churned their way up the shallow waters of the Missouri, Ohio, and Mississippi Rivers. Their hulls were flat, without room for cargo. The cargo was carried on the main deck or on the superstructure, one or two floors above the main deck. More efficient and dangerous high-pressure engines were used and often burned up to 32 cords of wood a day.

FIGURE 3.3. Concept Map for the Steamboat Paragraph Example.

Write your summary below:

The diagram you created is a type of graphic organizer, which is a spatial arrangement of the key words in the lesson based on a structure such as a

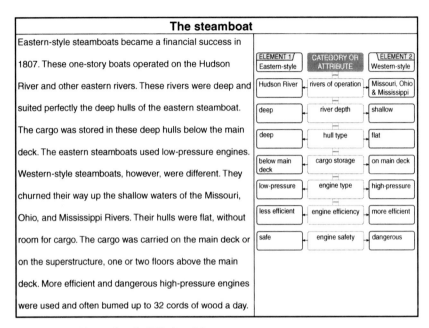

The steamboat	
Eastern-style steamboats became a financial success in 1807. These one-story boats operated on the Hudson River and other eastern rivers. These rivers were deep and suited perfectly the deep hulls of the eastern steamboat. The cargo was stored in these deep hulls below the main deck. The eastern steamboats used low-pressure engines. Western-style steamboats, however, were different. They churned their way up the shallow waters of the Missouri, Ohio, and Mississippi Rivers. Their hulls were flat, without room for cargo. The cargo was carried on the main deck or on the superstructure, one or two floors above the main deck. More efficient and dangerous high-pressure engines were used and often burned up to 32 cords of wood a day.	

FIGURE 3.4. Example of a Filled-in Matrix.

matrix. A matrix can be used to represent a common prose structure called compare-and-contrast in which two or more elements are compared along several dimensions. In this case, the matrix consists of two types of steamboats that are compared along several dimensions, such as type of hull and type of engine. Did your filled-in matrix look anything like Figure 3.4?

If you are like most students in a study by Ponce and Mayer (2014), filling in the matrix as you read the steamboat passage helped you perform better on a comprehension test than if you took conventional notes or simply read the passage. Filling in the matrix is a type of learning strategy called mapping, in which you translate printed or spoken text into a spatial arrangement of key words. Mapping is intended to help you focus on the key concepts and the relations among them. In this chapter, we consider the research evidence for learning by mapping, including when it works best and how it can be applied to improving student learning.

WHAT IS LEARNING BY MAPPING?

As you can see from the examples in the previous section, mapping is a learning strategy in which the learner converts a presented text lesson into a spatially arranged collection of words. In classic books on concept

TABLE 3.2. *Three types of mapping*

Type of mapping	Description	Level of constraint
Concept mapping	Spatial arrangement of nodes and links	Least constrained
Knowledge mapping	Spatial arrangement of nodes and links with a predetermined set of links (such as "part of" or "leads to")	Somewhat constrained
Graphic organizer mapping	Spatial arrangement of nodes within a predetermined structure (such as a matrix or flow chart)	Most constrained

learning, Novak and Gowin (1984) and Novak (1998) proposed that concept maps can be used (1) as learning strategies in which learners create concept maps during learning, (2) as adjuncts to learning by providing teacher-generated concept maps with lessons, or (3) as evaluation tools in which drawing a concept map is a way to evaluate what students know. In this book, we focus only on the first function of concept maps – as a generative learning activity in which the act of creating concept maps can facilitate learning. As summarized in Table 3.2, in this chapter we examine three types of mapping: concept mapping, knowledge mapping, and graphic organizer mapping.

In concept mapping, as exemplified by the first example in the previous section, students read a text or listen to a lecture as they construct a spatial arrangement consisting of nodes represented by words that describe the key concepts and links represented by lines between the nodes. The words in the nodes can be encapsulated in boxes of various shapes (such as in the example) or stand alone without any boxes. The lines can contain relational words, such as "consists of" or "leads to," or can be unlabeled. Concept maps can be drawn by hand (usually with pencil and paper), created on a computer (usually using a mapping tool that does the drawing), or even created physically by arranging cutouts of the nodes on a desktop or magnetic board. As an aid to drawing, in some cases learners may be given a list of key concepts for the nodes and a list of relations between nodes. The act of creating concept maps can be done individually or in a group. Importantly, students often need training in how to create concept maps before being given a lesson and sometimes need guidance during learning, such as being given a list of key concepts or key relationships or even a partially completed map.

Knowledge mapping is a special kind of concept mapping in which the possible relations among nodes are predetermined. For example, in an early paper, Holley and colleagues (1979) specified six kinds of links: "part of" and "type of" create a hierarchy structure; "leads to" creates a chain structure; and "analogous to," "characteristic of," or "is evidence of" create a cluster structure. As you can see, knowledge mapping (also called *networking*) is a more constrained version of concept mapping because the types of links and structures are predetermined.

Graphic organizer mapping increases the level of constraint by using predetermined spatial structures such as a matrix (for compare-and-contrast structures or what Holley and colleagues call a cluster structure), flow chart (for a process structure or what Holley and colleagues call a chain structure), or hierarchy (for a set-subset structure or what Holley and colleagues call a hierarchy structure). Of these three kinds of graphic organizers, matrix structures have received the most attention in educational research (Jairam et al., 2012; Kauffman & Kiewra, 2010). Graphic organizers and knowledge mapping are based on the idea that there are several basic prose structures commonly used in expository text (Chambliss & Calfee, 1998; Cook & Mayer, 1988).

HOW DOES MAPPING FOSTER LEARNING?

We propose that mapping can be an effective learning strategy to the extent that it primes generative learning processes that the learner would not otherwise perform. Table 3.3 summarizes how mapping is intended to prime the cognitive processes of selecting (in which learners must focus on the key concepts to be used as nodes), organizing (in which learners arrange

TABLE 3.3. *How mapping works: three cognitive processes activated by mapping*

Cognitive process	How mapping primes the process
Selecting	Learners focus on or choose which concepts to use as nodes.
Organizing	Learners physically arrange the nodes to show the relationships among them.
Integrating	Learners translate from one mode of representation into another, such as from linear words to spatially arranged words, which requires connecting incoming information with prose structures stored in long-term memory, such as compare-and-contrast.

the nodes spatially to show the relationships among them), and integrating (in which learners activate and use prose structures such as compare-and-contrast).

The act of converting linear text into spatially arranged text is intended to encourage the learner to make sense of the presented information. As Novak (1998, p. 226) aptly noted: "information does not automatically translate into knowledge." Asking students to engage in mapping is one way to help learners convert information into usable knowledge.

WHAT IS THE EVIDENCE FOR MAPPING?

Does mapping help students learn more deeply? We can address this question by examining research on the effectiveness of asking students to engage in concept mapping, knowledge mapping, and matrix graphic organizer mapping. Although there is a substantial research literature showing that students learn better when text is supplemented with concept maps or graphic organizers (Horton et al., 1993; Lambiotte et al., 1989; Nesbit & Adesope, 2006; O'Donnell, Dansereau, & Hall, 2002), our focus in this chapter is on whether learning from text can be improved when students engage in the learning activity of mapping. In particular, in this review we include published experiments that compare a group that received a lesson without instructions to engage in mapping (the control group) versus a group that received the same lesson along with instructions to engage in mapping (the mapping group), and in which the dependent measure taps a learning outcome, with the paper reporting sufficient information to compute Cohen's *d*. In some cases, the control group engaged in another learning strategy (such as note-taking), whereas in other cases the control group engaged no overt learning strategy.

What Is the Evidence for Concept Mapping?

The first section in Table 3.4 summarizes twenty-five published experimental comparisons between the test performance of students who were asked to generate a concept map during learning from text (the mapping group) versus students who were asked to take conventional notes during learning or simply to study the lesson during learning (the control group). In twenty-three of the twenty-five comparisons, the mapping group performed better than the control group on a learning outcome test, yielding a median effect size of $d = 0.62$, which is in the medium-to-large range.

TABLE 3.4. *Summary of research on mapping*

Citation	Population	Subject	Medium	Outcome	Effect size
Concept mapping					
Lehman, Carter, & Kahle (1985)	High school	Biology	Paper & class	Comprehension	0.02
Prater & Terry (1988, Expt. 1)	Elementary school	Stories	Paper	Comprehension	0.79
Prater & Terry (1988, Expt. 2)	Elementary school	Stories	Paper	Comprehension	0.58
Prater & Terry (1988, Expt. 3)	Elementary school	Stories	Paper	Comprehension	0.46
Heinze-Fry & Novak (1990)	High school	Biology	Paper & class	Comprehension	0.64
Okebukola (1990)	High school	Biology	Paper & class	Comprehension	1.62
Stensvold & Wilson (1990)	High school	Chemistry	Paper & class	Comprehension	0.35
Guastello, Beasley, & Sinatra (2000)	Middle school	Science	Paper & class	Comprehension	6.02
Chang, Sung, & Chen (2002, no support)	Elementary school	Science	Computer	Comprehension	0.20
Chang, Sung, & Chen (2002, medium support)	Elementary school	Science	Computer	Comprehension	0.34
Chang, Sung, & Chen (2002, strong support)	Elementary school	Science	Computer	Comprehension	0.86
Chang, Sung, & Chen (2002, no support)	Elementary school	Science	Computer	Recall	0.37
Chang, Sung, & Chen (2002, medium support)	Elementary school	Science	Computer	Recall	0.83
Chang, Sung, & Chen (2002, strong support)	Elementary school	Science	Computer	Recall	1.13
Chularut & DeBacker (2004; low ESL proficiency)	College & high school (ESL)	Science, history	Paper	Comprehension	1.33
Chularut & DeBacker (2004; high ESL proficiency)	College & high school (ESL)	Science, history	Paper	Comprehension	4.00

(continued)

TABLE 3.4. (*continued*)

Citation	Population	Subject	Medium	Outcome	Effect size
Chiou (2009; individual mapping)	College	Statistics	Paper	Comprehension	
Chiou (2009; collaborartive mapping)	College	Statistics	Paper	Comprehension	1.82
Liu, Chen, & Chang (2010; poor readers)	College (ESL)	Expository text	Computer	Comprehension	0.62
Liu, Chen, & Chang (2010; good readers)	College (ESL)	Expository text	Computer	Comprehension	−0.09
Haugwitz, Nesbit, & Sandmann (2010, low ability)	High school	Biology	Paper	Comprehension	0.57
Haugwitz, Nesbit, & Sandmann (2010, high ability)	High school	Biology	Paper	Comprehension	−0.07
Passmore, Owen, & Prabakaran (2011)	College	Medicine	Computer	Comprehension	2.65
Redford et al. (2012, Expt. 1)	Middle school	Science	Paper	Comprehension	0.28
Redford et al. (2012, Expt. 2)	Middle school	Science	Paper	Comprehension	0.68
MEDIAN					0.62
Knowledge mapping					
Holley et al. (1979; low-achieving students)	College	Geology	Paper	Recall & recognition	0.91
Holley et al. (1979; high-achieving students)	College	Geology	Paper	Recall & recognition	0.40
Chmielewski & Dansereau (1998, Expt. 1)	College	Science	Paper	Recall	0.47
Chmielewski & Dansereau (1998, Expt. 2)	College	Science	Paper	Recall	0.75

Study	Level	Subject	Format	Measure	Effect size
Roberts & Dansereau (2008; note-taking control, low ability)	College	Health	Paper	Recall & recognition	0.33
Roberts & Dansereau (2008; note-taking control, high ability)	College	Health	Paper	Recall & recognition	−0.35
MEDIAN					0.43
Graphic organizer mapping					
Kauffman (2004, note-taking control)	College	Statistics	Computer & paper	Comprehension	0.81
Kauffman (2004, note-taking control)	College	Statistics	Computer & paper	Transfer	0.46
Jairam & Kiewra (2010, Expt 2, note-taking control)	College	Biology	Computer	Comprehension	0.78
Kauffman, Zhao, & Yang (2011, Expt. 1, note-taking control)	College	Biology	Computer	Comprehension	1.05
Kauffman, Zhao, & Yang (2011, Expt. 2, note-taking control)	College	Statistics	Computer	Comprehension	1.82
Kauffman, Zhao, & Yang (2011, Expt. 2, note-taking control)	College	Statistics	computer	Transfer	1.54
Ponce & Mayer (2014; read-only control)	College	History	Computer	Retention	1.55
Ponce & Mayer (2014, note-taking control)	College	History	Computer	Retention	1.10
MEDIAN					1.07

In a set of three early experiments by Prater and Terry (1988), fifth grade students in the mapping group read six stories using concept maps generated together by the students and the teacher, whereas students in the control group read the same stories and engaged in oral discussion with the teacher using questions intended to improve comprehension. In each of the three experiments, the mapping group outperformed the control group on comprehension tests covering the content of the stories ($d = 0.79$, $d = 0.58$, and $d = 0.46$, respectively). It should be noted that the concept maps were partly generated by the teacher, so this study does not offer independent evidence for student-generated mapping. The remaining studies in Table 3.4 focus on scientific text rather than narrative text.

In an early study by Lehman, Carter, and Kahle (1985), high school students learned to create concept maps of their textbook chapter and laboratory exercises across four units (the mapping group) or used outlining techniques on the same material (the control group). The groups did not differ on subsequent comprehension tests covering the material ($d = 0.02$), suggesting that in some cases outlining can be as effective as mapping.

In contrast, studies in which the control group is not asked to engage in an alternative strategy (such as outlining) tend to produce positive effects for mapping. For example, Heinze-Fry and Novak (1990) asked students taking a biology course to create concept maps and receive feedback for three textbook units (the mapping group), whereas another group of students (the control group) did not. On subsequent comprehension tests, the mapping group outperformed the control group, yielding an average effect size of $d = 0.64$. Similarly, Okebukola (1990) taught genetics and ecology to high school students in Nigeria with in-class lessons that included student-generated concept maps (the mapping group) or did not (the control group). Across the two topics, the mapping group outperformed the control group on comprehension tests, yielding a large effect size ($d = 1.62$). Also in line with these findings, in a study by Stensvold and Wilson (1990), ninth graders who were taught to use concept maps in their chemistry class (the mapping group) performed better on a comprehension test than students who did not receive training in mapping (the control group), yielding a small-to-medium effect ($d = 0.35$).

In a study by Guastello, Beasley, and Sinatra (2000), low-achieving seventh graders received a classroom presentation and read textbook sections on the human circulatory system (the control group) or received the same lessons but also were taught how to create concept maps and worked on creating a map for the lesson with teacher assistance during class (the mapping group). On a twenty-item comprehension test, the mapping group greatly outperformed the control, with $d = 6.02$.

In some cases, learners may need guidance or practice in how to create concept maps. For example, in a study by Chang, Sung, and Chen (2002), fifth graders in Taiwan received reading comprehension training over seven weeks on generating concept maps for seven scientific texts using a computer-based mapping system (the mapping group) or no mapping training (the control group). Other students received a scaffolded approach in which a teacher-generated map was given for the first passage, with fading so that the middle passages were partially student-generated and the final two passages were completely student-generated (medium support), or students received an incorrect map with each passage and had to correct it (strong support). The mapping groups outperformed the control group on a subsequent test in which students read a new science passage and took a comprehension test and a retention test, but the strong support group performed best, followed by the medium support group. This pattern of results suggests that beginning readers may need extra scaffolding in learning how to generate concept maps.

Chularut and DeBacker (2004) asked English-as-a-Second-Language (ESL) students from high school and college to read several expository passages involving history and science and take a delayed comprehension test. Some students were trained in concept mapping and generated maps for each passage with feedback from instructors over five sessions (the mapping group), whereas others engaged in individual study and discussion for each passage (the control group). The mapping group outperformed the control group on a fifty-two-item comprehension test covering the material in the passages, both for students with low English proficiency ($d = 1.33$) and students with high English proficiency ($d = 4.00$).

In Chiou (2009), college students in Taiwan took a twelve-hour training program in concept mapping for a college course in statistics (the mapping group). Students in the mapping group learned to generate concept maps for class material each week after the course lecture either individually or in collaborative groups, whereas control students worked on exercises covering the same material. On a subsequent achievement test at the end of the course that included ten multiple-choice questions and four calculation problems, the mapping group outperformed the control group both for individual mapping ($d = 0.90$) and collaborative mapping ($d = 1.82$).

The positive effects of mapping may be strongest for less able students. In Liu, Chen, and Chang (2010), college students who were not native English speakers took an English class in which they learned to use a computer-based tool for creating concept maps as they read three sets of three magazine articles in English or read the articles without concept mapping. On subsequent comprehension tests, the mapping group outperformed the control group for poor readers ($d = 0.62$) but not for good readers ($d = -0.09$).

Haugwitz, Nesbit, and Sandmann (2010) asked high school students in Germany to read information about the human circulatory system and work in collaborative groups to construct a concept map (the mapping group) or write an essay based on the material (the control group). Similar to the Liu, Chen, and Chang (2010) study, the mapping group outperformed the control group for low cognitive ability learners ($d = 0.57$) but not for high cognitive ability learners ($d = -0.07$).

More recent research has also produced strong effects for mapping. For example, in a study by Passmore, Owen, and Prabakaran (2011), some college students taking an online course in nuclear medicine technology were asked to create concept maps based on their readings or course activities at three points during the course based on earlier training with concept mapping (the mapping group). Other students received the same lessons without being asked to create concept maps (the control group). On the final examination, the mapping group greatly outperformed the control group, with $d = 2.65$.

In two experiments, Redford and colleagues (2012) provided training in concept mapping to seventh graders across several days. Later the students read three science texts either with or without generating concept maps and then took comprehension tests on each. The mapping group outperformed the control group in each experiment ($d = 0.28$ in Experiment 1, which contained three lessons on mapping; $d = 0.68$ in Experiment 2, which contained eight lessons in mapping).

Overall, concept mapping appears to be an effective learning strategy, yielding a median effect size of $d = 0.62$. Importantly, constructing concept maps produced medium-to-large effects for poor readers or low-ability students but negligible or negative effects for good readers and high-ability students. In some cases, training and guidance in how to generate concept maps was needed.

What Is the Evidence for Knowledge Mapping?

The second section of Table 3.4 summarizes six comparisons of the learning outcome scores of students who were asked to engage in knowledge mapping while reading a text versus those who took conventional notes or simply studied the presented text. Positive effects of knowledge mapping were obtained in five out of six comparisons, yielding a median effect size of $d = 0.43$.

First, in a pioneering study by Holley and colleagues (1979), college students received 5.5 hours of training across four sessions in creating knowledge maps for expository texts such as passages from a psychology textbook (the mapping group) or they received no training (the control group). Then, students read a three thousand–word passage on geology while creating a knowledge map or taking notes, and five days later took recall and recognition tests on the main ideas in the passage. Overall, the mapping group outperformed the control group ($d = 0.66$), with lower grade point average (GPA) students showing a strong benefit of mapping ($d = 0.91$) and higher GPA students showing a small-to-medium effect of mapping ($d = 0.40$).

Next, Chmielewski and Dansereau (1998) taught college students how to create knowledge maps for expository passages in a two-hour training program (the mapping group) or gave no training (the control group). Subsequently, all students were asked to read two new passages without taking any notes and take a delayed recall test. Across two experiments, the mapping group recalled more important propositions than the control group ($d = 0.47$ in Experiment 1; $d = 0.75$ in Experiment 2). This is one of the few studies to test whether training with one set of materials transfers to learning with a different set of materials, and indicates the robustness of training in knowledge mapping.

Finally, Roberts and Dansereau (2008) asked college students to read a three thousand–word lesson on stress while creating a knowledge map (the mapping group) or taking summary notes (the control group) based on training in a prior session. The mapping group outscored the control group on a retention test for low verbal ability learners ($d = 0.33$) but not for high verbal learners ($d = -0.35$).

Overall, knowledge mapping appears to produce similar results to concept mapping, yielding a median effect size of $d = 0.43$ and showing stronger effects for lower-ability learners than for higher-ability learners. More research is needed on the value of constraining the types of links allowed, as all the studies on knowledge mapping were conducted in the same lab.

What Is the Evidence for Graphic Organizer Mapping?

The third section of Table 3.4 summarizes studies comparing the test performance of students who created matrix graphic organizers while reading a passage versus students who did not. In eight of eight comparisons, the

mapping group outperformed the control group on learning outcome post-
tests, yielding a median effect size of $d = 1.07$.

The first two lines of this section summarize a study by Kauffman (2004),
in which college students read a 3,500-word online statistics lesson consisting of separate web pages for levels of measurement, central tendency and
dispersion, and distribution of scores. Some students (the mapping group)
were given matrix sheets for each lesson with the topic names across the
top (e.g., levels of measurement: nominal, ordinal, interval, or ratio) and
the categories along the left side (e.g., purpose, characteristics, limitations,
or example). Other students (the control group) were given a sheet to take
notes as they wished. The mapping group outscored the control group on
a comprehension test consisting of multiple-choice items ($d = 0.81$) and
on a transfer test consisting of solving problems and applying knowledge
($d = 0.46$). In a follow-up study, Kauffman, Zho, and Yang (2011) were able
to replicate these results for the statistics lesson using an online note-taking
tool ($d = 1.82$ for comprehension and $d = 1.54$ for transfer) and for a two
thousand–word biology lesson about the species of wildcats ($d = 1.05$ on a
comprehension test).

In a related study, Jairam and Kiewra (2010) asked college students to
read an online 1,500-word lesson on the characteristics of six different types
of wildcats. Some students (the control group) took notes using a window
on the screen, whereas others (the mapping group) took notes by filling in
an onscreen matrix consisting of the types of wildcats across the top and the
various categories of characteristics on the left side. Both groups had twenty
minutes to read and twenty minutes to study their notes. The mapping
group outscored the control group on a thirty-item multiple-choice test on
the facts in the lesson ($d = 1.16$) and on a fourteen-item test on relationships
between two types of wildcats ($d = 0.40$), yielding an average effect size of
$d = 0.81$.

In a more recent study, Ponce and Mayer (2014) asked college students to
read an online paragraph about steamboats presented on the left side of the
screen while filling in a matrix organizer on the right side of the screen for
a maximum of five minutes (the mapping group). On a subsequent test in
which students wrote a summary and took a modified cloze test, the mapping group performed better than a group that read the paragraph without
taking any notes with the same time limit ($d = 1.94$ for summary, $d = 1.69$ for
cloze) or a group that typed in conventional notes on the right side of the
screen ($d = 1.17$ for summary, $d = 0.52$ for cloze), yielding an average effect
size of $d = 1.55$ when compared to the read-only control group, and $d = 1.10$
when compared to the note-taking control group.

It should be noted that these studies, which yielded a strong median effect size of $d = 1.07$, are all based on matrix organizers and all involved texts that had an underlying compare-and-contrast structure. In a study involving other kinds of graphic organizers and text structures, Stull and Mayer (2007) found that mapping was not effective when students had to complete multiple graphic organizers of various types, perhaps because the amount of required work was overwhelming.

WHAT ARE THE BOUNDARY CONDITIONS FOR MAPPING?

The research summarized in Table 3.4 suggests two important boundary conditions for the mapping effect. First, mapping appears to be more effective for lower-ability students than for higher-ability learners. The mapping effect is medium for lower-ability learners ($d = 0.45$ based on four comparisons) and negligible for higher ability learners ($d = -0.08$ based on four comparisons).

Second, mapping appears to be more effective for young readers when more support is provided during learning ($d = 1.00$ based on two comparisons) than when little support is provided during learning ($d = 0.28$ based on two comparisons). More research is needed to examine this observation, which is based on a single article.

Across all three kinds of mapping strategies, there is consistent evidence from published studies that students learn better when they are asked to engage in mapping during learning than when they are not. Does this result represent a file drawer effect in which published studies yield stronger effects than nonpublished studies such as dissertations and conference papers (Ellis, 2010)? A classic review of the effects of student-generated concept maps by Horton and colleagues (1993) yielded a median effect size of $d = 0.28$, with a median effect size of $d = 0.12$ for unpublished studies based on eight comparisons and $d = 0.45$ for published studies based on six comparisons. More recently, Nesbit and Adesope (2006) reported an average weighted effect size of $d = 0.82$ favoring self-generated mapping, with a median effect size of $d = 0.23$ for unpublished studies based on nine comparisons and $d = 0.87$ for published papers based on eighteen comparisons. Overall, there is some reason to suspect that published studies yield higher effect sizes, although the published and unpublished studies may differ on many characteristics, including the degree to which they employ acceptable experimental controls, provide sufficient training in mapping, and employ sensitive tests of learning outcome. More careful comparisons between published and unpublished studies are needed to determine the robustness of mapping effects.

Finally, as you can see in the tables, some studies rely on recall or recognition as the main dependent variable, but mapping effects are still strong for studies using measures of comprehension and transfer. Further research is needed on the effects of mapping strategies on comprehension and transfer test performance in addition to recall and recognition, particularly for knowledge mapping.

HOW CAN WE APPLY MAPPING?

What are some practical implications of research on mapping? Based on the review of mapping research summarized in Table 3.4, there is reason to encourage students to learn how to map expository text they are reading and to use the techniques on text material they encounter. A practical problem is that mapping is a time-consuming process, so students need to see how mapping will improve their learning – perhaps with some in-class demonstrations of learning without and then with mapping. To further combat this problem, students may use mapping sparingly or in abbreviated form or with scaffolds, such as partially constructed maps to be completed.

Research with beginning or less able readers shows that some students may need substantial training before learning and may need some guidance during initial learning. Once students have several hours of training and practice, they are likely to be able to using mapping techniques on their own.

There is preliminary evidence that school-based training in how to engage in mapping using worksheets with community college students (Cook & Mayer, 1988) or computer-based graphic organizer tools for middle school students (Ponce, Lopez, & Mayer, 2013) can transfer to improved reading comprehension performance in new contexts. Additional studies are needed to extend this promising line of research and to determine how best to establish a training program for study skills such as mapping.

CONCLUSION

Overall, research on mapping as a learning strategy that began in the 1970s has had a burst of new activity since 2000 across diverse labs. Although much of the research on mapping has focused on using teacher-provided concept maps and graphic organizers as aids to learning from text (Horton et al., 1993; Lambiotte et al., 1989; Nesbit & Adesope, 2006; O'Donnell, Dansereau, & Hall, 2002), there is now solid research demonstrating that mapping can also be an effective learning strategy if students are properly trained and supported. In short, this chapter demonstrates the progress that has been made in fulfilling the visionary promise of spatial learning strategies articulated a generation ago (Holley & Dansereau, 1984; Novak & Gowin, 1984). In the future, research is needed that helps pinpoint the conditions under which mapping is most effective, such as the amount of training and guidance that is needed for different kinds of learners. Finally, additional research is needed that examines how school-based training in mapping as a learning strategy transfers to reading new texts.

REFERENCES

Chambliss, M. J., & Calfee, R. C. (1998). *Textbooks for Learning*. Oxford, UK: Blackwell.

Chang, K., Sung, Y., & Chen, I. (2002). The effect of concept mapping to enhance text comprehension and summarization. *Journal of Experimental Education*, 71, 5–23.

Chiou, C. (2009). Effects of concept mapping strategy on learning performance in business and economics statistics. *Teaching in Higher Education*, 14, 55–69.

Chmielewski, T. L., & Dansereau, D. F. (1998). Enhancing the recall of text: knowledge mapping training promotes implicit transfer. *Journal of Educational Psychology*, 90, 407–13.

Chularut, P., & DeBacker, T. K. (2004). The influence of concept mapping on achievement, self-regulation, and self-efficacy in students of English as a Second Language. *Contemporary Educational Psychology*, 29, 248–63.

Cook, L. K., & Mayer, R. E. (1988). Teaching readers about the structure of scientific text. *Journal of Educational Psychology*, 80, 448–56.

Ellis, P. D. (2010). *The Essential Guide to Effect Sizes*. New York, NY: Cambridge University Press.

Guastello, E. F., Beasley, T. M., & Sinatra, R. C. (2000). Concept mapping effects on science content comprehension of low-achieving inner-city seventh graders. *Remedial and Special Education*, 21, 356–64.

Haugwitz, M., Nesbit, J. C., & Sandmann, A. (2010). Cognitive ability and the instructional efficacy of collaborative concept mapping. *Learning and Individual Differences*, 20, 536–43.

Heinze-Fry, J. A., & Novak, J. D. (1990). Concept mapping brings long-term movement toward meaningful learning. *Science Education*, 74, 461–72.

Holley, C. D., & Dansereau, D. F. (Eds.). (1984). *Spatial Learning Strategies*. Orlando, FL: Academic Press.

Holley, C. D., Dansereau, D. F., McDonald, B. A., Garland, J. C., & Collins, K. W. (1979). Evaluation of a hierarchical mapping technique as an aid to prose processing. *Contemporary Educational Psychology*, 4, 227–37.

Horton, P. B., McConney, A. A., Gallo, M., Woods, A. L., Senn, G. J., & Hamelin, D. (1993). An investigation of the effectiveness of concept mapping as an instructional tool. *Science Education*, 77, 95–111.

Jairam, D., & Kiewra, K. A. (2010). Helping students soar to success on computers: an investigation of the SOAR study method for computer-based learning. *Journal of Educational Psychology*, 102, 601–614.

Jairam, D., Kiewra, K. A., Kauffman, D. F., & Zhao, R. (2012). How to study a matrix. *Contemporary Educational Psychology*, 37, 128–35.

Kauffman, D. F. (2004). Self-regulated learning in web-based environments: instructional tools designed to facilitate cognitive strategy use, metacognitive processing, and motivational beliefs. *Journal of Educational Computing Research*, 30, 139–61.

Kauffman, D. F., & Kiewra, K. A. (2010). What makes a matrix so effective? An empirical test of the relative benefits of signaling, extraction, and localization. *Instructional Science*, 38, 679–705.

Kauffman, D. F., Zhao, R., & Yang, Y. (2011). Effects of online note taking formats and self-monitoring prompts on learning from online text: using technology to enhance self-regulated learning. *Contemporary Educational Psychology*, 36, 313–22.

Lambiotte, J. G., Dansereau, D. F., Cross, D. R., & Reynolds, S. B. (1989). Multirelational semantic maps. *Educational Psychology Review*, 1, 331–67.

Lehman, J. D., Carter, C., & Kahle, J. B. (1985). Concept mapping, vee mapping, and achievement: results from a field study with black high school students. *Journal for Research in Science Teaching*, 22, 663–73.

Liu, P., Chen, C., & Chang, Y. (2010). Effects of a computer-assisted concept mapping learning strategy on EFL college students' English reading comprehension. *Computers & Education*, 54, 436–45.

Nesbit, J. C., & Adesope, O. O. (2006). Learning with concept and knowledge maps: a meta-analysis. *Review of Educational Research*, 76, 413–48.

Novak, J. D. (1998). *Learning, Creating, and Using Knowledge*. Mahwah. NJ: Erlbaum.

Novak, J. D., & Gowin, D. B. (1984). *Learning How to Learn*. New York, NY: Cambridge University Press.

O'Donnell, A. M., Dansereau, D. F., & Hall, R. H. (2002). Knowledge maps as scaffolds for cognitive processing. *Educational Psychology Review*, 14, 71–86.

Okebukola, P. A. (1990). Attaining meaningful learning of concepts in generics and ecology: an examination of the potency of the concept-mapping technique. *Journal of Research in Science Teaching*, 27, 493–504.

Passmore, G. G., Owen, M. A., & Prabakaran, K. (2011). Empirical evidence of the effectiveness of concept mapping as a learning intervention for nuclear medicine technology students in a distance learning radiation protection and biology course. *Journal of Nuclear Medicine Technology*, 39, 284–9.

Ponce, H. R., Lopez, M. J., & Mayer, R. E. (2012). Instructional effectiveness of a computer-supported program for teaching reading comprehension strategies. *Computers & Education*, 59, 1170–83.

   (2013). A computer-based spatial learning strategy approach that improves reading comprehension and writing. *Educational Technology Research & Development*, 61, 819–40.

Ponce, H. R., & Mayer, R. E. (2014). Qualitatively different cognitive processing during online reading primed by different study activities. *Computers in Human Behavior*, 30, 121–30.

Prater, D. L., & Terry, C. A. (1988). Effects of mapping strategies on reading comprehension and writing performance. *Reading Psychology*, 9, 101–20.

Redford, J. S., Thiede, K. W., Wiley, J., & Griffin, T. D. (2012). Concept mapping improves metacomprehension accuracy among 7th graders. *Learning and Instruction*, 22, 262–70.

Roberts, F. W., & Dansereau, D. F. (2008). Studying strategy effects on memory, attitudes, and intentions. *Reading Psychology*, 29, 552–80.

Stensvold, M. S., & Wilson, J. T. (1990). The interaction of verbal ability with concept mapping in learning a chemistry laboratory activity. *Science Education*, 74, 473–80.

Stull, A., & Mayer, R. E. (2007). Learning by doing versus learning by viewing: three experimental comparisons of learner-generated versus author-provided graphic organizers. *Journal of Educational Psychology*, 99, 808–20.

4

Learning by Drawing

SUMMARY

Learning by drawing occurs when learners are asked to create drawings that illustrate the content of a text-based lesson. Learning by drawing includes determining which components to include in an illustration and how to arrange them spatially to show their structural and causal connections. For example, learners who read a lesson on how the human central nervous system works can be asked to make a drawing corresponding to text about how a neuron communicates with a neighboring neuron. The theoretical rationale for learning by drawing is that the act of constructing illustrations that correspond to text can prime the generative processes of selecting (in which learners choose which components to include), organizing (in which learners arrange the components in a spatial layout), and integrating (in which learners translate from words to pictures). Although drawing is intended to foster generative processing, the mechanics of drawing can create extraneous processing, which can reduce or eliminate the benefits of drawing. The empirical rationale for drawing is that asking students to create self-generated drawings improved performance on transfer and comprehension tests in twenty-six out of twenty-eight comparisons against a control group that did not draw, yielding a median effect size of $d = 0.40$. Some important boundary conditions are that the self-generated drawing effect is strongest when learners receive guidance in what to draw, when learners work with partially drawn illustrations intended to reduce cognitive load, or when learners are asked to compare their drawing with an instructor-provided drawing. In terms of practical applications, self-generated drawing can be an effective learning strategy for learning scientific explanations presented in words, as long as students receive appropriate guidance regarding what to draw and support in the mechanics of drawing.

BOX 1. *Overview of Learning by Drawing*

Definition	Learners create a drawing to illustrate the content of a lesson.
Example	Learners are asked to read a lesson on how the human central nervous system works and generate a drawing for each section of the lesson as if making illustrations for a science book.
Theoretical rationale	Asking learners to create drawings is intended to encourage them to identify key components in the text (i.e., engage in the cognitive process of selecting), spatially arrange the components (i.e., engage in the cognitive process of organizing), and relate them to prior knowledge through translating from verbal to visual forms of representation (i.e., engage in the cognitive process of integrating). Although drawing is intended to foster generative processing (involving selecting, organizing, and integrating), the mechanics of drawing can create extraneous cognitive processing, which can offset the advantages.
Empirical rationale	The self-generated drawing effect is upheld in twenty-six of twenty-eight tests, yielding a median effect size of $d = 0.40$.
Boundary conditions	The self-generated drawing effect may be strongest when learners receive explicit instruction in what to draw, when extraneous cognitive load is reduced by providing partially drawn illustrations, or when learners receive more support such as comparing one's self-generated drawing with an author-provided drawing.
Applications	Self-generated drawing applies to learning from scientific text within paper-based learning environments, but students may need guidance in what to draw and support in the mechanics of drawing.

CHAPTER OUTLINE

1. Example of Drawing as a Learning Strategy
2. What Is Learning by Drawing?
3. How Does Drawing Foster Learning?
4. What Is the Evidence for Drawing?
5. What Are the Boundary Conditions for Drawing?
6. How Can We Apply Drawing?
7. Conclusion

Please read the following portion from a lesson on how the human central nervous system works:

> Each of the parts of the nervous system is made of billions of specialized cells called **neurons.** A neuron is a type of cell found only in the nervous system. All of the neurons have three parts. The neurons' microscopic **cell body** is where all cellular functions take place. An **axon** extends out of the cell body like a branch. It carries messages from the cell body to other neurons. The cell body may also have more branches called **dendrites.** These dendrites receive messages from other neurons and carry them to the cell body.

Now, in the box below, please take the role of a textbook illustrator and make a drawing that illustrates the content of what you read, including each of the important elements, as you would see in a science textbook.

Make a drawing that includes the important elements:

Finally, without looking at the text or your drawing, please write down what you learned about how the central nervous system works.

Write down what you remember from the text you read:

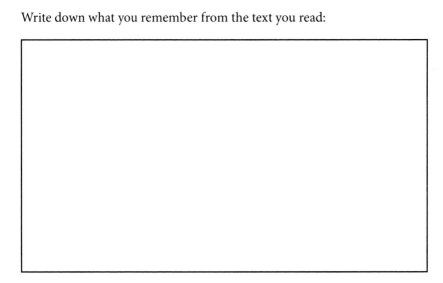

This is a sample modified from a groundbreaking study by Van Meter (2001). The next section in the lesson contains a description of how neurons send impulses across synapses. In Van Meter's study, elementary school students were given training in how to make useful drawings and then were asked to make drawings that illustrated the content of each of two pages of a text about the human central nervous system. If you are like most students in Van Meter's study, the act of generating a drawing helped you understand and remember the text better than simply reading the text, as indicated by performance on a post-test.

In this chapter, we explore the idea that students learn more deeply when they generate drawings while reading instructional text. In short, we want to determine whether drawing can serve as a generative learning strategy – that is, a technique that improves deep learning.

WHAT IS LEARNING BY DRAWING?

An important first step is to define what counts as a learner-generated drawing, or as Van Meter and Garner (2005, p. 288) aptly put it: "The phrase *learner-generated drawing* demands explanation of what is meant by both *drawing* and *learner-generated*."

First, let's consider some characteristics of a drawing – purpose, function, and content. The purpose of a drawing can be artistic expression or educational communication. We focus on drawings that have an educational purpose rather than an artistic purpose.

According to Mayer (1993) and Levin and Mayer (1993), the function of drawings can be:

- *decorative* – appealing illustrations that fill space on the page or screen without enhancing the content of the lesson (such as a drawing of superhero with a white cape embossed with a red "N" in a lesson on how neurons work)
- *representational* – simple illustrations that portray a single element in the lesson (such as a drawing of the shape of a neuron in a lesson on how neurons work)
- *organizational* – maplike illustrations that depict the locations of elements within a system (such as a line drawing of neuron and its parts with each part labeled in a lesson on how neurons work)
- *explanative* – causal-chain illustrations that explain how a system works by showing how a change in one part affects a change in another part (such as a series of frames showing the steps in how a neuron fires in a lesson on how neurons work)

We focus on explanative and organizational drawings (which are intended to prime the cognitive processes of organizing and/or integrating that are needed for understanding) rather than decorative drawings (which prime extraneous processing) or representational drawings (which prime only the cognitive process of selecting).

The content of drawings can be pictorial (e.g., depictions of a neuron and its parts, with each part labeled) or verbal (e.g., in which words about neurons are spatially arranged in a matrix table or a concept map). We focus on drawings with visual content rather than verbal content, although visual drawings can have verbal labels.

Second, let's consider what is meant by *learner-generated*. Drawings can be produced by hand (such as with a pencil and paper) or by computer (such as with a computer-based drawing tool on a computer screen). For purposes of this chapter, both formats for rendering drawings constitute what we mean by learner-generated. Whether learners draw by hand on paper or by using a computer-based drawing tool on a screen, what they are doing is learner-generated. An important research issue concerns whether the effectiveness of drawing as a learning strategy depends on the medium in which the drawing is generated.

Drawings can be generated with various levels of assistance, such as:

- *unsupported* – with no direction or help
- *guided* – with learners given training in how to produce drawings and/ or being told what content to include in their drawings

- *partial* – with learners asked to complete a partially drawn illustration
- *supported* – with learners being given an author-provided illustration and asked to make comparisons between their drawing and the provided drawing

We include all of these levels of assistance in our definition of *learner-generated*, because in each case the learner generates a drawing (or part of one). An important research issue concerns whether the level of assistance alters the effectiveness of drawing as a learning strategy.

HOW DOES DRAWING FOSTER LEARNING?

As shown in Table 4.1, learning by drawing is intended to foster generative processing by priming the cognitive processes of selecting, organizing, and integrating. Selecting is involved when learners must decide which components to include in their drawing. Organizing is involved when learners must arrange the components within a spatial layout in a way that conveys their relations with one another. Integrating is involved when learners must use their prior knowledge to translate from a verbal mode of representation (i.e., the instructional text) to a visual/spatial mode of representation (i.e., an illustration). In addition, in some cases learners may add verbal annotations to their illustrations, which also involves the cognitive process of integrating between words and pictures.

Although drawing is intended to encourage generative processing, there is also the potential that learner difficulties with the mechanics of drawing can create extraneous processing – cognitive processing that wastes limited processing capacity without serving the instructional goal. When learners struggle with using a computer-based drawing tool or with their ability to draw by hand, they are wasting processing capacity that could be used for

TABLE 4.1. *Three cognitive processes activated by drawing*

Cognitive process	How drawing primes the process
Selecting	Learners choose which components to include in their drawing.
Organizing	Learners arrange the components in a spatial layout.
Integrating	Learners translate from a verbal to a visual/spatial mode of representation, and may add verbal annotations to visual/spatial representations.

generative processing. Similarly, when learners are uncertain about what to draw or how to make sense of their drawings, they are wasting processing capacity that could be used for generative processing. Thus, an important challenge for instructors is to provide an appropriate level of guidance and training for each learner to prime generative processing during learning without creating excessive amounts of extraneous processing.

WHAT IS THE EVIDENCE FOR DRAWING?

Table 4.2 lists twenty-eight experimental comparisons on learning outcome tests between students who are asked to make a drawing that represents the key ideas in an instructional passage (the drawing group) and students who are asked to study the passage (the control group). In some cases, the control group is asked to engage in another activity (such as rereading), whereas in others the control group is not given instructions about what to do during learning. We list only published studies that include sufficient information to allow the computation of effect size comparing the drawing group versus the control group based on Cohen's *d*, with a test of learning outcome as the dependent measure (preferably a measure of transfer). The table lists the citation source, the age group of the students, the subject of the lesson, the presentation medium, the type of learning outcome measure, and the effect size. Overall, the drawing group outperformed the control group in twenty-six of twenty-eight comparisons, yielding a median effect size of *d* = 0.40, which is in the small-to-medium range.

The modern era of research on the instructional effects of student-generated drawings began with a study by Alesandrini (1981) in which college students read a lesson that explained fourteen concepts about the chemistry of electric batteries, as summarized in the first three lines of Table 4.2. Some students were asked to make drawings to illustrate each of the fourteen components (the drawing group), whereas other students were asked to reread each of the fourteen sections (the control group). On a comprehension post-test, the drawing group performed better than the control group (*d* = 0.41). The drawing effect was stronger when students were given more detailed drawing instructions to generate drawings that show how each component contributed to the overall workings of the battery (*d* = 0.64) or when they were told to make drawings that focused on the specific characteristics of each component (*d* = 0.48).

In a useful replication using different materials, Hall, Bailey, and Tillman (1997) conducted a study in which college students read a six

TABLE 4.2. *Summary of comparisons between drawing and control groups*

Citation	Population	Subject	Medium	Outcome	Effect size
Alesandrini (1981, untimed, unguided drawing)	College	Chemistry	Paper	Comprehension	0.41
Alesandrini (1981, untimed, analytic drawing)	College	Chemistry	Paper	Comprehension	0.48
Alesandrini (1981, untimed, holistic drawing)	College	Chemistry	Paper	Comprehension	0.64
Hall, Bailey, & Tillman (1997, untimed, guided drawing)	College	Pump	Paper	Transfer	0.71
Gobert & Clement (1999, untimed, guided drawing)	Elementary school	Plate tectonics	Paper	Transfer	1.02
Van Meter (2001, untimed)	Elementary school	Nervous system	Paper	Retention	0.37
Van Meter (2001, untimed, extra support)	Elementary school	Nervous system	Paper	Retention	0.94
Van Meter et al. (2006, untimed)	Elementary school	Bird wings	Paper	Transfer	0.23
Van Meter et al. (2006, untimed, extra support)	Elementary school	Bird wings	Paper	Transfer	0.71
Van Meter et al. (2006, untimed)	Elementary school	Bird wings	Paper	Retention	0.05
Van Meter et al. (2006, untimed, extra support)	Elementary school	Bird wings	Paper	Retention	0.15
Leutner, Leopold, & Sumfleth (2009, timed)	High school	Chemistry	Paper	Comprehension	0.23
Schwamborn et al. (2010a, timed, reduced load)	High school	Chemistry	Paper	Transfer	0.91
Schwamborn et al. (2010a, timed, reduced load)	High school	Chemistry	Paper	Comprehension	0.87
Schwamborn et al. (2010b, Expt. 1, timed, reduced load)	High school	Chemistry	Paper	Transfer	−0.05
Schwamborn et al. (2010b, Expt. 1, timed, reduced load)	High school	Chemistry	Paper	Comprehension	0.55
Schwamborn et al. (2010b, Expt. 1, timed, extra support)	High school	Chemistry	Paper	Transfer	0.39

(continued)

TABLE 4.2. (*continued*)

Citation	Population	Subject	Medium	Outcome	Effect size
Schwamborn et al. (2010b, Expt. 1, timed, extra support, reduced load)	High school	Chemistry	Paper	Comprehension	0.91
Schwamborn et al. (2010b, Expt. 2, untimed, reduced load)	High school	Chemistry	Paper	Transfer	0.40
Schwamborn et al. (2010b, Expt. 2, untimed, reduced load)	High school	Chemistry	Paper	Comprehension	0.81
Schwamborn et al. (2010b, Expt. 2, untimed, reduced load, extra support)	High school	Chemistry	Paper	Transfer	0.12
Schwamborn et al. (2010b, Expt. 2, untimed, reduced load, extra support)	High school	Chemistry	Paper	Comprehension	0.57
Schwamborn et al. (2011, timed, increased load)	High school	Chemistry	Computer	Transfer	0.17
Schwamborn et al. (2011, timed, increased load)	High school	Chemistry	Computer	Comprehension	−0.16
Leopold & Leutner (2012, Expt. 1, timed)	High school	Chemistry	Paper	Transfer	0.32
Leopold & Leutner (2012, Expt. 1, timed)	High school	Chemistry	Paper	Comprehension	0.15
Leopold & Leutner (2012, Expt. 2, timed)	High school	Chemistry	Paper	Transfer	0.69
Leopold & Leutner (2012, Expt. 2, timed)	High school	Chemistry	Paper	Comprehension	0.15
MEDIAN					0.40

hundred–word text explaining how a pump works. Some students were asked to draw a representation of the pump based on explicit instructions for how to draw a cylinder, rod, and handle (the drawing group), whereas others were not told to make a drawing (the control group). On a problem-solving transfer test, the drawing group greatly outperformed the control group ($d = 0.71$).

In some cases, the benefits of drawing as a learning strategy may be enhanced by providing guidance to students on how to draw, particularly when the students are in elementary school. For example, Gobert and Clement (1999) asked fifth graders to read a two-page text about plate tectonics. In the drawing group, students received an expectancy prompt before each section of the text (such as, "After this paragraph, you will be asked to draw a picture [on the next page] of the different layers of the earth") and a drawing prompt after each section (such as, "Thinking back to what you just read, draw a picture of the different layers of the earth. Include and label all the information about these layers that you can"). In this case, the student is given support during drawing in the form of explicit guidance concerning the content of the illustration. In the control group, students simply read the two-page text, without being asked to engage in any learning activities. To assess how well students understood the lesson (i.e., how well they were able to build a mental model of the cause-and-effect system underlying plate tectonics), they were asked open-ended transfer questions, such as, "The movement in the crust of the earth is caused by _____?" and, "Rock from the floor of the Atlantic Ocean tests to be younger than rock from the middle of the North American continent because _____?" Based on a scoring rubric that allocated points for correct statements about the steps in the causal chain, the drawing group performed much better than the control group on the transfer test ($d = 1.02$). The common theme in these first three publications on the self-generated drawing effect all converge on the point that drawing can be an effective learning strategy when the learner is given explicit guidance in what to draw. These promising early findings motivate a more detailed search for the conditions under which drawing can serve as an effective learning strategy.

The next study in Table 4.2 was conducted by Van Meter (2001), in which fifth and sixth graders read a two-page text on the human central nervous system. Students in the drawing group were asked to construct a drawing after each page on a blank sheet of paper provided after each page of text in a booklet, whereas students in the control group read the two-page booklet without any extra blank pages or instructions to make drawings. The drawing treatment involved minimal support because little guidance was provided concerning what to draw. The drawing group outperformed the control group on recall (prompted by, "How does the central nervous system work?") and recognition (consisting of five low-level multiple choice items such as, "What are neurons?" followed by six choices, half of which were true), which we average into a single measure of comprehension ($d = 0.37$). However, Van Meter notes that the drawing group spent more than twice as much learning time as the control group.

In an effort to provide more support to learners in the drawing group, Van Meter (2001) included a group that made a drawing after each page, but then saw the author's illustration and was prompted to make changes based on prompts such as, "In the illustration, what are the parts of a neuron? In your drawing, what are the parts of a neuron? In the illustration, how are the parts of the neuron connected to one another? In your drawing, how are the parts of the neuron connected to one another? Should you change anything in your drawing to make it more accurate?" This high-support version of the drawing treatment resulted in much better post-test performance than the control group achieved ($d = 0.94$), although it also required more than triple the learning time.

In a follow-up study, Van Meter and colleagues (2006) asked fourth and sixth graders to read a two-page scientific text on bird wings, using the same treatment groups as in the previous study. Students in the drawing group performed better than the control group on a transfer test (with open ended questions such as, "There is a bird that is experiencing a lot of turbulence in flight. What is wrong with this bird? Can it be fixed?"), but not on a comprehension test (involving five multiple-choice items testing specific names or facts). When supports were added to guide the drawing process as in the previous study, performance was greatly improved. Overall, this set of studies by Van Meter and colleagues shows that the strongest effects of drawing are found when extra support is provided and when the learning outcome test assesses problem-solving transfer (indicating deeper understanding of the material).

The next line in Table 4.2 summarizes a study by Leutner, Leopold, and Sumfleth (2009), in which tenth graders were given thirty-five minutes to read a 1,600-word booklet (in German) on the chemistry of water molecules, either with or without instructions to "draw a picture that represents the content of the paragraph" after each of thirteen paragraphs. The drawing group slightly outperformed the control group on a twenty-two–item multiple-choice test ($d = 0.23$), although the drawing group reported substantially more cognitive load.

The authors note the need to mitigate difficulties with the mechanics of drawing, which create extraneous cognitive load, because students are less able to learn deeply when they are focused on the mechanics of making drawings. One way to minimize cognitive load during drawing is to provide a readymade labeled background scene along with readymade labeled elements on the side that students can copy within the background scene. This is the approach taken by Schwamborn and colleagues (2010a). Ninth grade students received a computer-based one thousand–word lesson for thirty-five minutes on the chemistry of washing with soap and water, either with or without instructions to create a drawing using a sheet with the premade background scene and readymade elements on the side. These partially drawn sheets provide a way to reduce extraneous cognitive load for creating drawings by virtue of presenting readymade elements that can be copied onto a readymade background scene. Students took a transfer test consisting of three open-ended problem-solving questions (such as, "Suppose you would like to clean a table which is soiled with marker lint. If you would try to clean it with water nothing will happen; using acetone, however, it will work. Please explain why it works with acetone") and a comprehension test consisting of thirteen multiple-choice items. On both tests, the drawing group outperformed the control group (d = 0.91 for transfer and d = 0.87 for comprehension).

The foregoing studies show that drawing can be a powerful learning strategy, particularly when students are given appropriate support during the drawing process. The next eight lines in Table 4.2 summarize a series of follow-up experiments by Schwamborn and colleagues (2010b) using the same basic materials as in the previous study. In Experiment 1, students had thirty minutes with the lesson, and the drawing group outperformed the control group on comprehension (d = 0.55) but not transfer (d = -0.05). In Experiment 2, there was no time limit, and the drawing group outperformed the control group on comprehension (d = 0.40) and transfer (d = 0.81). Apparently, students may need more time (as in Experiment 2) to use the drawing activity most effectively as a learning strategy for improving deep understanding.

What happens when we add more support in the form of asking students to draw, then view the author's drawing and systematically compare it with his or her self-generated drawing? As shown for the other "extra support" lines in Table 4.2, the drawing group outperformed the control group on comprehension (d = 0.91) and transfer (d = 0.39) in Experiment 1, and on comprehension (d = 0.57) and transfer (d = 0.12) in Experiment 2. Thus, there is some evidence that adding drawing support in the form of asking students to compare their drawings to the author's drawings can boost learning.

In the next two lines of Table 4.2, Schwamborn and colleagues (2011) examine whether the effects replicate when the material is presented as a computer-based lesson, with drawing carried out using a drag-and-drop tool for moving premade elements onto a premade on-screen background scene. In this case, the mechanics of using the drag-and-drop tool may create increased extraneous cognitive load, particularly when time is limited. Consistent with this analysis, the drawing group performed slightly worse than the control group on comprehension (d = -0.16) and slightly better on transfer (d = 0.17). Apparently, the advantages of the drawing activity in fostering generative processing were offset by the disadvantages of the mechanics of using the drawing tool in creating extraneous processing.

Finally, the final four lines in Table 4.2 summarize two experiments by Leopold and Leutner (2012), in which tenth graders read a 1,600-word lesson on water molecules for thirty-five minutes. Students in the drawing group were asked to draw a sketch representing the main idea in the paragraph in the box provided on a sheet of paper for each of seven paragraphs. Across both studies, the drawing group outperformed the control group on transfer (d = 0.32 and 0.69, respectively) and on comprehension (d = 0.15 in both experiments).

Overall, research on drawing as a generative learning strategy is encouraging, yielding a median effect size of d = 0.40. We can conclude that under appropriate conditions, learner-generated drawing can be a generative activity that promotes deeper learning. These conclusions are consistent with an earlier literature review by Van Meter and Garner (2005) and a recent overview by Ainsworth, Prain, and Tytler (2011), which stated: "Emerging research suggests that drawing should be explicitly recognized as a key element in science education" (p. 1096).

This review does not include studies in which learners were asked to select and arrange words in a spatial array, such as a matrix sometimes called a graphic organizer (Igo & Kiewra, 2007; Kauffman, Zhao, & Yang, 2011; Ponce & Mayer, 2014; Stull & Mayer, 2007) or a network in which the nodes are words and the links are labeled lines sometimes called a concept map or a knowledge map (Holley et al., 1979; Nesbit & Adesope, 2006; Novak, 1998), because mapping strategies are examined in Chapter 3. However, creating spatial summaries such as graphic organizers or concept maps can be seen as a generative learning strategy that shares some of the features of drawing.

WHAT ARE THE BOUNDARY CONDITIONS FOR DRAWING?

A more detailed inspection of the research summarized in Table 4.2 shows that the median effect size for drawing is greater when we focus on drawing treatments that provide explicit instruction in what to draw, reduced cognitive load by providing partially drawn illustrations, or more support such as comparing one's self-generated drawing with an author-provided drawing. In short, drawing has the potential to promote generative processing by encouraging the student to make sense of the text, but drawing also has the potential to create extraneous processing by virtue of the difficulties in the mechanics of how to draw and the lack of a clear idea of exactly what to draw. Thus, drawing is most effective when learners know what to draw and do not have excessive technical problems in the act of drawing.

HOW CAN WE APPLY DRAWING?

The research reviewed in this chapter suggests that drawing should be added to each student's learning strategy toolbox. To date, generating drawings has been successfully used in paper-based learning environments with scientific text across a range of age groups. Thus, it makes sense to ask students to create illustrations for a small portion of science text from their textbook or, perhaps, an in-class presentation. The text should convey how a scientific system works, such as how the nervous system works, how a pump works, or how plate tectonics work. The drawings should be intended as instructional devices (that show the spatial and causal connections among the elements) rather than as artistic expressions. In workforce training, drawing strategies may be helpful for topics that deal with spatial relations, such as troubleshooting electrical schematics or understanding how a piece of equipment works.

As drawing can be a tedious and confusing activity for some learners, it is worthwhile to provide some pretraining in how to generate drawings and to provide explicit guidance in what to draw during learning. In some cases, it may be worthwhile to provide partially completed drawings in order to minimize extraneous processing, while leaving enough work to be done so that the learner engages in the generative processes of selecting, organizing, and integrating. A related approach is to ask learners to compare their illustrations to an author-provided illustration, although this approach should be used sparingly because it can be a time-consuming and laborious activity. Students could benefit from a discussion in which they compare their drawings with those of other students as a way of improving their skill in using drawing as a generative learning strategy. Finally, it is useful for students to develop productive beliefs about the usefulness of learning strategies such as drawing.

CONCLUSION

Overall, research on drawing as a learning strategy has a long history dating back more than thirty years, but a more recent explosion of research within the past ten years (mainly by Leutner and colleagues) has helped create a research base that simply cannot be ignored. There is strong evidence that learner-generated drawing can help students learn more deeply from science text, under appropriate conditions, so drawing has earned a place in the arsenal of learning strategies (Leutner & Schmeck, 2014; Pashler et al., 2007; Weinstein & Mayer, 1986; Wittrock, 1990). More work is needed to determine the robustness of learner-generated drawing effects beyond the monumental and continuing work of Leutner and colleagues. In addition, work is needed to determine the optimal level of guidance and support for various kinds of learners, and the degree to which drawing can enhance learning in domains other than the sciences.

REFERENCES

Ainsworth, S., Prain, V., & Tytler, R. (2011). Drawing to learn in science. *Science*, 333, 1096–7.

Alesandrini, K. L. (1981). Pictorial-verbal and analytic-holistic learning strategies in science learning. *Journal of Educational Psychology*, 73, 358–68.

Gobert, J. D., & Clement, J. J. (1999). Effects of student-generated diagrams versus student-generated summaries on conceptual understanding of causal and dynamic knowledge in plate tectonics. *Journal of Research in Science Teaching*, 36, 39–53.

Hall, V. C., Bailey, J., & Tillman, C. (1997). Can student-generated illustrations be worth ten thousand words? *Journal of Educational Psychology*, 89, 677–81.

Holley, C.D., Dansereau, D. F., McDonald, B. A., Garland, J. C., & Collins, K. W. (1979). Evaluation of a hierarchical mapping technique as an aid to prose processing. *Contemporary Educational Psychology*, 4, 227–37.

Igo, B. L., & Kiewra, K. A. (2007). How do high-achieving students approach web-based, copy and paste note taking? Selective pasting and related learning outcomes. *Journal of Advanced Academics*, 18, 512–29.

Kauffman, D. F., Zhao, R., & Yang, Y. (2011). Effects of online note taking formats and self-monitoring prompts on learning from online text: using technology to enhance self-regulated learning. *Contemporary Educational Psychology*, 36, 313–22.

Leopold, C., & Leutner, D. (2012). Science text comprehension: drawing, main idea selection, and summarizing as learning strategies. *Learning and Instruction*, 22, 16–26.

Leutner, D, Leopold, C., & Sumfleth, E. (2009). Cognitive load and science text comprehension: effects of drawing and mental imagining text content. *Computers in Human Behavior*, 25, 284–9.

Leutner, D., & Schmeck, A. (2014). The drawing principle in multimedia learning. In R. E. Mayer (Ed.), *The Cambridge Handbook of Multimedia Learning* (pp. 433–48). New York, NY: Cambridge University Press.

Levin, J. R., & Mayer, R. E. (1993). Understanding illustrations in text. In B. Britton, A. Woodward, & M. Binkley (Eds.), *Learning from Textbooks: Theory and Practice* (pp. 95–113). Hillsdale, NJ: Erlbaum.

Mayer, R. E. (1993). Illustrations that instruct. In R. Glaser (Ed.), *Advances in Instructional Psychology* (vol. 4; pp. 253–84). Hillsdale, NJ: Erlbaum.

Nesbit, J. C., & Adesope, O. O. (2006). Learning with concept and knowledge maps: a meta-analysis. *Review of Educational Research*, 76, 413–48.

Novak, J. D. (1998). *Learning, Creating, and Using Knowledge: Concept Maps as Facilitative Tools in Schools and Corporations*. Mahwah, NJ: Erlbaum.

Pashler, H., Bain, P., Bottage, B., Graesser, A. Koedinger, K., McDaniel, M., & Metcalfe, J. (2007). *Organizing Instruction and Study to Improve Student Learning*. Washington, DC: National Center for Educational Research.

Ponce, H. R., & Mayer, R. E. (2014). Qualitatively different cognitive processing during online reading primed by different study activities. *Computers in Human Behavior*, 30, 121–30.

Schwamborn, A., Mayer, R. E., Thillmann, H., Leopold, C., & Leutner, D. (2010a). Drawing as a generative activity and drawing as a prognostic activity. *Journal of Educational Psychology*, 102, 872–9.

Schwamborn, A., Thillmann, H., Leopold, C., Sumfleth, E., & Leutner, D. (2010b). Der Einsatz von vorgegebenen und selbst generierten Bildern als Textverstehenshilfe beim Lernen aus einem naturwissenschaftlichen Sachtext [Using presented and self-generated pictures as learning aids for learning from science text]. *Zeitschrift fur Padagogische Psychologie*, 24, 221–33.

Schwamborn, A., Thillmann, H., Opfermann, M., & Leutner, D. (2011). Cognitive load and instructionally supported learning with provided and learner-generated visualizations. *Computers in Human Behavior*, 27, 89–93.

Stull, A., & Mayer, R. E. (2007). Learning by doing versus learning by viewing: three experimental comparisons of learner-generated versus author-provided graphic organizers. *Journal of Educational Psychology*, 99, 808–20.

Van Meter, P. (2001). Drawing construction as a strategy for learning from text. *Journal of Educational Psychology*, 69, 129–40.

Van Meter, P., Aleksic, M., Schwartz, A., & Garner, J. (2006). Learner-generated drawing as a strategy for learning from content area text. *Contemporary Educational Psychology*, 31, 142–66.

Van Meter, P., & Garner, J. (2005). The promise and practice of learner-generated drawing: literature review and synthesis. *Educational Psychology Review*, 17, 285–325.

Weinstein, C. E., & Mayer, R. E. (1986). The teaching of learning strategies. In M. C. Wittrock (Ed.), *Handbook of Research on Teaching* (pp. 315–27). New York, NY: Macmillan.

Wittrock, M. C. (1990). Generative processes of comprehension. *Educational Psychologist*, 24, 345–76.

5

Learning by Imagining

SUMMARY

Learning by imagining occurs when learners are asked to form mental images that illustrate the content of a text-based lesson. Learning by imagining includes determining which components to include in an image and how to arrange them spatially to show their structural and causal connections. For example, learners who read a lesson on how the human respiratory system works can be asked to form a mental image corresponding to text about the structure or process of the system. The theoretical rationale for imagining as a learning strategy is that the act of forming mental images that correspond to text can prime the generative processes of selecting (in which learners choose which components to include), organizing (in which learners arrange the components in a spatial layout), and integrating (in which learners translate words to pictures). Although imagining is intended to foster generative processing, an important consideration is that learners need a high level of motivation to persist on a task that requires no overt activity. The empirical rationale for imagining is that asking students to create mental images for a lesson improved performance on transfer and retention tests in sixteen out of twenty-two cases as compared against a control group that was not asked to imagine, yielding a median effect size of $d = 0.65$. Regarding boundary conditions, the imagination effect is stronger for learners who are high in experience and when the materials are well designed ($d = 0.77$ based on sixteen comparisons). In terms of practical applications, imagining may serve as a powerful alternative to drawing as a generative learning strategy, as long as students receive appropriate guidance in what to imagine and have sufficient knowledge to carry out the task.

BOX 1. *Overview of Learning by Imagining*

Definition	Learners form mental images to illustrate the content of a lesson.
Example	Learners are asked to read a lesson on chemical processes in washing with soap and water and mentally imagine the content of each section of the lesson while reading.
Theoretical rationale	Asking learners to create mental images is intended to encourage them to identify key components in the text for their image (i.e., engage in the cognitive process of selecting), spatially arrange the components in their image (i.e., engage in the cognitive process of organizing), and relate them to prior knowledge through translating from verbal to visual forms of representation (i.e., engage in the cognitive process of integrating). Although imagining is intended to foster generative processing (involving selecting, organizing, and integrating), it requires high levels of motivation for completion because there is no overt activity as there is in drawing.
Empirical rationale	The imagination effect is upheld in sixteen of twenty-two tests, yielding a median effect size of $d = 0.65$.
Boundary conditions	The imagination effect is strongest when learners are high in experience and when the materials are well designed ($d = 0.77$ based on sixteen comparisons).
Applications	Imagining applies to learning from well-designed procedural manuals or scientific text within paper-based learning environments, but students may need to possess enough prior knowledge to create useful images.

CHAPTER OUTLINE

1. Example of Imagining as a Learning Strategy
2. What Is Learning by Imagining?
3. How Does Imagining Foster Learning?
4. What Is the Evidence for Imagining?
5. What Are the Boundary Conditions for Imagining?
6. How Can We Apply Imagining?
7. Conclusion

EXAMPLE OF IMAGINING AS A LEARNING STRATEGY

Suppose you are reading a lesson on how the human respiratory system works. Please read the following paragraph on the left side, and on the right side please imagine an illustration to accompany the text.

The thoracic cavity is the space in the chest that contains the lungs. It is surrounded by the rib cage, which can move slightly inward or outward, and has the diaphragm on the bottom, which has a dome that can move downward. The main muscles involved in respiration are the diaphragm and the rib muscles. The diaphragm is located underneath the lungs. It lines the lower part of the thoracic cavity, sealing it off air-tight from the rest of the body. The rib muscles are attached to the ribs, which in turn encircle the lungs. When in the relaxed position, the ribs are slightly inward and the diaphragm dome curves upward	**Please imagine the structure of the thoracic portion, consisting of the thoracic cavity, lungs, rib cage, and diaphragm.**

Next, read the following paragraph on the left side, and on the right side please imagine an illustration to accompany it.

During inhaling, a signal from the brain to inhale causes the dome of the diaphragm to contract downward and the rib cage to move slightly outward creating more space in the thoracic cavity into which the lungs can expand. Air is drawn in through the nose or mouth and moves down through the windpipe and bronchial tubes to tiny air sacs in the lungs.	**Please imagine the steps in the thoracic cavity when the diaphragm and rib muscles receive a signal to inhale.**

Now, using what you have read, please explain how this portion of the human respiratory system works.

Please write your explanation of how this portion of the human respiratory system works, in the box below.

```
┌─────────────────────────────────────────────────────────┐
│                                                           │
│                                                           │
│                                                           │
│                                                           │
│                                                           │
│                                                           │
│                                                           │
│                                                           │
│                                                           │
│                                                           │
└─────────────────────────────────────────────────────────┘
```

If you are like most people in a recent study by Leopold and Mayer (in press), the act of imagining the content of a text helped you understand the lesson. As you can see, the first paragraph described the structure of the thoracic cavity, so imagining could help you understand and remember the main components and their spatial relations. In contrast, the second paragraph described the step-by-step process of events in the thoracic cavity, so imagining could help you understand and remember the causal relations between a change in one component and a change in another component. Across two experiments, students who were given pretraining in how to form useful mental images for scientific text and who were given specific prompts to form images as they read about the structure or process of a portion of the respiratory system performed better on tests of retention and transfer than students who read the text without being asked to imagine. In this chapter, we examine whether imagining the content of a lesson can be an effective learning strategy.

WHAT IS LEARNING BY IMAGINING?

Learning by imagining occurs when learners form mental images that illustrate the content of a lesson. For purposes of this chapter, the content of the lesson can be an expository text passage that describes or explains an academic topic (such as imagining illustrations to accompany a lesson on how the human respiratory system works), a manual that shows how to carry out a task (such as how to use a spreadsheet program), or a table or graph that shows the relation between two variables (such as a bus timetable or a time-temperature graph). In this chapter, we do not focus on the role of the learner's imagery in lessons whose content consists of paired associates (such as using imagery mnemonics for foreign language vocabulary or word definitions) or a motor skill (such as mental practice for golf swings), although there is some evidence for imagination effects within each of these related domains.

The act of imagining can occur with different presentation media and imagination media. Concerning the presentation medium, the lesson can be presented on paper (such as in a textbook) or via computer (such as in an online encyclopedia). Concerning the imagination medium, learners can be asked to form an image within a space on the page or screen (such as in an empty box or window) or to look away and form a "picture in your head."

The act of imagining can occur with different formats and content. Concerning the format of what is imagined, learners can form static images (such as a mental illustration) or dynamic images (such as a mental movie). Concerning the content of what is imagined, learners can visualize the steps in carrying out a procedure (such as what happens when you program a spreadsheet to compute with a formula), the structure of a system (such as how the parts of the human respiratory system fit together), or the causal process of a system (such as the cause-and-effect relations between how a change in one part causes a change in another part of the system). In this chapter, we do not focus on decorative images (which are not relevant to the instructional goal) or representational images (which are simple pictures of one element in the lesson).

Finally, the act of imagining can be supported by different levels of guidance: (a) imaginers can receive general prompts (e.g., "make a picture in your head") or specific prompts (e.g., "imagine a textbook illustration to accompany this paragraph that shows the lungs, rib cage, and diaphragm within the thoracic cavity"); (b) imaginers can have or not have pretraining or practice in how to form useful images; and (c) imaginers can not ever see an author-generated drawing or later see an author-generated drawing to which they can compare their mental image.

Thus, learning by imagining is a collection of learning strategies that can be implemented in different ways and in different contexts, some of which are examined in the research base summarized in this chapter. The most common scenario is to ask learners to form images with some guidance after each section of a short academic lesson and then take an immediate learning outcome test.

HOW DOES IMAGINING FOSTER LEARNING?

Generative learning occurs when learners engage in appropriate cognitive processing during learning, including selecting the relevant information in the lesson, organizing it into a coherent mental representation, and integrating it with relevant knowledge activated from long-term memory. According to the multimedia learning principle (Butcher, 2014; Mayer, 2009), generative learning is epitomized by asking learners to make connections between verbal and visual representations. This is exactly what happens when learners are asked to translate verbal lessons into mental images. Thus, asking learners to create mental images is intended to encourage them to identify key components in the text for their image (i.e., engage in the cognitive process of selecting), generate an image and spatially arrange the components in their image (i.e., engage in the cognitive process of organizing), and relate these components to prior knowledge through translating from verbal to visual forms of representation (i.e., engage in the cognitive process of integrating). These three processes are summarized in Table 5.1.

Imagining may have some cognitive advantages as compared to drawing, because it does not depend on the mechanics of drawing – that is, learners do not need to be able to use a computer drawing interface or to be artistically proficient in making drawings. By reducing extraneous cognitive load caused by the mechanics of drawing, imagining strategies may be able to prime generative processes without taking away the capacity to implement them. Similarly, imaginers may be able to persist through longer lessons because they do not suffer from the physical fatigue of using their hands to make drawings. On the other hand, imaginers may need higher levels of motivation and conscientiousness to not cut corners because there is no overt indication that the mental drawing is completed. This is why some level of guidance may be useful to helping imaginers know what

TABLE 5.1. *Why imaging works: three cognitive processes activated by imagining*

Cognitive process	How imagining primes the process
Selecting	Learners choose which components to put into their image.
Organizing	Learners mentally arrange the components into a spatial layout.
Integrating	Learners translate from one mode of representation into another, such as from words to pictures, which requires connecting incoming information with knowledge activated from long-term memory.

to do. Imagining may be more cognitively demanding than drawing (as discussed in Chapter 4), because pictorial images must be continuously held in working memory, whereas drawing offloads some of the cognitive work onto the paper or screen.

WHAT IS THE EVIDENCE FOR IMAGINING?

Can we achieve some of the advantages of drawing without having to deal with the mechanics of drawing? One emerging approach is to ask learners to imagine a visualization that corresponds to the text in a lesson. This approach is encouraged by a rich tradition of previous research in other learning domains showing the benefits of (a) imagery mnemonics for memorizing word lists and paired associates (e.g., Dunlosky et al., 2013; Jones et al., 2000; Raugh & Atkinson, 1975); (b) the role of mental practice in improving motor skill performance (e.g., Driskell, Copper, & Moran, 1994); and (c) the effectiveness of forming a "picture in your head" as students read stories (e.g., De Koning and van der Schoot, 2013; Dunlosky, et al., 2013; Pressley, 1977).

Imagination Effects in Comprehension of Stories

Although this chapter focuses on imagination effects in learning of academic content, a closely related literature examines imagination effects in comprehension of stories. For example, Bender and Levin (1978) asked ten-to-sixteen-year-old students who were designated as developmentally delayed to listen to a twenty-sentence story while generating "mental pictures of the story" (the imagining group) or not (the control group). Imagining instructions did not result in significantly better performance on a comprehension post-test, but insufficient information was presented to allow computation of effect size. Adding author-drawn pictures greatly improved post-test performance, suggesting that the students had difficulty in generating useful images on their own. In contrast, Giesen and Peeck (1984) found that for college students, instructions to form mental images while reading a story resulted in better comprehension test performance.

As a complement to early research with stories, Anderson and Kulhavy (1972) asked twelfth graders to form mental images of the content as they read a two thousand–word expository text about the characteristics of a fictitious tribe (the imagining group) or to read carefully (the control group). Imagining instructions did not significantly improve performance on a comprehension test, but many students in the imagining group reported not forming images and many control students did. Means and standard deviations were not reported, so it is not possible to compute effect size, but it appears that students may need some guidance in imagining.

The foregoing studies suggest that some students may have difficulty in forming mental images that help them learn, so let's consider what happens when students are given basic training and practice in how to form images for narrative prose (i.e., stories). In a landmark study, Pressley (1976) asked third-graders to read a 950-word story while making "pictures in your head" of the events in the story (the imagining group) or "doing whatever you can in order to remember" (the control group). The imagining group received pretraining and practice in how to form images for sentences, paragraphs, and a short story. The imagining group (which received pretraining) performed better than the control group on a comprehension post-test ($d = 0.54$).

Gambrell and Jawitz (1993) asked fourth graders to read a 925-word story while making "as many pictures as you can in your head about the things you read" (the imagining group) or trying "very hard to remember what you read" (the control group). The imagining group greatly outperformed the control group on a free recall test ($d = 0.92$) and a cued recall test ($d = 0.41$), which we combined into a retention score ($d = 0.66$). Oakhill and Patel (1991) reported that imagery training was helpful for poor comprehenders but not for good comprehenders, suggesting a possible boundary condition.

What would happen if beginning readers were given extensive training in how to form mental images as they listen to stories? In a study by Center and colleagues (1999), seven-year-olds received training and practice in how to form useful mental images of spoken stories across twelve practice lessons (the imagining group) or simply received practice in comprehending spoken stories across twelve practice lessons (the control group). On subsequent standardized listening and reading comprehension tests, the imagining group outperformed the control group, yielding a median effect size of $d = 0.46$.

In a recent review of research on the effects of imagery strategies on comprehension of stories, De Koning and van der Schoot (2013) concluded that "make a picture in your head" instruction "is most likely to result in improved reading comprehension for elementary school children and readers identified as poor comprehenders" (p. 269) and pointed to the need for explicit instruction in how to mentally visualize. In another recent review, Dunlosky and colleagues (2013) pointed out that imagination effects are most common for stories that can easily be visualized and for tests that do not require extensive transfer. These encouraging results with imagination effects for story comprehension suggest the value of examining imagining effects in academic learning.

Imagination Effects in Academic Learning

Following this tantalizing overview on the effects of imagining on story comprehension, in this section, we explore whether imagining techniques can improve academic learning beyond remembering the content of narratives. Table 5.2 summarizes twenty-two experimental comparisons on measures of learning outcome between a group that read an academic text or academic material and a group that read and also formed a mental image of sections of the presented content. The comparisons were published in research journals and provide sufficient information to compute Cohen's d. Overall, in sixteen of twenty-two comparisons, engaging in imagining as a learning strategy improved learning, with a median effect size of $d = 0.65$.

A pioneering study by Rasco, Tennyson, and Boutwell (1975) found some evidence that asking students to "form as many mental images as you can to help you recall the information" as they read an expository text resulted in better performance on a comprehension post-test than not asking students to form mental images of the material. However, the study is not included in Table 5.2 because not enough information was provided to allow for computation of effect size.

A set of studies by Cooper and colleagues (2001) initiated current efforts to understand the cognitive consequences of imagining during academic learning. Seventh graders received a three-part computer-based lesson on how to set up a spreadsheet to solve formulas, in which each section contained a text description followed by a worked example. As pretraining, students in the imagining group were instructed to "try to imagine the procedures presented" in the text before proceeding to the worked example. For example, students in the imagining group were asked to consider a simple example such as $(25 + 10)/5$ by "imagining in your mind the steps required to add 25 to 10 together and then divide the answer by 5." Then, within each section of the lesson, they were asked to "turn away from the screen and imagine performing the steps demonstrated." In contrast, students in the control group where asked to "try to understand and remember the procedures presented." As can be seen in Table 5.2, for high-knowledge learners and high-achieving students, the imagining group greatly outperformed the control group ($ds = 0.63, 1.50$, and 0.94) on a transfer test

TABLE 5.2. *How well does imagining work: summary of comparisons between imagining and control groups*

Citation	Population	Subject	Medium	Outcome	Effect size
Cooper et al. (2001, Expt. 1, untimed, high knowledge)	Middle school	Spreadsheet	Computer	Transfer	0.63
Cooper et al. (2001, Expt. 2, untimed, high knowledge)	Middle school	Spreadsheet	Computer	Transfer	1.50
Cooper et al. (2001, Expt. 3, untimed, low knowledge)	Middle school	Spreadsheet	Computer	Transfer	−1.13
Cooper et al. (2001, Expt. 4, untimed, higher achieving)	Middle school	Spreadsheet	Computer	Transfer	0.94
Cooper et al. (2001, Expt. 4, untimed, lower achieving)	Middle school	Spreadsheet	Computer	Transfer	−0.95
Ginns et al. (2003, Expt. 1, untimed, low knowledge)	College	Programming	Computer	Transfer	−0.83
Ginns et al. (2003, Expt. 2, untimed, high knowledge)	Middle school	Geometry	Paper	Transfer	1.14
Leahy & Sweller (2004, Expt. 1, timed)	Adults	Contour maps	Paper	Transfer	0.54
Leahy & Sweller (2004, Expt. 2a, timed, integrated)	Elementary school	Temperature graphs	Paper	Transfer	1.25
Leahy & Sweller (2004, Expt. 2b, timed, split)	Elementary school	Temperature graphs	Paper	Transfer	−0.35
Leahy & Sweller (2005, Expt. 1, timed, high experience)	Elementary school	Bus timetables	Paper	Transfer	0.57
Leahy & Sweller (2005, Expt. 2, timed, low experience)	Elementary school	Bus timetables	Paper	Transfer	−0.62

Study	Level	Topic	Medium	Measure	Effect size
Leahy & Sweller (2005, Expt. 2, timed, high experience)	Elementary school	Temperature graphs	Paper	Transfer	0.67
Leahy & Sweller (2005, Expt. 2, timed, low experience)	Elementary school	Temperature graphs	Paper	Transfer	−0.89
Leahy & Sweller (2008, timed)	Elementary school	Bus timetables	Paper	Transfer	0.80
Leutner et al. (2009, timed)	High school	Water molecules	Paper	Comprehension	0.57
Leopold & Mayer (in press, Expt. 1a, untimed)	College	Respiratory system	Computer	Transfer	1.30
Leopold & Mayer (in press, Expt. 1a, untimed)	College	Respiratory system	Computer	Retention	0.80
Leopold & Mayer (in press, Expt. 1b, untimed, supported)	College	Respiratory system	Computer	Transfer	0.61
Leopold & Mayer (in press, Expt. 1b, untimed, supported)	College	Respiratory system	Computer	Retention	0.44
Leopold & Mayer (in press, Expt. 2, untimed)	College	Respiratory system	Computer	Transfer	0.86
Leopold & Mayer (in press, Expt. 2, untimed)	College	Respiratory system	Computer	Retention	0.74
MEDIAN					0.65

involving solving new spreadsheet problems. In contrast, for low-knowledge or low-achieving students, the opposite pattern emerged ($ds = -1.13$ and -0.95). The authors conclude that imagining can be an effective learning strategy when learners possess prerequisite schemas.

A complementary set of experiments by Ginns, Chandler, and Sweller (2003) using different materials also found that imagination strategies are more effective for high-knowledge learners rather than low-knowledge learners. In Experiment 1, non–computer science college students who had minimal prior knowledge learned to write programs using the programming language HTML in a computer-based lesson. At the end of each example in the lesson, students in the imagining group were told: "Now look away from the screen and try to imagine the steps involving [a given web page effect]. You will have one minute." In contrast, at the end of each example, students in the control group were told: "Now study the steps used to create [a given web page effect]. You will have one minute." On a subsequent transfer test involving new programming problems, the control group outperformed the imagination group ($d = -0.83$).

In Experiment 2 of the Ginns, Chandler, and Sweller (2003) paper, seventh graders who had prior knowledge in geometry received a lesson in which they learned two rules for solving geometry problems, with each section describing the rule and then providing a worked example. Students were given pretraining in imagining using the arithmetic problem $(25 + 10)/5$ as described for the Cooper and colleagues (2001) study. For each worked example, students in the imagining group were asked to imagine each of the steps in the worked example for three minutes, whereas students in the control group were asked to study each of the steps in the worked example for three minutes. On a subsequent transfer test involving new geometry problems, the imagining group outperformed the control group ($d = 1.14$). Thus, as in the Cooper and colleagues (2001) study, Ginns, Chandler, and Sweller (2003) found that imagining can be an effective learning strategy when learners possess prerequisite knowledge.

Leahy and Sweller (2005) provide replication evidence for the boundary condition concerning prior knowledge, in which imagination effects were positive for high-knowledge learners ($ds = 0.57$ and 0.67) but negative for low-knowledge learners ($ds = -0.62$ and -0.89) in studies involving elementary school children learning to read temperature graphs and bus timetables, respectively. In a replication by Leahy and Sweller (2008), elementary school students who learned to read bus timetables by imagining the steps described in numbered annotations on each timetable performed much better on a transfer post-test than those who learned by studying the steps (d = 0.80). Overall, this line of research provides strong and consistent support for the imagination effect in learning the steps in a procedure.

To examine the robustness of the imagining effect, Leahy and Sweller (2004) conducted a set of experiments involving new learning tasks – reading contour maps and reading temperature graphs. In Experiment 1, elementary school teachers read a two-page lesson from a high school geometry curriculum on contour maps, in which they saw contour maps along with five numbered text annotations describing the steps in creating the graph. Students in the imagining group were asked to avert or close their eyes and imagine the actions involved in each step, whereas students in the control group were asked to study the steps. Across a set of four transfer test problems, the imagining group outperformed the control group (d = 0.54), thus providing additional evidence for the imagination effect.

In Experiment 2 of the Leahy and Sweller (2004) paper, fourth graders learned to read five temperature graphs showing the relation between time of day on the x-axis and temperature on the y-axis, along with numbered text annotations explaining each step in interpreting the graph. Students in the imagining group were asked to turn away or close their eyes and imagine the actions involved in each step, whereas students in the control group were asked to study each step. When the annotations were embedded in the graph (i.e., an integrated format), the imagining group performed much better than the control group on a subsequent transfer test (d = 1.25), but not when the annotations were separated from the graphs and placed on a separate page (d = –0.35). Thus, this study complements previous ones by adding another important boundary condition: imagining is more effective for presentation formats that minimize rather than maximize extraneous cognitive load, thereby leaving cognitive capacity for the deeper processing involved in imagining.

How does imagining work for a text lesson that explains how a scientific system works, similar to the materials in much of the research on drawing as a generative activity in the previous chapter? Leutner, Leopold, and Sumfleth (2009) asked German tenth grade students to read a 1,600-word text (in German) on water molecules, broken into thirteen paragraphs, and to imagine the content of each paragraph (the imagining group) or to study the paragraph (the control group). The imagining group scored higher than the control group on a comprehension post-test (d = 0.57). In contrast, as described in Chapter 4 on drawing, Leutner, Leopold, and Sumfleth (2009) reported that asking students to draw a picture of the content of each paragraph produced only a small positive effect (d = 0.23). Thus, in the only study to compare the effectiveness of drawing and imagining directly, the more powerful learning strategy is imagining, perhaps because imagining avoids the extraneous processing created by the mechanics of drawing.

In another extension of the imagination effect to learning with scientific text, Leopold and Mayer (in press) asked college students to read an eight hundred–word lesson broken into nine paragraphs on how the human respiratory system works. The lesson was presented one paragraph at a time via a computer with the learner told to press a continue key to go on to the next paragraph. Some students (the imagining group) were given pretraining in how to form useful mental images of scientific text and were given specific prompts along with each paragraph to imagine an illustration in a space provided on the right side of the screen. Across two experiments, the imagining group outperformed students who were not instructed to imagine (the control group) on both transfer tests (ds = 1.30 and 0.86) and retention tests (ds = 0.80 and 0.74). When extra support was provided to the imagining group by showing them an instructor-generated drawing after they formed an image, the imagination effect was diminished (d = 0.61 for transfer and d = 0.44 on retention in Experiment 1). Presumably, students in the imagining group did not work as hard to create mental images because they knew they would be shown the "correct" illustration. Although the results of Leopold and Mayer's study add support for the imagination effect with scientific text, it should be noted that the imagining group also took more time with the lesson than the control group.

Overall, this line of research provides strong and consistent support for the idea that imagining can increase transfer and comprehension performance, yielding an effect size in the medium-to-large range (d = 0.65). The effect size is greatest when we discard studies with inexperienced learners or poorly designed instruction, both of which tend to create extraneous cognitive load that can interfere with the imagination process (d = 0.77 based on sixteen comparisons). There is initial evidence that imagining can be more effective than drawing (Leutner, Leopold, & Sumfleth, 2009), perhaps because it eliminates any difficulties with the mechanics of drawing. Thus, this review shows that within the last ten to fifteen years, evidence has accumulated showing the potential benefits of imagining as a generative learning strategy. Imagining can take its place among evidence-based learning strategies for academic learning, indicating an extension beyond classic evidence on imagery mnemonics for improving memory of word lists and paired associates (e.g., Levin et al., 1982; Pressley, 1977; Raugh & Atkinson, 1975) and imaginary practice for improving motor skill learning (e.g., Driskell, Copper, & Moran, 1994).

WHAT ARE THE BOUNDARY CONDITIONS
FOR IMAGINING?

A careful review of Table 5.2 reveals two important barriers to the imagination effect: low experience and poor instructional design. In the five comparisons involving students with low experience, low prior knowledge, or low proficiency, the imagination effect reverses with a median effect size of $d = -0.89$ (based on five comparisons) in which imagining hurts test performance. Students who lack the knowledge or skill to create useful images may engage in extraneous processing that reduces the cognitive capacity needed to make sense of the material. In one comparison involving poorly designed materials (i.e., a separated presentation in which printed words are far away from corresponding graphics), the imagination effect reverses with an effect size of $d = -0.35$, indicating that imagining hurts test performance. In this case, extraneous cognitive load created by poorly designed materials may have interfered with the learner's capacity to engage in productive imagining. Overall, imagining improves transfer and comprehension performance when the learners are not low in experience and the instructional materials are not poorly designed ($d = 0.77$ based on sixteen comparisons). These boundary conditions are summarized in Table 5.3. Another potential boundary condition ripe for future research concerns the amount of training in how to imagine.

It should be noted that most of the studies in Table 5.2 come from the lab of Sweller and colleagues and focus on procedural tasks, such as using a

TABLE 5.3. *When does imagining work: boundary conditions for imagining*

	Median imagination effect	Explanation
Conditions that hurt		
Students lack prior knowledge or proficiency	$d = -0.89$ based on five comparisons	Act of imagining creates too much extraneous cognitive processing
Instructional materials are poorly designed	$d = -0.35$ based on one comparison	Extraneous processing caused by poor design leaves insufficient capacity for imagining
Conditions that help		
Students have sufficient knowledge and proficiency, and instructional materials are well designed	$d = 0.77$ based on sixteen comparisons	Learners have sufficient cognitive capacity to engage in imagining

spreadsheet or bus timetable. Research is needed to examine the robustness of the imagination effect within different research labs and with different kinds of instructional content, such as explanations of how scientific systems work. Leutner, Leopold, and Sumfleth's (2009) study is a useful preliminary step in that direction, as is the recent paper by Leopold and Mayer (in press).

HOW CAN WE APPLY IMAGINING?

Although imagining has been shown to be an effective learning strategy in some assorted short-term laboratory experiments, you might wonder how the imagining strategy should be applied in authentic learning environments, such as helping students study from textbooks, online lessons, or face-to-face presentations. Based on the research reviewed in this chapter, there is some justification for judiciously applying the imagining strategy to some everyday learning situations, particularly those in which students learn about scientific systems from reading a scientific text or learn the steps in how to carry out a procedure from reading a manual or an annotated chart. So far, we only know that imagining can help in the short term when used on a short lesson, so a good place initially to apply the imagining strategy is to short lessons or to part of a longer module.

Three important considerations in applying the imagining strategy concern the need to provide training, to use specific prompts, and to ensure that students have sufficient knowledge and proficiency. First, students may need explicit training and practice in how to form useful mental images for printed (or even spoken) text, which should include practice with feedback. Second, students may need focused prompts during learning that specify the content of the to-be-formed images. Third, students need to have sufficient knowledge and skill in the domain of the lesson so that the task of imagining does not overload working memory. Thus, imagining might not be the best technique when students are just starting out on the first section of a highly unfamiliar topic.

CONCLUSION

The research reviewed in this chapter provides some preliminary encouragement to continue to pursue the intriguing idea that imagining can be a useful learning strategy. However, further work is needed to address issues such as (a) how much and what kind of activity should be included in imagination training, (b) how imagining strategies can be effectively applied across an entire course rather than a one- or two-page lesson, (c) how well imagining works in learning from face-to-face presentations, and (d) what role is played by individual differences in spatial ability and visualizer-verbalizer learning style. It is also worthwhile to determine whether the effects of imagining can be attributed to increased study time, by incorporating control groups that study the material for the same amount of time as the imagining group. An important and understudied ingredient underlying the imagination effect concerns the role of learner motivation to form images. Overall, we see imagining strategies as having potential for improving learning, and therefore imagining deserves to be included in the learning strategy toolbox.

REFERENCES

Anderson, R. C. & Kulhavy, R. W. (1972). Imagery and prose learning. *Journal of Educational Psychology*, 63, 242–3.

Bender, B. G., & Levin, J. R. (1978). Pictures, imagery, and retarded children's prose learning. *Journal of Educational Psychology*, 70, 583–8.

Butcher, K. (2014). Multimedia principle. In R. E. Mayer (Ed.), *The Cambridge Handbook of Multimedia Learning* (pp. 174–205). New York, NY: Cambridge University Press.

Center, Y., Freeman, L., Robertson, G., & Outred, L. (1999). The effect of visual imagery training on the reading and listening comprehension of low listening comprehenders in year 2. *Journal of Research in Reading*, 22, 241–56.

Cooper, G., Tindall-Ford, S., Chandler, P., & Swller, J. (2001). Learning by imagining. *Journal of Experimental Psychology: Applied*, 7, 68–82.

De Koning, B. B., & van der Schoot, M. (2013). Becoming part of the story! Refueling interest in visualization strategies for reading comprehension. *Educational Psychology Review*, 25, 261–87.

Driskell, J.E., Copper, C., & Moran, A. (1994). Does mental practice enhance performance? *Journal of Applied Psychology*, 79, 481–92.

Dunlosky, J., Rawson, K. A., Marsh, E. J., Nathan, M. J., & Willingham, D. T. (2013). Improving students' learning with effective learning techniques: promising directions from cognitive and educational psychology. *Psychological Science in the Public Interest*, 14(1), 3–58.

Gambrell, L. B., & Jawitz, P. B. (1993). Mental imagery, text illustrations, and children's story comprehension and recall. *Reading Research Quarterly*, 28, 264–76.

Giesen, C., & Peeck, J. (1984). Effects of imagery instruction on reading and retaining literary text. *Journal of Mental Imagery*, 8, 79–90.

Ginns, P., Chandler, P., & Sweller, J. (2003). When imagining is effective. *Contemporary Educational Psychology*, 28, 229–51.

Jones, M. L., Levin, M. E., Levin, J. R., & Beitzel, B. D. (2000). Can vocabulary-learning strategies and pair-learning formats be profitably combined? *Journal of Educational Psychology*, 92, 256–62.

Leahy, W., & Sweller, J. (2004). Cognitive load and the imagination effect. *Applied Cognitive Psychology*, 18, 857–75.

(2005). Interactions among the imagination, expertise reversal, and element interactivity effects. *Journal of Experimental Psychology: Applied*, 11, 266–76.

(2008). The imagination effect increases with an increased intrinsic cognitive load. *Applied Cognitive Psychology*, 22, 273–83.

Leopold, C., & Mayer, R. E. (in press). An imagination effect in learning from scientific text. *Journal of Educational Psychology*, 106, 000–000.

Leutner, D, Leopold, C., & Sumfleth, E. (2009). Cognitive load and science text comprehension: effects of drawing and mental imagining text content. *Computers in Human Behavior*, 25, 284–9.

Levin, J. R., McCormick, C. B., Miller, G. E., Berry, J. K., & Pressley, M. (1982). Mnemonic versus nonmnemonic vocabulary learning strategies for children. *American Educational Research Journal*, 19, 121–36.

Mayer, R. E. (2009). *Multimedia Learning* (2nd ed.). New York, NY: Cambridge University Press.

Oakhill, J., & Patel, S. (1991). Can imagery training help children who have comprehension problems? *Journal of Research in Reading*, 14, 106–15.

Pressley, M. (1976). Mental imagery helps eight-year olds remember what they read. *Journal of Educational Psychology*, 68, 355–9.

(1977). Children's use of the keyword method to learn simple Spanish vocabulary words. *Journal of Educational Psychology*, 69, 465–72.

Rasco, R. W., Tennyson, R. D., & Boutwell, R. C. (1975). Imagery instructions and drawings in learning prose. *Journal of Educational Psychology*, 67, 188–92.

Raugh, M. R., & Atkinson, R. C. (1975). A mnemonic method for learning a second language vocabulary. *Journal of Educational Psychology*, 67, 1–16.

6

Learning by Self-Testing

SUMMARY

Self-testing involves answering practice questions about previously studied material to enhance long-term learning. For example, after reading a chapter in a textbook, a student answers practice questions on the material without referring back to the chapter. In forty-four out of forty-seven experimental tests, students who studied material and then took a practice test performed better on a later test than students who only studied the material (median d = 0.62). Further, in twenty-six of twenty-nine additional comparisons, self-testing was more effective than restudying or otherwise receiving extended study time (median d = 0.43). Concerning boundary conditions, self-testing is most effective when it involves generative tests such as free-recall or cued-recall, when students repeatedly take practice tests, when testing is coupled with corrective feedback, and when there is a relatively close match between the practice test and the final test. Testing can be applied broadly across subject areas and lesson formats, including learning from text, multimedia, and lectures. Overall, there is strong support that self-testing enhances long-term recall of previously learned material; however, more research is needed on the effects of self-testing with more complex learning materials (such as how a scientific process works) and deeper learning outcomes (such as problem-solving transfer).

BOX 1. *Overview of Learning by Self-Testing*	
Definition	Learners test themselves on previously studied material by answering practice questions.
Example	Learners are asked to read an expository text describing a scientific process and then to take a practice cued-recall test about important facts and concepts from the passage.
Theoretical rationale	Asking students to self-test allows students to practice accessing previously learned material from long-term memory (i.e., engage in retrieval practice), which may facilitate the processes of organizing and integrating the material with their existing knowledge, resulting in enhanced long-term memory. Although testing is intended to foster generative processing, the benefits of self-testing may depend on how well learners initially learned the to-be-learned material.
Empirical rationale	Self-testing yielded positive effects in forty-four of forty-seven tests (compared to only studying), yielding a median effect size of $d = 0.62$; and positive effects in twenty-six of twenty-nine tests (compared to extended studying), yielding a median effect size of $d = 0.43$. Overall, the self-testing effect is upheld in seventy of seventy-six tests, yielding a median effect size of $d = 0.57$.
Boundary conditions	The self-testing effect may be strongest when learners receive corrective feedback following practice testing, when practice tests are in a free-recall or cued-recall format (e.g., short-answer) rather than a recognition format (e.g., multiple-choice), when learners repeatedly take practice tests, and when there is a close match between practice test items and the final test.
Applications	Self-testing applies to learning from expository texts within paper-based learning environments, learning from computer-based multimedia, and learning from lecture-based instruction.

CHAPTER OUTLINE

1. Example of Self-Testing as a Learning Strategy
2. What Is Learning by Self-Testing?
3. How Does Self-Testing Foster Learning?
4. What Is the Evidence for Self-Testing?
5. What Are the Boundary Conditions for Self-Testing?
6. How Can We Apply Self-Testing?
7. Conclusion

EXAMPLE OF SELF-LEARNING AS A
LEARNING STRATEGY

Please read the following short passage, which describes important facts about the sun:

The Sun

The Sun today is a yellow dwarf star. It is fueled by thermonuclear reactions near its center that convert hydrogen to helium. The Sun has existed in its present state for about 4 billion, 600 million years and is thousands of times larger than the Earth. By studying other stars, astronomers can predict what the rest of the Sun's life will be like. About 5 billion years from now, the core of the Sun will shrink and become hotter. The surface temperature will fall. The higher temperature of the center will increase the rate of thermonuclear reactions. The outer regions of the Sun will expand approximately 35 million miles, which is about the distance to Mercury. The Sun will then be a red giant star. Temperatures on the Earth will become too hot for life to exist. Once the Sun has used up its thermonuclear energy as a red giant, it will begin to shrink. After it shrinks to the size of the Earth, it will become a white dwarf star. The Sun may throw off huge amounts of gases in violent eruptions called nova explosions as it changes from a red giant to a white dwarf. After billions of years as a white dwarf, the Sun will have used up all its fuel and will have lost its heat. Such a star is called a black dwarf. After the sun has become a black dwarf, the Earth will be dark and cold. If any atmosphere remains there it will have frozen onto the Earth's surface.

Now, without referring back to the passage, please write down everything you can remember from the passage in the following box:

You may think that you have just engaged in an assessment activity –
that is, a test of your ability to recall the passage from memory. However,
research suggests that self-testing is also a powerful *learning* strategy. In
fact, one experiment by Roediger and Karpicke (2006b) found that students
later recalled significantly more facts from passages (such as the preceding
one) for which they took a practice free-recall test than from passages they
read twice without self-testing. This study and many others indicate that
when students practice remembering recently learned material, they are
more likely to be able to access the information in the future.

In this chapter, we explore the available research evidence on the learning benefits of self-testing. In particular, we are concerned with how
testing can be used as a learning strategy to improve learning of meaningful academic materials such as learning from scientific texts, and to promote meaningful learning outcomes as indicated by comprehension and
transfer tests.

WHAT IS LEARNING BY SELF-TESTING?

Self-testing occurs when learners answer practice questions about previously studied material. Although testing is often seen as an assessment tool,
it can also serve as a powerful learning strategy – a finding that is referred
to as the *testing effect* (Roediger & Karpicke, 2006a). Research on the testing
effect is often concerned with studying basic memory processes by asking

participants to memorize word lists (Karpicke & Roediger, 2007b; Zaromb & Roediger, 2010) or paired associates (Kang, McDaniel, & Pashler, 2011; Karpicke & Roediger, 2007a; Vaughn & Rawson, 2011). For example, many studies have shown that people remember word pairs best when they practice using one of the words as a cue and generate the other word on their own, compared to studying both words being presented together (e.g., Karpicke & Roediger, 2007a; Karpicke & Roediger, 2008). While such research demonstrates the importance of retrieval practice for basic memory tasks, its implications for educational practice are somewhat limited (e.g., acquiring foreign language vocabulary; Karpicke & Roediger, 2008; Pavlik & Anderson, 2005). Fortunately, recent research has extended the testing effect to more meaningful learning materials, such as learning from prose passages (e.g., Roediger & Karpicke, 2006b), and more meaningful learning outcomes, such as the ability to transfer knowledge to new situations (e.g., Butler, 2010; Johnson & Mayer, 2009). In this chapter, we focus on how testing can be used to promote meaningful learning of academic material such as prose passages.

According to the testing effect, taking practice tests promotes long-term learning. In a typical experiment, students first study the to-be-learned material once, such as by reading a brief prose passage. Then they take a practice test without referring back to the study materials, such as by taking a multiple-choice quiz or answering short-answer questions. Such practice tests may target the recollection of basic facts, comprehension of important concepts, or the ability to apply concepts to help solve novel problems. Finally, students take a final test of the material (typically days after initial learning), which again assesses students' ability to recall, comprehend, or transfer. Research on the testing effect indicates that students who take practice tests after initial studying generally outperform those who do not take a practice test or those who study the same material again (Roediger & Karpicke, 2006a). This chapter explores the research evidence on the testing effect, its boundary conditions, and how it can be applied to improve academic learning.

HOW DOES SELF-TESTING FOSTER LEARNING?

The testing effect has its roots in the study of basic human memory processes (e.g., Allen, Mahler, & Estes, 1969). For example, many early studies showed that memory is enhanced when people practice retrieving previously studied items (such as words from a word list) compared to restudying the items. Retrieval practice is thought to facilitate memory in part because

---

BOX 2. *Three Cognitive Processes Activated by Self-Testing*

Cognitive process	How self-testing primes the process
Selecting	Learners access essential prior knowledge required to respond to a question.
Organizing	Learners rearrange elements of activated knowledge into a coherent response.
Integrating	Learners restructure activated prior knowledge when responding to a question by connecting it with other relevant knowledge stored in long-term memory.

---

the process of retrieving information reconstructs and strengthens the memory trace for the information. In particular, retrieval creates links with other stored knowledge, allowing the information to be accessed through additional retrieval routes. This process of reconstruction makes it more likely for learners to retrieve the information successfully when provided with similar cues in the future. Thus, the effects of self-testing are often most pronounced on delayed tests (such as one week after initial learning) rather than immediate tests.

When students learn from more meaningful learning materials, such as a prose passages, self-testing may serve to prime the cognitive processes of selecting, organizing, and integrating, as shown in Box 2. Selecting involves activating relevant information from long-term memory that can be used to answer questions from the practice test. Organizing involves rearranging and making connections between the elements of information activated to formulate a coherent response. Integrating involves making connections between the elements of information activated and other relevant knowledge stored in long-term memory. In short, accessing information from long-term memory in order to respond to a question restructures that knowledge in a way that makes it more accessible in the future.

If self-testing enhances long-term learning, its effects are likely to depend somewhat on whether learners possess the necessary knowledge for constructing a coherent response. Thus, the testing effect may bear on whether learners have sufficiently acquired the to-be-learned information during initial studying and therefore are able to access the material successfully while taking a practice test. Further, if testing supports the ability to access the information again in the future, the effect is also likely to depend somewhat on the relationship between the initial testing conditions and the conditions of the final test. For example, taking a practice recall test is likely to facilitate subsequent recall performance, whereas taking a practice transfer test is likely to facilitate subsequent transfer performance. Overall, self-testing provides learners with practice using recently learned material so that they are better able to access it under similar circumstances in the future.

WHAT IS THE EVIDENCE FOR SELF-TESTING?

Table 6.1 presents the effect sizes of forty-seven experimental comparisons investigating the effects of self-testing on learning of meaningful material (i.e., an educationally relevant lesson rather than a word list). Studies included in Table 6.1 consisted of a experimental condition in which students were exposed to the learning material once (e.g., by reading a passage) and then took a practice test on the material (e.g., by taking a cued-recall test), and a control condition in which students were exposed to the information only once and did not receive a practice test. Performance was compared on delayed final tests of the material. Studies that did not involve meaningful learning materials, did not include a control group, did not isolate the effects of testing, or did not include sufficient statistics to calculate effect size were not included in this analysis. The analysis revealed positive effects for self-testing (compared to only studying) in forty-four of forty-seven tests, yielding a median effect size of $d = 0.62$.

Table 6.2 presents the effect sizes of twenty-nine additional comparisons in which self-testing was compared to an active control condition in which students restudied the material – for example, by reading the same passage twice or by studying a summary of the material. Positive effects for self-testing compared to restudying were found in twenty-six of twenty-nine tests, yielding a median effect size of $d = 0.43$. Overall, there is strong evidence for the positive benefits of taking practice tests on long-term learning. In the following subsections, we take a closer look at this evidence, discuss boundary conditions, and describe how testing can be applied to maximize student learning.

Early Evidence for Self-Testing

Early research on self-testing mostly focused on improving recall of short text passages. In an early study by Duchastel (1981), high school students read a prose passage about the Victorian era and then either took a practice short-answer, multiple-choice, or free-recall test on the material, or they

TABLE 6.1. *Effect sizes for learning by self-testing (vs. study-only control)*

Citation	Population	Materials	Practice test	Outcome	Effect size
Duchastel (1981)	High school	Prose passage	Short-answer	Recall	0.60
Duchastel (1981)	High school	Prose passage	Recognition or free-recall	Recall	-0.32
Nungester & Duchastel (1982), previously tested items	High school	Prose passage	Recognition and recall	Recall	1.23
Nungester & Duchastel (1982), new items	High school	Prose passage	Recognition and recall	Recall	0.04
Foos & Fisher (1988)	College	History passage	Recognition	Recognition, recall	0.30
Foos & Fisher (1988)	College	History passage	Recall	Recognition, recall	0.71
Glover (1989, Expt. 1)	College	Prose passage or diagram of flower	Recall	Recall	1.95
Glover (1989, Expt. 2), immediate practice test	College	Prose passage	Recall	Recall	-0.10
Glover (1989, Expt. 2), delayed practice test	College	Prose passage	Recall	Recall	3.05
Glover (1989, Expt. 3)	College	Diagram of flower	Recall	Recall	1.06
Glover (1989, Expt. 4)	College	Prose passage or diagram of flower	Recall	Recall, recognition	1.88
Glover (1989, Expt. 4)	College	Prose passage or diagram of flower	Recognition	Recall, recognition	1.06
Kang, McDermott, & Roediger (2007, Expt. 1), without feedback	College	Scientific articles	Recognition	Recognition	0.61
Kang, McDermott, & Roediger (2007, Expt. 1), without feedback	College	Scientific articles	Recognition	Recall	1.03
Kang, McDermott, & Roediger (2007, Expt. 1), without feedback	College	Scientific articles	Recall	Recall	0.55

Study	Population	Material			Effect size
Kang, McDermott, & Roediger (2007, Expt. 1), without feedback	College	Scientific articles	Recall	Recognition	0.25
Kang, McDermott, & Roediger (2007, Expt. 2), with feedback	College	Scientific articles	Recognition	Recognition	0.78
Kang, McDermott, & Roediger (2007, Expt. 2), with feedback	College	Scientific articles	Recognition	Recall	0.93
Kang, McDermott, & Roediger (2007, Expt. 2), with feedback	College	Scientific articles	Recall	Recall	1.18
Kang, McDermott, & Roediger (2007, Expt. 2), with feedback	College	Scientific articles	Recall	Recognition	1.18
Butler & Roediger (2008), without feedback	College	Prose passages	Recognition	Recall	0.97
McDaniel et al. (2007)	College	Psychology	Recognition	Recognition	0.27
McDaniel et al. (2007)	College	Psychology	Recall	Recall	0.51
McDaniel et al. (2011, Expt. 1), identical items	Middle school	Science topics	Recognition	Recognition	0.81
McDaniel et al. (2011, Expt. 2a), identical items	Middle school	Science topics	Recognition	Recognition	0.65
McDaniel et al. (2011, Expt. 2b), identical items	Middle school	Science topics	Recognition	Recognition	0.42
McDaniel et al. (2012, Expt. 1), identical items	College	Psychology	Recognition	Recognition	1.00
McDaniel et al. (2012, Expt. 1), identical items	College	Psychology	Recall	Recall	1.37
McDaniel et al. (2012, Expt. 1), related items	College	Psychology	Recognition	Recognition	0.52
McDaniel et al. (2012, Expt. 1), related items	College	Psychology	Recall	Recall	0.50
McDaniel et al. (2012, Expt. 2), identical items	College	Psychology	Recognition	Recognition	2.08
McDaniel et al. (2012, Expt. 2), identical items	College	Psychology	Recall	Recall	1.80
McDaniel et al. (2012, Expt. 2), related items	College	Psychology	Recognition	Recognition	0.62
McDaniel et al. (2012, Expt. 2), related items	College	Psychology	Recall	Recall	0.60

(continued)

TABLE 6.1. *(continued)*

Citation	Population	Materials	Practice test	Outcome	Effect size
Balch (1998)	College	Psychology	Recognition	Comprehension	0.37
Lyle & Crawford (2011)	College	Statistics	Recall	Comprehension	0.68
Daniel & Broida (2004), in-class quizzes	College	Human development	Recognition	Comprehension	2.28
Daniel & Broida (2004), online quizzes	College	Human development	Recognition	Comprehension	2.51
Leeming (2002)	College	Learning and memory	Recall	Comprehension	0.47
Cranney et al. (2009, Expt. 1), identical items	College	Psychology	Recognition, recall	Recognition, recall	0.50
Cranney et al. (2009, Expt. 1), new items	College	Psychology	Recognition, recall	Recognition, recall	−0.21
Cranney et al. (2009, Expt. 2), identical items	College	Psychology	Recognition, recall	Recognition, recall	1.33
Cranney et al. (2009, Expt. 2), related items	College	Psychology	Recognition, recall	Recognition, recall	0.51
Agarwal & Roediger (2011, Expt. 1), open-book test	College	Prose passages	Comprehension	Comprehension	0.58
Agarwal & Roediger (2011, Expt. 1), open-book test	College	Prose passages	Comprehension	Transfer	0.42
Agarwal & Roediger (2011, Expt. 1), closed-book test	College	Prose passages	Comprehension	Comprehension	0.54
Agarwal & Roediger (2011, Expt. 1), open-book test	College	Prose passages	Comprehension	Transfer	0.39
MEDIAN					0.62

Citation	Population	Materials	Practice test	Outcome	Effect size
Nungester & Duchastel (1982), previously tested items	High school	Prose passage	Recognition, recall	Recall	0.97
Nungester & Duchastel (1982), new items	High school	Prose passage	Recognition, recall	Recall	−0.25
Roediger & Karpicke (2006b, Expt. 1), without feedback	College	Prose passages	Recall	Recall	0.89
Kang, McDermott, & Roediger (2007, Expt. 1), without feedback	College	Scientific articles	Recognition	Recognition	−0.06
Kang, McDermott, & Roediger (2007, Expt. 1), without feedback	College	Scientific articles	Recognition	Recall	0.37
Kang, McDermott, & Roediger (2007, Expt. 1), without feedback	College	Scientific articles	Recall	Recall	0.11
Kang, McDermott, & Roediger (2007, Expt. 1), without feedback	College	Scientific articles	Recall	Recognition	−0.40
Kang, McDermott, & Roediger (2007, Expt. 2), with feedback	College	Scientific articles	Recognition	Recognition	0.27
Kang, McDermott, & Roediger (2007, Expt. 2), with feedback	College	Scientific articles	Recognition	Recall	0.23
Kang, McDermott, & Roediger (2007, Expt. 2), with feedback	College	Scientific articles	Recall	Recall	0.40
Kang, McDermott, & Roediger (2007, Expt. 2), with feedback	College	Scientific articles	Recall	Recognition	0.62
Butler & Roediger (2007)	College	Art history lectures	Recognition	Recall	0.02
Butler & Roediger (2007)	College	Art history lectures	Recall	Recall	1.24
Weinstein, McDermott, & Roediger (2010, Expt. 1), immediate final test	College	Prose passages	Comprehension	Comprehension	0.96

(continued)

TABLE 6.2. (*continued*)

Citation	Population	Materials	Practice test	Outcome	Effect size
Weinstein, McDermott, & Roediger (2010, Expt. 2), delayed final test	College	Prose passages	Comprehension	Comprehension	0.51
Weinstein, McDermott, & Roediger (2010, Expt. 3), immediate final test	College	Prose passages	Comprehension	Recall	0.33
Johnson & Mayer (2009)	College	Lightning formation	Recall	Recall	0.44
Johnson & Mayer (2009)	College	Lightning formation	Transfer	Transfer	0.56
McDaniel et al. (2007), previously tested items	College	Psychology	Recall	Recognition	0.43
McDaniel et al. (2007), previously untested items	College	Psychology	Recall	Recognition	0.05
McDaniel et al. (2007), tested and untested items	College	Psychology	Recognition	Recognition	0.03
McDaniel et al. (2012, Expt. 1), identical items	College	Psychology	Recall	Recall	0.83
McDaniel et al. (2012, Expt. 2), identical items	College	Psychology	Recognition	Recognition	1.23
McDaniel et al. (2012, Expt. 2), identical items	College	Psychology	Recall	Recall	1.00
Cranney et al. (2009, Expt. 1), identical items	College	Psychology	Recognition, recall	Recognition, recall	0.39
Cranney et al. (2009, Expt. 1), untested items	College	Psychology	Recognition, recall	Recognition, recall	0.06
Cranney et al. (2009, Expt. 2), identical items	College	Psychology	Recognition, recall	Recognition, recall	0.95
Cranney et al. (2009, Expt. 2), related items	College	Psychology	Recognition, recall	Recognition, recall	0.49
Carpenter & Kelly (2012)	College	Spatial skills	Recall	Transfer	0.68
MEDIAN					0.43

took did not take a practice test (the control group). On a subsequent delayed cued-recall test, students who took a short-answer practice test significantly outperformed the control group ($d = 0.60$), but the other test groups did not significantly outperform the control group (average $d = -0.32$). This study suggests that the testing effect may be strongest when students take more generative practice tests.

A follow-up study by Nungester and Duchastel (1982) tested whether the benefits of testing hold when compared to a control group that reviews the material. High school students read a short history passage and then either took a practice test on the passage (the test group), spent additional time studying the passage (the additional study group), or engaged in an unrelated task (the study-only group). Results indicated that the test group significantly outperformed the additional study group ($d = 0.97$) and the study-only group ($d = 1.23$) on previously tested items on a final test; however, the test group did not outperform the additional study group ($d = -0.25$) or the study-only group ($d = 0.04$) on new items (i.e., items that were not previously tested). This suggests that the benefits of self-testing hold when compared to receiving additional study time, but may also be somewhat limited to items that have already been explicitly tested.

In a study by Foos and Fisher (1988), college students read a short essay about the American Civil War. Some students then took a practice test on the material that was either fill-in-the-blank or multiple-choice, and which contained either verbatim or inference-based questions, whereas other students did not take a practice test. Results indicated that in general both test groups outperformed the no-test group on a subsequent retention test; however, this effect was strongest for those who took a fill-in-the-blank test (average $d = 0.71$) compared to a multiple-choice test (average $d = 0.30$). There was also some evidence that this difference was partly due to the fact that taking a practice multiple-choice test did not enhance performance on fill-in-the-blank items on the final test.

In a series of experiments by Glover (1989), college students read a short passage about a fictitious nation or studied a labeled diagram of the parts of a flower. Some students then took a practice test on the material, whereas other students did not take a practice test. Results of Experiments 1a and 1b found that taking a practice test two days after initial learning significantly enhanced performance on a final recall test four days after initial learning (average $d = 1.95$). Experiment 2 found that taking an immediate practice test did not improve final recall performance compared to the control ($d = -0.10$), but taking a spaced practice test (two days after initial learning) greatly enhanced recall performance ($d = 3.05$). Experiment 3 replicated the effect of taking a spaced practice test (d = 1.06), and also found additional benefits for taking a second practice test when it was spaced after the first, but not when it was taken directly after the first. Finally, Experiments 4a, 4b, and 4c found that taking various types of practice tests (free-recall, cued-recall, and recognition) generally improved final test performance, regardless of whether the final test assessed free-recall, cued-recall, or recognition. The most notable pattern from these several comparisons is that taking practice recall tests was generally more effective (average d = 1.88) than taking practice recognition tests (average d = 1.06), although both practice tests produced large effects. Overall, the study provides consistent support that practice testing improves long-term retention, particularly when the practice tests require learners to engage in generative processing.

Core Evidence for Self-Testing

More recent investigations of the testing effect have focused on developing a better understanding of how testing influences learning and when it works best. However, many studies continue to use relatively basic learning materials and measures of rote learning. Roediger and Karpicke (2006b) asked students to read short prose passages about the sun or about sea otters, and then either to take a practice free-recall test on the passage (study-test) or restudy the passage (study-study). Students were then given final recall tests either immediately or following a two-day or one-week delay. Results indicated that restudied passages were better recalled on the immediate test; however, tested passages were better recalled on the delayed tests (average d = 0.89). A follow-up experiment found that repeated practice testing resulted in better long-term learning than repeated studying, despite the fact that restudying resulted in greater judgments of learning (i.e., self-ratings of how much was learned) than repeated testing. Overall, this study provides strong support for the idea that taking practice recall tests can improve long-term recall of educationally relevant materials such as prose passages.

Kang, McDermott, and Roediger (2007) tested several possible moderators of the testing effect, including the format of the practice and final tests (e.g., recognition or recall) and the provision of feedback. In Experiment 1, college students read short scientific articles from psychology research journals and then either took a practice test on the article without feedback (study-test), read a list of summary statements about the article (study-study), or only read the article (study-only). The practice and final tests were either in recognition (multiple-choice) or recall (short-answer) format. Compared to the study-only condition, taking a practice recognition test resulted in better performance on both types of final tests (recognition: $d = 0.61$, recall: $d = 1.03$); however, taking a practice recall test only led to significantly better performance on a final recall test ($d = 0.55$), but not on a final recognition test ($d = 0.25$). Compared to the study-study condition, taking a practice recognition test only enhanced performance marginally on a final recall test ($d = 0.37$), but not on a final recognition test ($d = -0.06$); further, taking a practice recall test did not enhance final recall performance ($d = 0.11$) and actually significantly hurt final recognition performance ($d = -0.40$).

One explanation for these mixed results is that participants may not have been able to retrieve the material during the practice test. Thus in Experiment 2, participants received corrective feedback following each of their responses to either the recognition or recall test. In this experiment, compared to the study-only condition, taking either type of practice test resulted in improved performance on both a final recognition test and a final recall test. Compared to the study-study condition, however, only taking a practice recall test led to significantly better final test performance; taking a practice recognition test did not significantly enhance learning. Overall, the study by Kang, McDermott, and Roediger provides two important implications for the testing effect: (1) practice testing may need to be coupled with corrective feedback; and (2) more generative practice tests (such as free-recall rather than recognition) may lead to the best long-term learning.

A study by Butler and Roediger (2007) provides further evidence for the power of generative practice tests. In their experiment, students viewed a series of lectures on art history in a simulated classroom environment over the course of three days. After each lecture, they studied a summary of the lecture (study-study), took a multiple-choice test (study-recognition test), or took a short-answer test (study-recall test) on the material. On a final recall test (i.e., a short-answer test) administered a month later, lectures for which students took practice short-answer tests led to greater recall than lectures for which students studied a lecture summary ($d = 1.24$). Taking a practice multiple-choice test did not significantly improve learning compared to the study-study condition ($d = 0.02$). Both testing conditions did outperform a read-only control group; however, insufficient statistics were provided to calculate effect size. The provision of feedback was also manipulated in this study but did not influence final recall performance, likely because performance on the practice test was high. Overall, this suggests answering short-answer recall questions may enhance long-term retention of lecture-based material, whereas practice recognition tests may have limited benefits.

Another study by Butler and Roediger (2008) tested the implications of taking multiple-choice practice tests on subsequent learning. One potential drawback of multiple-choice tests is that "lure" items (i.e., incorrect alternatives) may cause learners to develop false knowledge. In the experiment, college students read short prose passages and then took a practice multiple-choice test with immediate feedback, delayed feedback, or no feedback. In control conditions, students either simply read the passage once or twice (without practice tests). First, a basic testing effect was found such that the test without feedback condition group significantly outperformed the no-test condition on a cued-recall test ($d = 0.97$). Further, both feedback conditions (immediate and delayed) outperformed the no feedback condition and were much less likely to respond with incorrect lures on the cued-recall test. This study suggests that practice multiple-choice tests coupled with feedback can greatly improve long-term retention and can help prevent the acquisition of false knowledge.

So far, we have seen that self-testing can greatly improve recall of facts and concepts. Can self-testing also be used to help students apply their knowledge to new situations? In a study by Johnson and Mayer (2009), college students learned about lightning formation by watching a short narrated animation. Students then watched the lesson a second time (the study-restudy group), took a practice retention test on the material (the study-practice recall test group), or took a transfer test on the material (the study-practice transfer test group). Results indicated testing effects in which students who took a practice retention test outperformed the restudy group on a delayed recall test ($d = 0.44$), and students who took a practice transfer test outperformed the restudy group on a delayed transfer test ($d = 0.56$). Further, the findings were consistent with a transfer-appropriate processing account of the testing effect, in that the practice transfer group outperformed the practice recall group on the delayed transfer test, but the practice recall group outperformed the practice transfer group on the delayed recall test. Apparently, the effects of self-testing depend somewhat on whether the practice tests and final tests assess similar learning outcomes. Overall, this study demonstrates that the testing effect extends to learning from multimedia materials and can be used to enhance transfer performance.

In a study by Weinstein, McDermott, and Roediger (2010), college students read short prose passages and then answered practice comprehension questions (the test condition) or reread the passage (the additional study condition). Across three experiments, results indicated that the test condition consistently outperformed the additional study condition on a final immediate short-answer comprehension test (Experiment 1: $d = 0.96$), a delayed short-answer test (Experiment 2: d = 0.51), and an immediate free-recall test (Experiment 3: d = 0.33). A third condition was also included in the experiment that both generated and answered practice comprehension questions. This group also outperformed the additional study group, but took considerably more learning time and did not outperform the testing group. Overall, this study provides further support for the benefits of self-testing on recalling and comprehending short prose passages.

One key implication of the testing effect for classroom instruction is that assigning low-stakes practice quizzes should improve performance on subsequent exams. In a study by McDaniel and colleagues (2007), students enrolled in a web-based undergraduate psychology course took weekly multiple-choice (the recognition test condition) or short-answer (the recall test condition) quizzes and received corrective feedback. On some weeks, students did not take quizzes but instead were given additional reading (the additional study condition). Items on subsequent practice unit and final exams were either previously quizzed or not previously quizzed (the study-only condition). First, results indicated that students performed better on subsequent unit exams for previously quizzed items compared to items not previously quizzed, for both types practice quizzes (multiple-choice: average d = 0.27; short-answer: average d = 0.51). Second, when compared to additional study, taking short-answer quizzes improved performance for previously quizzed items (average d = 0.43) but not for items that were not previously quizzed (average d = 0.05). Taking multiple-choice quizzes did not improve unit test performance for either type of test item (i.e., quizzed or not quizzed; average d = 0.03). Similar effects of taking practice quizzes were found for performance on a subsequent final exam; however, insufficient statistics were provided to calculate effect size. Overall, this finding suggests that asking students to take practice quizzes periodically may enhance the effectiveness of web-based courses, but this benefit may not hold when students are presented with new test items.

Another study by McDaniel and colleagues (2011) tested whether quizzing eighth grade students in a science class enhanced performance on subsequent unit and final exams. In Experiment 1, students were given multiple-choice quizzes with feedback spaced over a unit of material. On unit and final exams, some multiple-choice items were previously quizzed, whereas some items were new (i.e., not previously quizzed) items. Results indicated that students performed better on quizzed items compared to non-quizzed items on unit, end-of-semester, and end-of-year multiple-choice exams (average d = 0.81), yet this effect declined over time (unit d = 1.58; semester d = 0.56; year d = 0.28).

In Experiments 2a and 2b, students were given quizzes with feedback on some content before the lecture (pre-lesson), some immediately after the lecture (post-lesson), and some as a review before the final unit exam (review). The post-lesson condition is the most relevant for the purposes of this analysis. In Experiment 2a, results indicated that items on post-lesson quizzes were better remembered on a unit (recognition) test than items that were not quizzed ($d = 0.65$); in Experiment 2b, this effect held for both the unit and end-of-semester exam (average $d = 0.42$). There was evidence that review quizzing (before the unit exam rather than after each lesson) resulted in the greatest performance on final tests, and minimal benefits were found for pre-lesson quizzing. Thus, the timing of practice tests may modulate the long-term effects of testing. Overall, these results suggest that taking practice multiple-choice quizzes with feedback may be a useful instructional tool in the science classroom. Again, it is important to note that this research shows benefits of testing when the items on practice tests are identical to those on the final tests.

McDaniel and colleagues (2012) found similar support for quizzing with feedback in a web-based college psychology course. In Experiment 1, quizzed items (either on multiple-choice or short-answer quizzes) were better remembered than nonquizzed items (multiple choice $d = 1.00$; short-answer, $d = 1.37$). The effects were also maintained (yet somewhat reduced) when items on the final test were *related* to previously quizzed items (multiple-choice $d = 0.52$; short-answer $d = 0.50$). Further, compared to a read-facts control condition, the short-answer quizzes improved performance on identical final test items ($d = 0.83$); the advantage for multiple-choice quizzes did not reach statistical significance. When test items were related to quizzed items, the effects of practice quizzing (either multiple choice or short answer) compared to the read-facts condition did significantly enhance learning.

Similarly, Experiment 2 found that identical quizzed items were better remembered compared to nonquizzed items (multiple-choice $d = 2.08$; short-answer $d = 1.80$) and compared to additional study (multiple-choice $d = 1.23$; short-answer $d = 1.00$). When quizzed items were related to the final exam items, both types of quizzes enhanced performance compared to nonquizzed items (multiple-choice $d = 0.62$; short-answer $d = 0.60$), but not compared to additional study. Unfortunately, this study did not provide sufficient statistics to calculate effect sizes for nonsignificant comparisons. Overall, this study further emphasizes that the benefits of taking practice recognition and recall tests may be somewhat limited to when identical items are presented on a subsequent test (particularly when compared to a condition receiving additional study time).

In a study by Cranney and colleagues (2009), college students watched a video on psychobiology; the students then were either tested on the material (the test group), highlighted the video transcript (the additional study group), or did not receive additional time with the material (the study-only group). In Experiment 1, the test group outperformed the study-only group on previously tested items appearing on a final test ($d = 0.50$), but not on new test items ($d = -0.21$). Further, the test group did not significantly outperform the additional study group on previously tested items ($d = 0.39$) or on new test items ($d = 0.06$). However, in Experiment 2 the test group outperformed the study-only group on both previously tested and related items (tested items: $d = 1.33$; related items: $d = 0.51$). This effect was also found when comparing the test group to the additional study group (tested items: $d = 0.95$; related items: $d = 0.49$). Taken together, this set of studies are consistent with the idea that recognition- and recall-based practice tests enhance long-term retention for identical items and may facilitate memory for related but not entirely new test items.

Several other studies have investigated the testing effect within classroom environments. For example, in an earlier study by Balch (1998), introductory psychology students either took a practice multiple-choice exam (the test group) or reviewed the exam key (the study-only group). The test group significantly outperformed the study-only group on a final exam administered one week later ($d = 0.37$). Importantly, the final exam consisted of new items that were related to those on the practice exam. A more recent study by Lyle and Crawford (2011) found that quizzing students after each lecture in a statistics for psychology course led to greater performance on exams than that of students who were not quizzed ($d = 0.68$), similar to a finding from Leeming (2002) in a course on learning and memory. Finally, Daniel and Broida (2004) found large benefits for both in-class and online practice quizzing on final exam performance in a college course on child and adolescent development (in-class: $d = 2.28$; online: $d = 2.51$). These studies suggest that taking low-stakes quizzes throughout the duration of a course can cause considerable gains in student achievement on later tests.

Related Evidence for Self-Testing

In this section, we focus on additional considerations for incorporating learning by self-testing, such as using different types of learning materials or manipulating the timing or frequency of practice testing. Much of the research on self-testing has focused on its effects with verbal learning materials. A recent study by Carpenter and Kelly (2012) investigated whether the testing effect can be applied to acquiring spatial skills. College students studied an arrangement of objects within a three-dimensional virtual environment. After studying, students were asked to imagine that they were standing at one object, facing a second object, and to point to a third object. Some students were told the relative location of the third object (the study group), whereas other students had to determine the location of the third object from memory (the test group). On a subsequent transfer test involving a new arrangement of objects, the test group showed fewer pointing errors than the study group, regardless of whether or not they received corrective feedback during initial learning (average $d = 0.68$). This result suggests that the benefits of self-testing extend to transfer performance on nonverbal tasks. Apparently, practice accessing relevant material, whether verbal or spatial, can lead to be better performance on new problems faced in the future.

Several studies have also explored variations on the traditional testing effect to provide insight into how self-testing can be used most effectively. For example, how does the testing effect apply to learning from open- or closed-book tests? In two experiments by Agarwal and colleagues (2008), students read prose passages and either restudied the material or took an open- or closed-book test (with or without feedback) on the material. Results indicated a testing effect for both open- and closed-book tests when the tests included feedback, but no testing effect was found when the tests were given without feedback. However, the study did not provide sufficient statistics to calculate effect size. These findings provide further evidence for the value of testing with feedback and suggest that the testing effect applies to both open- and closed-book tests.

In a related study by Agarwal and Roediger (2011), college students read short prose passages and then either took a closed-book comprehension test with feedback or an open-book comprehension test, or they only studied the passage. Results of Experiment 1 indicated that both testing conditions outperformed the study-only condition on subsequent comprehension (open-book $d = 0.58$; closed-book $d = 0.54$) and transfer tests (open-book $d = 0.42$; closed-book $d = 0.39$). A follow-up experiment that manipulated test expectancy found that students performed best on final closed-book comprehension and transfer tests if they read passages with the expectation of taking a closed-book test compared to when they read with the expectation of taking an open-book test. Apparently, students invest more effort when they expect to take a closed-book test.

Another consideration is whether taking more practice tests offers additive benefits beyond taking only one practice test. In one experiment of the study by Roediger and Karpicke (2006b) mentioned previously, students either repeatedly studied passages four times, studied three times and then took a practice recall test, or studied once and took a practice recall test three times. Results indicated that taking a practice recall test (either once or three times) led to better performance on a final recall test than only repeatedly reading the material. Further, repeated practice testing was more effective than only taking one practice test. This result suggests that there are added benefits from repeatedly retrieving recently studied material from memory.

If repeated testing enhances long-term learning, how should the tests be sequenced over time? In one study, Karpicke and Roediger (2010) compared the effects of equally spaced and expanding retrieval practice schedules on retention of text passages. First, an overall testing effect was found such that taking an immediate practice test led to greater long-term retention. Repeated testing also resulted in greater retention over taking one test, and testing with feedback was superior to testing without feedback. However, there were no differences on a final recall between retrieval practice schedules evenly spaced in time compared to practice schedules that progressively expanded over time. Thus, this study suggests that the spacing of practice tests did not significantly modulate the testing effect.

Butler (2010) explored whether repeated testing can be used to help students transfer important facts and concepts when learning from prose. In a series of experiments, college students read short prose passages and either repeatedly restudied or repeatedly took practice tests consisting of factual and conceptual questions. Then all students took a delayed test on the passages that contained either the same factual and conceptual questions as the practice tests (Experiment 1a), new inferential questions within the same knowledge domain (Experiment 1b and Experiment 2), or new inferential questions within a different knowledge domain (Experiment 3). The results indicated that practice testing enhanced students' retention of important facts and concepts and their ability to transfer this knowledge to new conceptual questions and new domains.

Does the testing effect apply to pretesting? In a series of five experiments, Richland, Kornell, and Kao (2009) asked some students to take pretests before reading an essay about vision, whereas other students received extended study time. Results consistently found a pretesting effect such that performance on a post-test was greatest for those who were tested before studying. Importantly, this effect holds even though only items that were incorrect on the pretest were included in the analysis. This study suggests that unsuccessful retrieval attempts may enhance future learning, although as reported by previously discussed study by McDaniel and colleagues (2011), pretesting alone may not be sufficient to enhance learning in more authentic educational contexts. This research on placement of test items within a lesson extends classic research on adjunct questions in text (Mayer, 1975; Rothkopf, 1970; Rothkopf & Bisbicos, 1967).

In a study by Rohrer, Taylor, and Sholar (2010), fourth graders learned how to assign region names to map locations. Some students were tested on the location of each region before studying its location, whereas other students studied only the location of the regions. Results indicated that students who were tested outperformed those who only studied on delayed retention and transfer tests. The retention test involved filling in an unlabeled map with a given list of the region names, whereas the transfer test involved filling in an unlabeled map without a list provided (the transfer test was completed first). In a follow-up experiment, the transfer test included more conceptual items, and students who were tested again outperformed those who only studied on both the delayed retention and transfer tests. These findings suggest that pretesting can help young students retain and apply their knowledge to new situations.

Does taking a practice test improve how students restudy the material? In two experiments by McDaniel, Howard, and Einstein (2009), college students learned from educational texts by engaging in one of three learning strategies: rereading, note-taking, or a read-recite-review (3R) strategy. The rereading group read each text twice, the note-taking group read each text twice and took notes on a sheet of paper, and the 3R group read each text once, took an immediate free-recall test, and then read the text again. In Experiment 1, students read relatively basic educational texts, whereas in Experiment 2, students read more complicated texts about how pumps and brakes work. Results of both experiments indicated that the 3R group significantly outperformed the reread group on delayed free-recall tests. For Experiment 1, which involved reading basic texts, the 3R group did not outperform the read group on delayed multiple-choice or short-answer tests. However, for Experiment 2, which involved reading more complicated texts, the 3R group outperformed the reread group on the delayed multiple-choice and short-answer tests. Overall, these results suggest that combining practice testing with review (i.e., the 3R strategy) can be an effective strategy for promoting meaningful learning.

How does the testing effect compare to other learning strategies, such as creating a concept map? In a study by Karpicke and Blunt (2011), college students read a short scientific text one time, read the passage repeatedly, read the passage and then created a concept map while viewing the passage, or alternated reading and self-testing by taking a free-recall test on the passage. Total learning time was matched across the four conditions. Results indicated that the self-testing group performed better than the other three conditions on a delayed recall test of the passage. Thus, self-testing was more effective than creating a concept map when students were assessed on free recall. Importantly, a follow-up study indicated that the advantage of self-testing over concept mapping held even when participants were assessed on a final concept mapping test. This finding provides strong support for the benefits of self-testing over other study strategies.

WHAT ARE THE BOUNDARY CONDITIONS FOR SELF-TESTING?

Self-testing works best when testing is followed by corrective feedback, particularly when performance on the practice test is relatively poor. For example, feedback after multiple-choice items helps reinforce correct responses and reduces the likelihood of responding with lure items on a later recall test (e.g., Fazio et al., 2010; Roediger & Marsh, 2005). In general, free-recall, cued-recall, or otherwise open-response practice tests appear to be more effective than practice recognition tests, such as a multiple-choice test. Thus, the research evidence suggests that learning is maximized when the testing requires learners to generate responses to questions from memory rather than merely recognize the correct response on a multiple-choice test. There is also evidence that taking multiple practice tests may lead to additive learning benefits beyond taking only one practice test.

The vast majority of research on the testing effect has used practice and final tests that assess recall or recognition of facts. Much of this research indicates that the testing effect can be somewhat limited to items that were previously tested explicitly or to items that are very similar or require only minor inferences. Although a few studies have attempted to address this issue, it remains relatively unclear the extent to which taking practice recall or recognition tests transfers to novel test items. Further research is needed to explore the possibility that taking more meaningful practice tests (such as comprehension or transfer) helps students apply their knowledge toward solving novel problems on a final test.

HOW CAN WE APPLY SELF-TESTING?

Self-testing can be applied as a learning strategy for students to use at home or as an instructional strategy for teachers to employ within the classroom. For example, students are likely to benefit from activities such as answering practice questions after reading a chapter in a textbook, solving practice math problems and receiving feedback, and self-testing using flashcards.

The effectiveness of such techniques depends on the extent to which learners exert effort to generate appropriate answers. Further, teachers can take advantage of the learning benefits of testing by incorporating low-stakes practice quizzes in-class or online, following lessons or as a review before exams. For example, there is preliminary evidence that asking students to respond to in-class questions via a remote student response system (i.e., handheld clickers) following a lesson can improve exam performance on similar and new test items (Mayer et al., 2009). Feedback and discussion of how to answer the questions may also be helpful.

Self-testing can also be applied across various learning environments and subject areas and to achieve various learning goals. For example, there is strong evidence that testing can help students acquire new vocabulary or recall important facts from text passages. There is also some evidence that testing can help students apply their knowledge to solving novel problems, such as when learning how a scientific process works. Overall, the cognitive activity required by the self-testing should be similar to the cognitive activity required on the final test.

CONCLUSION

Self-testing is a highly versatile learning strategy supported by considerable research evidence. When students practice accessing recently studied material, they are more likely to access it successfully in the future under similar conditions. In short, self-testing promotes learning outcomes that persist over time. Students should be encouraged to use self-testing frequently as a study strategy rather than merely restudying the same information. Research on the testing effect suggests teachers should incorporate low-stakes testing into the curriculum as both an assessment tool and as a learning tool. Although testing has been shown to improve retention of important facts and concepts, further research is needed on how testing can be used to help students apply their knowledge to help solve novel problems. Overall, learning by self-testing offers students and teachers a simple but promising strategy for promoting meaningful learning.

REFERENCES

Agarwal, P. K., Karpicke, J. D., Kang, S. H. K., Roediger, H. L., III, & McDermott, K. B. (2008). Examining the testing effect with open- and closed-book tests. *Applied Cognitive Psychology, 22,* 861–76.

Agarwal, P. K., & Roediger, H. L., III (2011). Expectancy of an open-book test decreases performance on a delayed closed-book test. *Memory, 19,* 836–52.

Allen, G. A., Mahler, W. A., & Estes, W. K. (1969). Effects of recall tests on long-term retention of paired-associates. *Journal of Verbal Learning and Behavior*, 8(4), 463–70.

Balch, W. R. (1998). Practice versus review exams and final exam performance. *Teaching of Psychology*, 25(3), 181–5.

Butler, A. C. (2010). Repeated testing produces superior transfer of learning to repeated studying. *Journal of Experimental Psychology: Learning, Memory, and Cognition*, 36(5), 1118–33.

Butler, A. C., & Roediger, H. L. III (2007). Testing improves long-term retention in a simulated classroom setting. *European Journal of Cognitive Psychology*, 19, 514–27.

(2008). Feedback enhances the positive effects and reduces the negative effects of multiple-choice testing. *Memory & Cognition*, 36(3), 604–16.

Carpenter, S. K., & Kelly, J. W. (2012). Tests enhance retention and transfer of spatial learning. *Psychonomic Bulletin Review*, 19, 443–8.

Cranney, J., Ahn, M., McKinnon, R., Morris, S., & Watts, K. (2009). The testing effect, collaborative learning, and retrieval-induced facilitation in a classroom setting. *European Journal of Cognitive Psychology*, 21, 919–40.

Daniel, D. B., & Broida, J. (2004). Using web-based quizzing to improve exam performance: lessons learned. *Teaching of Psychology*, 31, 207–8.

Duchastel, P. C. (1981). Retention of prose following testing with different types of tests. *Contemporary Educational Psychology*, 6, 217–26.

Fazio, L. K., Agarwal, P. K., Marsh, E. J., & Roediger, H. L., III. (2010). Memorial consequences of multiple-choice testing on immediate and delayed tests. *Memory & Cognition*, 38, 407–18.

Foos, P. W., & Fisher, R. P. (1988). Using tests as learning opportunities. *Journal of Educational Psychology*, 80(2), 179–83.

Glover, J. A. (1989). The "testing" phenomenon: not gone but nearly forgotten. *Journal of Educational Psychology*, 81, 392–9.

Johnson, C. I., & Mayer, R. E. (2009). A testing effect with multimedia learning. *Journal of Educational Psychology*, 101(3), 621–9.

Kang, S. H. K., McDaniel, M. A., & Pashler, H. (2011). Effects of testing on learning of functions. *Psychonomic Bulletin & Review*, 18, 998–1005.

Kang, S. H. K., McDermott, K. B., & Roediger, H. L., III (2007). Test format and corrective feedback modify the effect of testing on long-term retention. *European Journal of Cognitive Psychology*, 19(4–5), 528–58.

Karpicke, J. D., & Blunt, J. R. (2011). Retrieval practice produces more learning than elaborative studying with concept mapping. *Science*, 331, 772–5.

Karpicke, J. D. & Roediger, H. L., III (2007a). Expanding retrieval practice promotes short-term retention, but equally spaced retrieval enhances long-term retention. *Journal of Experimental Psychology: Learning, Memory, and Cognition*, 33, 704–19.

(2007b). Repeated retrieval during learning is the key to long-term retention. *Journal of Memory and Language*, 57, 151–62.

(2008). The critical importance of retrieval for learning. *Science*, 319, 966–8.

(2010). Is expanding retrieval a superior method for learning text materials? *Memory and Cognition*, 38, 116–24.

Leeming, F. C. (2002). The exam-a-day procedure improves performance in psychology classes. *Teaching of Psychology*, 29(3), 210–12.

Lyle, K. B., & Crawford, N. A. (2011). Retrieving essential material at the end of lectures improves performance on statistics exams. *Teaching of Psychology*, 38(2), 94–7.

Mayer, R. E. (1975). Forward transfer of different reading strategies evoked by testlike events in mathematics text. *Journal of Educational Psychology*, 67, 165–9.

Mayer, R. E., Stull, A., DeLeeuw, K., Almeroth, K., Bimber, B., Chun, D., Bulger, M., Campbell, J., Knight, A., & Zhang, H. (2009). Clickers in the classroom: fostering learning with questioning methods in large lecture classes. *Contemporary Educational Psychology*, 34, 51–7.

McDaniel, M. A., Anderson, J. L., Derbish, M. H., & Morrisette, N. (2007). Testing the testing effect in the classroom. *European Journal of Cognitive Psychology*, 19(4/5), 494–513.

McDaniel, M. A., Howard, C. D., & Einstein, G. O. (2009). The read-recite-review study strategy: effective and portable. *Psychological Science*, 20, 516–22.

McDaniel, M. A., Agarwal, P. K., Huelser, B. J, McDermott, K. B., & Roediger, H. L., III (2011). Test-enhanced learning in a middle school science classroom: the effects of quiz frequency and placement. *Journal of Educational Psychology*, 103, 399–414.

McDaniel, M. A., Wildman, K. M., & Anderson, J. L. (2012). Using quizzes to enhance summative-assessment performance in a web-based class: an experimental study. *Journal of Applied Research in Memory and Cognition*, 1, 18–26.

Nungester, R. J., & Duchastel, P. C. (1982). Testing versus review: effects on retention. *Journal of Educational Psychology*, 74(1), 18–22.

Pavlik, P. I., & Anderson, J. R. (2005). Practice and forgetting effects on vocabulary memory: an activation-based model of the spacing effect. *Cognitive Science*, 29, 559–86.

Richland, L. E., Kornell, N., & Kao, L. S. (2009). The pretesting effect: do unsuccessful retrieval attempts enhance learning? *Journal of Experimental Psychology: Applied*, 15, 243–57.

Roediger, H. L., III, & Karpicke, J. D. (2006a). The power of testing memory: basic research and implications for educational practice. *Perspectives on Psychological Science*, 1, 181–210.

    (2006b). Test-enhanced learning: taking memory tests improves long-term retention. *Psychological Science*, 17, 249–55.

Rohrer, D., III, & Marsh, E. J. (2005). The positive and negative consequences of multiple-choice testing. *Journal of Experimental Psychology*, 31(5), 1155–9.

Rohrer, D., Taylor, K., & Sholar, B. (2010). Tests enhance the transfer of learning. *Journal of Experimental Psychology: Learning, Memory, and Cognition*, 36, 233–9.

Rothkopf, E. Z. (1970). The concept of mathemagenic activities. *Review of Educational Research*, 40, 325–36.

Rothkopf, E. Z., & Bisbicos, E. (1967). Selective facilitative effects of interspersed questions on learning from written material. *Journal of Educational Psychology*, 58, 56–61.

Vaughn, K. E., & Rawson, K. A. (2011). Diagnosing criterion level effects on memory: what aspects of memory are enhanced by repeated retrieval? *Psychological Science*, 22, 1127–31.

Weinstein, Y., McDermott, K. B., & Roediger, H. L., III. (2010). A comparison of study strategies for passages: rereading, answering questions, and generating questions. *Journal of Experimental Psychology: Applied*, 16(3), 308–16.

Zaromb, F. M., & Roediger, H. L., III. (2010). The testing effect in free recall is associated with enhanced organizational processes. *Memory & Cognition*, 38, 995–1008.

7

Learning by Self-Explaining

SUMMARY

Self-explaining occurs when students explain the content of a lesson to themselves during learning. For example, students may read a lesson on how the human circulatory system works and generate comments that explain how the system works in their own words, including how the information they are currently reading relates to previous information in the lesson and to their relevant prior knowledge. The theoretical rationale for self-explaining is that it causes learners to select relevant elements of information from the lesson, organize them into a coherent mental model, and relate them to their existing mental model. The empirical rationale for self-explaining is that in forty-four of fifty-four experimental comparisons, students who were asked to generate self-explanations during learning performed better on a subsequent test of the material than a control group that was not asked to generate self-explanations during learning, yielding a median effect size of $d = 0.61$. Regarding boundary conditions, self-explanation may be most effective for studying diagrams and conceptual materials, for learners with low prior knowledge, and for instances where self-explanation is focused rather than general. Regarding applications, the self-explanation strategy applies to learning from text, diagrams, and worked examples and to learning from paper-based and computer-based lessons.

> **BOX 1.** *Overview of Learning by Self-Explaining*
>
> | | |
> |---|---|
> | Definition | Learners explain the content of a lesson to themselves by elaborating upon the instructional material presented. |
> | Example | Students are asked to read a lesson on how the human circulatory system works and generate self-explanations after each sentence they read to help make sense out of the material. |
> | Theoretical rationale | Self-explanation involves selecting relevant material from the lesson and reorganizing it into a coherent cognitive representation that can be integrated with the learner's prior knowledge in order to fill in gaps or repair inaccurate mental models. |
> | Empirical rationale | The self-explanation effect is upheld in forty-four of fifty-four tests, yielding a median effect size of $d = 0.61$. |
> | Boundary conditions | The self-explanation effect may be strongest for studying diagrams and conceptual materials, for learners with low prior knowledge, and for instances where prompting is more focused rather than general. |
> | Applications | Self-explanation applies to learning from text, diagrams, and examples, and within paper-based and computer-based learning environments. |

CHAPTER OUTLINE

1. Example of Self-Explaining as a Learning Strategy
2. What Is Learning by Self-Explaining?
3. How Does Self-Explaining Foster Learning?
4. What Is the Evidence for Self-Explaining?
5. What Are the Boundary Conditions for Self-Explaining?
6. How Can We Apply Self-Explaining?
7. Conclusion

EXAMPLE OF SELF-EXPLAINING AS A LEARNING STRATEGY

Suppose we asked you to read a textbook lesson on how the human circulatory system works. In an effort to encourage you to make sense of the material, we ask you to read each sentence aloud and then explain aloud to yourself what it means. To help you keep on track, every once in a while we follow up your comment with a prompt such as, "Can you explain that?"

or, "What do you mean?" Here are your instructions for reading the lesson (as modified from Chi et al., 1994, p. 477):

> The following is a chapter on the human circulatory system, which was taken from a high school textbook. I will present the text one sentence at a time so that you will have time to really think about what information each sentence provides and how this relates to what you've already read. We would like you to read each sentence out loud and then explain what it means to you. That is, what new information does each sentence provide for you, how does it relate to what you've already read, does it give you a new insight into your understanding of how the circulatory system works, or does it raise a question in your mind? Tell us whatever is going through your mind, even if it seems unimportant. You may need to go back and reread parts of the text to really understand all the material. Let me know when you'd like to start a new sentence.

As you read the one hundred–sentence lesson, you come to the following sentences:

> Sentence 17: The septum divides the heart lengthwise into two sides.
> Sentence 18: The right side pumps blood to the lungs, and the left side pumps blood to the other parts of the body.

Please write down want you would say after reading sentence 18:

For purposes of comparison, let's look at what a student said in a study by Chi and colleagues (1994, p. 454).

> So the septum is a divider so that the blood doesn't get mixed up. So the right side is to the lungs, and the left side is to the body. So the septum is like a wall that divides the heart into two parts … it kind of like separates it so that the blood doesn't get mixed up … .

As you can see, the student has made an important inference – the septum acts as a wall so the blood on one side of the heart does not mix with blood from the other side of the heart. How did your self-explanation compare to this one?

In a landmark study by Chi and colleagues (1994), students who were asked to engage in generating self-explanations after each sentence performed better than students who read the lesson twice without generating self-explanations on measures of deep learning, indicating that generating self-explanations helped students build a more accurate mental model of how the human circulatory system works. This is an example of the *self-explanation effect* – the finding that generating explanations to oneself during learning results in a deeper understanding of the material, compared to engaging in more passive learning activities, such as rereading. The goal of this chapter is to present the available research evidence for the self-explanation effect and to discuss its theoretical and practical implications for generative learning.

WHAT IS LEARNING BY SELF-EXPLAINING?

Self-explaining occurs when learners generate explanations to themselves as they study material from a lesson. When students self-explain, they elaborate upon the presented material by integrating it with their prior knowledge and relating it to previously presented material, allowing them to generate inferences that extend the lesson's content. Thus, self-explanation is distinct from other nongenerative learning strategies, such as simply repeating or paraphrasing the information presented in lesson, because learners "go beyond" the instructional material presented. Overall, the purpose of generating self-explanations is to facilitate knowledge construction – that is, to help identify and fill in gaps in learners' knowledge and to repair inaccurate existing mental models (Chi, 2000). As a result, generating self-explanations is intended to result in deeper learning, improved self-regulation, and enhanced problem solving.

One promising feature of generating self-explanations is that it can be employed across a wide range of domains and lesson formats and can be used by students of all ages (Fonseca & Chi, 2011; Wylie & Chi, 2014). For example, students can self-explain while reading expository texts, studying scientific diagrams, seeing worked examples, or solving algebra problems. Self-explanation also generally requires relatively little training and can be applied to students ranging from pre-kindergarten to college. In short, self-explanation is a generative learning strategy with wide educational applicability.

Self-explanation is somewhat similar to another learning strategy, called *elaborative interrogation* (e.g., Pressley et al., 1987), which involves "generating an explanation for why an explicitly stated fact or concept is true" (Dunlosky et al., 2013, p. 6). However, elaborative interrogation has mainly been studied with learning materials that consist of a short series of facts rather than conceptual learning materials (such as lessons that explain how a scientific process works). For example, in a recent review Dunlosky and colleagues (2013) conclude that, "concerns remain about the applicability of elaborative interrogation to material that is lengthier or more complex than fact lists" (p. 11). Another similar learning strategy is *journal writing*, which involves asking students to "write down the main ideas of preceding lessons, give examples of new concepts, and indicate how they plan to overcome difficulties in understanding" (Glogger et al., 2012, p. 452). Thus, journal writing includes the use of many learning strategies, not strictly self-explanation. Since we are concerned with isolating the effects of learning strategies shown to promote meaningful learning, this chapter focuses on research investigating the effects of self-explanation on student understanding of academic material.

HOW DOES SELF-EXPLAINING FOSTER LEARNING?

An important theoretical framework underlying research on self-explanation comes from Chi's (2009; Fonseca & Chi, 2011) passive-active-constructive-interactive theory. According to this framework, learning environments can be classified into four basic categories: (1) *passive*: learning environments that involve no physical activity from the learner, such as listening to a lecture or reading a textbook; (2) *active*: learning environments that involve some form of physical activity from the learner, such as highlighting or underlining a textbook; (3) *constructive*: learning environments that involve the learner generating novel output, such as generating self-explanations, concept maps, or questions; or (4) *interactive*: learning environments

BOX 2. *Three Cognitive Processes Activated by Self-Explaining*

Cognitive process	How self-explaining primes the process
Selecting	Learners choose which elements of information need to be explained.
Organizing	Learners create inferences to fit the elements of information together into a coherent mental model.
Integrating	Learners generate inferences and search for consistencies and inconsistencies between the currently presented material and their relevant prior knowledge or previously presented material.

that involve learner dialogue with another person (e.g., a peer or expert) or system (e.g., a computer-based tutor). Based on this analysis, learning environments in which students generate self-explanations are classified as *constructive learning environments*. As such, these environments are associated with constructing and repairing learners' mental models, and therefore, are predicted to lead to better learning outcomes than passive or active learning environments do. Overall, Chi's framework predicts that students who engage in generating self-explanations during learning will develop a deeper understanding of the material than students who passively view the material during learning or otherwise engage in nongenerative activities, such as rereading the material.

According to the cognitive theory of multimedia learning (Mayer, 2009, 2014), self-explaining primes the cognitive processes of selecting, organizing, and integrating, as shown in Box 2. Selecting involves deciding which elements of information from the lesson need to be explained. Organizing involves making inferences about the material selected in order to fit the elements of information into a coherent cognitive representation. Integrating involves assimilating the developed cognitive representation with existing knowledge, or it involves repairing or replacing an inaccurate existing mental model. In short, self-explaining promotes deep learning when learners actively generate inferences about the material and modify their preconceptions of the material accordingly.

WHAT IS THE EVIDENCE FOR SELF-EXPLAINING?

Table 7.1 presents the effect sizes of fifty-four experimental comparisons testing the effects of generating self-explanations. These experiments directly compared the learning outcomes of students asked to generate self-

TABLE 7.1. *Effect sizes for learning by self-explaining*

Citation	Population	Subject	Outcome	Effect size
King (1992), immediate test	College	Social studies	Comprehension	0.67
King (1992) delayed test	College	Social studies	Comprehension	1.03
Chi et al. (1994)	College	Human circulatory system	Transfer	1.13
O'Reilly, Symons, & MacLatchey-Gaudet (1998)	College	Human circulatory system	Recall	0.78
Renkl et al. (1998)	College	Accounting	Near transfer	0.54
Renkl et al. (1998)	College	Accounting	Far transfer	0.63
Atkinson, Renkl, & Merrill (2003, Expt. 1),	College	Probability	Near transfer	0.70
Atkinson, Renkl, & Merrill (2003, Expt. 1)	College	Probability	Far transfer	0.67
Atkinson, Renkl, & Merrill (2003, Expt. 2)	High school	Probability	Near transfer	0.81
Atkinson, Renkl, & Merrill (2003, Expt. 2)	High school	Probability	Far transfer	0.73
Schworm & Renkl (2006), examples without provided explanations	College	Structuring worked examples	Transfer	1.09
Schworm & Renkl (2006), examples with provided explanations	College	Structuring worked examples	Transfer	0.19
Berthold, Eysink, & Renkl (2009), open prompts	College	Probability	Procedural	0.64
Berthold, Eysink, & Renkl (2009), assisted prompts	College	Probability	Procedural	0.49
Berthold, Eysink, & Renkl (2009), open prompts	College	Probability	Conceptual	0.72
Berthold, Eysink, & Renkl (2009), assisted prompts	College	Probability	Conceptual	1.16
Berthold & Renkl (2009)	High school	Probability	Procedural	−0.34
Berthold & Renkl (2009)	High school	Probability	Conceptual	0.70
Nokes-Malach et al. (2013)	College	Rotational motion	Far transfer	0.93
Gerjets, Scheiter, & Catrambone (2006, Expt. 2), modular worked examples	College	Probability	Transfer	0.28

Study	Level	Topic	Measure	Effect size
Gerjets, Scheiter, & Catrambone (2006, Expt. 2), molar worked examples	College	Probability	Transfer	-0.66
Grobe & Renkl (2006, Expt. 1), uniform solution	College	Probability	Conceptual	-0.04
Grobe & Renkl (2006, Expt. 2), multiple solutions	College	Probability	Conceptual	-0.69
Grobe & Renkl (2007, Expt. 1)	College	Probability	Near transfer	0.03
Grobe & Renkl (2007, Expt. 1)	College	Probability	Far transfer	-0.19
Schworm & Renkl (2007), exemplifying-domain prompts	College	Argumentation skills	Transfer	0.43
Schworm & Renkl (2007), learning-domain prompts	College	Argumentation skills	Transfer	0.97
Hilbert et al. (2008)	College	Geometry	Conceptual	0.44
Hilbert & Renkl (2009)	High school	Finance	Conceptual	0.29
Mayer & Johnson (2010), menu-based prompts	College	Electrical circuits	Transfer	0.91
Johnson & Mayer (2010, Expt. 1), menu-based prompts	College	Electrical circuits	Transfer	1.20
Johnson & Mayer (2010, Expt. 2), menu-based prompts	College	Electric circuits	Transfer	0.71
Johnson & Mayer (2010, Expt. 2), open prompts	College	Electric circuits	Transfer	-0.06
de Koning et al. (2011), cued animation	High school	Human circulatory system	Transfer	0.82
de Koning et al. (2011), uncued animation	High school	Human circulatory system	Transfer	0.04
Berthold et al. (2011), conceptual prompts	College	Tax law	Procedural	-0.97
Berthold et al. (2011), conceptual prompts	College	Tax law	Conceptual	0.57
Lin & Atkinson (2013, Expt. 1)	College	Human cardiovascular system	Comprehension	0.90
Lin & Atkinson (2013, Expt. 2), animated lesson	College	Human cardiovascular system	Comprehension	1.82
Lin & Atkinson (2013, Expt. 2), static lesson	College	Human cardiovascular system	Comprehension	0.22

(continued)

TABLE 7.1. (*continued*)

Citation	Population	Subject	Outcome	Effect size
Cho & Lee (2013)	College	Instructional design principles	Transfer	0.34
Mwangi & Sweller (1998, Expt. 3)	Elementary school	Arithmetic word problems	Transfer	−0.10
Rittle-Johnson (2006)	Elementary school	Mathematical equivalence	Procedural	0.38
Rittle-Johnson (2006)	Elementary school	Mathematical equivalence	Conceptual	−0.11
McEldoon, Durkin, & Rittle-Johnson (2013)	Elementary school	Mathematical equivalence	Procedural	0.58
McEldoon, Durkin, & Rittle-Johnson. (2013)	Elementary school	Mathematical equivalence	Conceptual	0.43
Hsu & Tsai (2011)	Elementary school	Light and shadow concepts	Comprehension	0.17
Hausmann & Chi (2002, Expt. 1)	College	Human circulatory system	Comprehension	0.11
Ainsworth & Burcham (2007), maximally coherent text	College	Human circulatory system	Transfer	1.41
Ainsworth & Burcham (2007), minimally coherent text	College	Human circulatory system	Transfer	0.68
de Bruin, Rikers, & Schmidt (2007)	College	Chess	Transfer	1.51
Chamberland et al. (2011), unfamiliar cases	Graduate	Diagnosing clinical cases	Transfer	0.75
Chamberland et al. (2011), familiar cases	Graduate	Diagnosing clinical cases	Transfer	−0.27
Larsen, Butler, & Roediger (2013)	Graduate	Clinical neurology	Transfer	0.68
MEDIAN				0.61

explanations during academic learning against a control group that engaged in more passive strategies such as rereading or normal studying. Studies that did not measure learning outcomes (such as comprehension), did not include a control group, did not isolate the effects of self-explaining, or did not include sufficient statistics to calculate effect size were not included in this analysis. The analysis reveals positive effects of generating self-explanations for forty-four of fifty-four tests, yielding a median effect size of $d = 0.61$. Overall, there is consistent evidence in the moderate-to-strong range that generating self-explanations promotes deep learning.

Early Evidence for Self-Explaining

In a classic study by Chi and colleagues (1989), college students were instructed to think aloud as they studied a lesson containing worked examples of physics problems related to the laws of motion. Data obtained from think-aloud protocols were then coded and analyzed based on whether students showed evidence of generating self-explanations while learning – that is, the degree to which students went beyond what was presented in the lesson by generating inferences about the material. Results indicated that those who generated more self-explanations while studying tended to perform better on a subsequent problem-solving test when compared to those who generated fewer self-explanations. Thus, this study provided preliminary evidence for an association between self-explaining and meaningful learning, a finding that has since been replicated within other learning domains (Ferguson-Hessler & de Jong, 1990; Pirolli & Recker, 1994; Renkl, 1997).

Building on the correlational approach of early research by Chi and others, researchers began to investigate whether training or prompting students to generate self-explanations resulted in deeper learning. To address this question, King (1992) trained underprepared college students on how to engage in self-questioning (i.e., a form of self-explanation) following lecture-based instruction. Students were trained on how to use general questions (e.g., "What conclusions can I draw from...?") to prompt, and then generate, their self-explanations after viewing a series of lectures of the course across several class periods. A control group was not trained on a learning strategy and instead practiced reviewing their notes after the lectures. All students then listened to a final lecture and engaged in their respective learning strategy (i.e., self-questioning or note-taking review). The results indicated that those who generated and responded to their own self-question prompts following the lecture outperformed those who only reviewed their notes on both immediate (d = 0.67) and delayed (d = 1.03) comprehension tests.

As a follow-up to their correlational study (Chi et al., 1989), Chi and colleagues (1994) tested whether prompting students to self-explain while reading a scientific text results in deeper learning. Eighth graders read a text-based lesson on the human circulatory system. Some students were prompted to self-explain after each sentence they read (self-explanation group), whereas other students read the same text twice, but were not prompted to self-explain (control group). On questions designed to assess deep understanding, the self-explanation group experienced greater learning gains from pretest to post-test than the control group (d = 1.13). Further, consistent with data from Chi and colleagues (1989), students who generated more explanations during learning developed a better understanding of the material than those who generated fewer explanations.

In a related study, O'Reilly, Symons, and MacLatchy-Gaudet (1998) asked college students to learn about the human circulatory system by either rereading each sentence or engaging in self-explanation after they read each sentence. The self-explanation group was prompted to explain what the sentence meant to them and to explain how any new information from the sentence related to their prior knowledge. The results indicated that the self-explanation group outperformed the reread group on both cued-recall and recognition tests, which we combined to form a single measure of recall (average d = 0.78). Interestingly, the self-explanation group also significantly outperformed a group of students who were prompted to engage in elaborative interrogation, which involves participants repeatedly asking themselves "why" the information in the text makes sense.

The studies discussed in this section provide encouraging support that generating quality self-explanations during learning promotes deep understanding. In the following sections, we explore how self-explanation can be applied across different learning environments and types of learners.

Learning by Self-Explaining Worked Examples

Self-explanation has been particularly popular as a supplement to learning from worked examples. Worked examples are designed to reduce extraneous processing (i.e., processing irrelevant for learning), yet there is no guarantee that students will use their remaining cognitive resources to engage in generative processing. As Chi and colleagues (1994) showed, most students do not spontaneously engage in self-explanations on their own (also see Renkl, 1997, 1999). Thus, prompting students to self-explain while studying worked examples is intended to help students allocate available cognitive resources toward generative processing.

To test this hypothesis, Renkl and colleagues (1998) had apprentices from a bank learn to calculate compound and real interest by studying a set of worked examples. Some participants were given brief self-explanation training and were prompted to generate self-explanations aloud during learning, whereas others were not prompted to self-explain, and instead only thought aloud. Further, some participants studied uniform examples, whereas others studied varied examples. The results indicated that students prompted to self-explain outperformed those who did not self-explain on both near and far transfer tests, regardless of the type of worked examples they studied (near transfer average $d = 0.54$; far transfer average $d = 0.63$). There was also evidence that being prompted to self-explain was particularly helpful for those with low prior knowledge. Overall, this study suggests that adding self-explanation prompts to worked examples can result in deep learning, presumably by priming generative processing in learners.

In a study by Atkinson, Renkl, and Merrill (2003), worked examples of probability problems were presented on a computer screen to college students. Instead of generating self-explanations aloud during learning, students in the self-explanation group were prompted to select rules or principles from a menu presented on the screen. Students in a control group did not receive self-explanation prompts. The format of the worked examples also varied; some were presented in a backward fading format (i.e., solution steps were progressively omitted), whereas other students were presented with fully worked-out examples (i.e., all solution steps provided) paired with conventional problems (i.e., no solution steps provided). Results indicated that those who received self-explanation prompts outperformed those who did not receive prompts on subsequent near and far transfer tests, regardless of whether they studied backward-faded examples or worked example problem pairs (near transfer average $d = 0.70$; far transfer average $d = 0.67$). This finding was then replicated in a follow-up experiment involving high school students who studied only backward-faded examples (near transfer: $d = 0.81$; far transfer: $d = 0.73$). Overall, this study suggests that selecting explanations from a menu can be an effective form of self-explanation when studying worked examples presented on a computer.

Schworm and Renkl (2006) investigated whether the effects of self-explaining worked examples were influenced by the presence of accompanying instructional explanations. In their experiment, student teachers learned about how to structure effective worked examples by studying a set of worked examples of high school geometry and physics problems. The worked examples were presented with or without accompanying instructional explanations, and student teachers were either prompted or not prompted to self-explain. The self-explanation groups typed their explanations in a text box for each problem. Results indicated that students asked to self-explain outperformed those who did not self-explain on a subsequent transfer test requiring students to select a particular format of worked examples from several options and generate a structured worked-out example set by combining multiple worked examples. Further, this self-explanation effect was strongest when it was not coupled with instructional explanations ($d = 1.09$) compared to when it was coupled with explanations ($d = 0.19$), suggesting that the presence of provided explanations in worked examples may inhibit or negate the need for student-generated self-explanations.

Berthold, Eysink, and Renkl (2009) tested whether students benefited from more assisted forms of self-explanation prompting over more open prompting. College students learned about probability theory from worked examples presented in multiple representations. Some students received open self-explanation prompts, in which they provided a free response to self-explanation prompts following each problem (e.g., "Why do you calculate the total possible outcomes by multiplying?"), whereas some students received assisted self-explanation prompts, in which they responded to the same questions by filling blanks in an explanation provided to them. A control group only studied the worked examples and received no prompting. The results indicated that both forms of self-explanation prompting facilitated the acquisition of procedural knowledge (open prompts: $d = 0.64$; assisted prompts: $d = 0.72$) and conceptual knowledge (open prompts: $d = 0.49$; assisted prompts: $d = 1.16$), although assisted prompting enhanced conceptual knowledge significantly more than open prompting. The authors concluded that assisted self-explanation prompts provide the most promise for generating quality self-explanations and achieving deep learning from multiple representations, perhaps because students are more likely to generate quality explanations.

In a study by Berthold and Renkl (2009), high school students studied multiple representations (e.g., diagrams or equations) of worked examples of probability problems presented on a computer. Some students received self-explanation prompts by typing responses into a text box (the self-explaining group), whereas other students could use the text box to take notes (the control group). Results indicated that the self-explaining group significantly outperformed the control group on a subsequent test of conceptual knowledge (average $d = 0.70$), but performed significantly worse on a test of procedural knowledge (average $d = -0.34$). This effect did not depend on the type of representations students studied. Apparently, self-explaining may have differential effects on different types of learning – in particular, self-explaining may be most beneficial for helping students develop a conceptual understanding of the material.

Finally, in a recent study by Nokes-Malach and colleagues (2013), students learned about physics concepts of rotational motion by studying worked examples and solving practice problems. Some students were prompted to self-explain aloud while studying the examples (self-explanation group), whereas other students only read the examples (control group). On a subsequent far transfer test, the self-explanation group significantly outperformed the control group ($d = 0.93$).

In summary, the evidence reported in this section suggests that learning from worked examples is enhanced when students self-explain during learning (although see Gerjets, Scheiter, & Catrambone, 2006; Grobe & Renkl, 2006). In particular, the self-explaining effect may be strongest for acquiring conceptual knowledge, when learners have relatively low prior knowledge, and when self-explanation prompts are more focused or guided rather than general or open.

Learning by Self-Explaining Within Computer-Based Learning Environments

Self-explanation activities have recently been incorporated into the design of computer-based learning environments such as animated lessons, intelligent tutors, and educational games and simulations. For example, Aleven and Koedinger (2002) tested the effects of adding self-explanation features to a computer-based cognitive tutor. High school students solved geometry problems using either the base version of the tutor (control group) or a version that also required students to type a reason for each solution step (self-explanation group). Results indicated that students who self-explained their answers during problem solving showed significantly greater pre- to post-test gains on problems requiring deep understanding compared to the control group. The study did not include sufficient statistics to calculate effect size; nonetheless, it provides evidence that adding self-explanation features such as typing one's reason for a solution step can enhance learning from an intelligent tutoring system.

Mayer and Johnson (2010; Johnson & Mayer, 2010) investigated the effects of adding self-explanation features to a gamelike environment. In their experiments, college students learned how electrical circuits work by playing a computer-based educational game. Some students learned by playing the base version of the game, which required them to solve various problems related to the flow rate of electrical circuits (the control group). Other students were asked to self-explain their response to each problem by selecting the appropriate explanation from a list (the menu-based prompt group) or openly typing their explanation into a text box (the open prompt group). The results indicated that students who received the menu-based form of prompting significantly outperformed the base group on an embedded transfer test (Mayer & Johnson, 2010: $d = 0.91$; Johnson & Mayer, 2010: Expt. 1, $d = 1.20$; Expt. 2, $d = 0.71$); however, students asked to generate their explanations openly did not benefit from prompting (Johnson & Mayer, 2010, Expt. 2, $d = -0.06$). This research suggests that within game-like environments, a more focused form of self-explanation prompting (i.e., in which students choose options from a menu) may be more effective than more open forms of prompting (i.e., in which students type in their explanations).

Several other studies have tested the effects of different types of self-explanation prompting. For example, in a study by Kwon, Kumalasari, and Howland (2011), students who generated their own responses to conceptual self-explanation prompts by typing into a text box outperformed students who selected responses from a menu. A study by van der Meij and de Jong (2011) found that more specific forms of prompting resulted in better learning than more general prompting. Similarly, Gadgil, Nokes-Malach, and Chi (2012) found that students who were asked to self-explain by comparing and contrasting diagrams outperformed those who received more general open prompting. Overall, this research suggests that when learners are required to generate responses on their own, more focused forms of prompting may be most effective.

De Koning and colleagues (2011) tested whether generating self-explanations may enhance learning from cued animations. With a rationale similar to that for self-explaining worked examples, cueing may effectively reduce extraneous processing caused by animations; however, it does not guarantee that students will use these spared resources to engage in generative processing. Therefore, adding self-explanation prompting to cued animations may help foster generative processing. To test this hypothesis, de Koning and colleagues asked high school students to learn about the human cardiovascular system from instructional animations that were visually cued (i.e., by spotlighting important elements of the animation) or not visually cued; further, some students were prompted to self-explain while watching the animation, whereas other students did not self-explain. Results indicated that students who self-explained during learning performed better on a transfer test when the animation was cued (d = 0.82), but not when the animation was not cued (d = 0.04). This result suggests that cueing animations may effectively reduce extraneous processing, allowing students to be more effective in generating appropriate self-explanations when prompted to self-explain.

In a study by Berthold and colleagues (2011), college students completed a complex e-learning module on tax law that contained instructional explanations, examples, and practice exercises. Some students were provided with five conceptually oriented prompts throughout the module, such as, "Does the [German] think-cap rule differentiate between interests that are paid to their shareholders by a co-entrepreneurship and interests that are paid to a bank by a corporation?" A control group did not receive self-explanation prompts. Similar to the study by Berthold and Renkl (2009) described previously, the results indicated "double-edged" (p. 69) effects of receiving conceptual prompts – that is, students receiving the prompts significantly outperformed the control group on a conceptual knowledge test (d = 0.57) but performed significantly worse than the control group on a procedural knowledge test (d = −0.97).

In two experiments by Lin and Atkinson (2013), college students learned about how the human cardiovascular system works from a multimedia lesson that was either animated or consisted of static visuals. Some students were prompted to self-explain throughout the lesson by typing their responses to open-ended questions such as, "Could you explain the function of blood in your own words?" Other students were not prompted to self-explain during the lesson. Results of Experiment 1 indicated that students prompted to self-explain significantly outperformed students who were not prompted to self-explain on a subsequent comprehension test, regardless of whether the lesson was animated or static (average d = 0.90). In Experiment 2, participants not prompted to self-explain were allowed to take notes during the lesson. Results indicated that, overall, the prompted students again outperformed the unprompted students on the comprehension test; however, this effect held only for those who learned from an animated lesson (animated lesson d = 1.82; static lesson d = 0.22). The authors concluded that prompting students to self-explain "may be the contributing factor that bridges the gap and enhances the coherence between external animations and internal mental models" (p. 105).

Finally, in a recent study by Cho and Lee (2013), pre-service teachers learned about principles of instructional design by studying examples presented on PowerPoint slides. Some participants wrote self-explanations of each slide on a worksheet (self-explanation group), whereas others only studied the slides and did not self-explain (control group). As a transfer task, both groups were then asked to evaluate the strengths and weaknesses of novel presentation slides in terms of content, layout, and illustrations. Across these six dimensions, results indicated some evidence that the self-explain group was better able to evaluate novel slides than the control group (average $d = 0.34$).

Prompting Younger Learners to Self-Explain

Does the self-explanation effect hold for younger learners? In one experiment by Mwangi and Sweller (1998), third graders learned how to solve arithmetic word problems by studying worked examples that were either integrated or involved split attention. Children either were asked to self-explain the examples (self-explanation group) or they were not asked to self-explain (control group). Results indicated no significant difference between the groups in the number of correct solutions provided on a delayed transfer test for children either studying integrated or split-attention examples (average $d = -0.10$). The authors concluded that the lack of benefit for self-explaining may be due to the procedural (rather than conceptual) nature of the learning materials.

In a study by Pine and Messer (2000), five-to-nine-year-old children learned a balance beam task by viewing a demonstration from the instructor. Some children were asked to self-explain how the instructor was able to get the beam balanced, whereas other children only observed the demonstration. Results indicated that children who asked to self-explain experienced significantly greater improvement in their understanding of how a balance beam works than those who only observed; however, the study did not include sufficient statistics to calculate effect size. Similar results were found in a study by Siegler and Chen (2008), in which children were better able to learn rules for solving a water displacement task when they were asked to explain why their answers were correct or incorrect.

Does the type of instruction children receive moderate the effects of self-explaining? A study by Rittle-Johnson (2006) tested whether self-explanation is more effective within a direct instruction or discovery-learning environment for teaching elementary school students about mathematical equivalence. In the experiment, students were either explicitly taught a procedure (i.e., direct instruction) or were asked to invent a procedure on their own (i.e., discovery learning). Some students were prompted to self-explain during learning, whereas others did not self-explain. The results indicated that students who self-explained during learning significantly outperformed those who did not self-explain on a procedural transfer test (d = 0.38), regardless of which form of instruction they received, but self-explaining did not result in greater gains in conceptual knowledge (average d = −0.11).

In a related study by Matthews and Rittle-Johnson (2009), children learned about mathematical equivalence from conceptual instruction on the meaning of the equal sign. Children asked to self-explain did not significantly outperform those not asked to self-explain on procedural transfer or conceptual knowledge tests. The study did not provide sufficient statistics to calculate effect size.

In a recent study by McEldoon, Drukin, and Rittle-Johnson (2013), children from second to fourth grade learned how to solve mathematical equivalence problems. Some children were prompted to self-explain during learning, whereas other children were not prompted to self-explain. Results indicated that children who self-explained outperformed children who did not self-explain on immediate and delayed measures of procedural (average d = 0.43) and conceptual (average d = 0.58) knowledge. However, when compared to a third condition that received additional problem-solving practice (to equate overall learning time), the benefits of self-explaining were considerably reduced. This result suggests that it is important to consider the extent to which self-explaining, which can be time-consuming, offers unique learning benefits beyond other uses of learning time.

In a study by Hsu and Tsai (2011), third-graders were taught concepts related to light and shadows within a digital game-based environment. Some students played the game with menu-based self-explanation prompts that required them to select the correct explanation to various questions (e.g., "Which option is the possible cause of the failure?"), whereas other students played the game without prompts. The results showed no major differences in post-test performance between the two groups (d = .17); however, only the students receiving self-explanation prompts demonstrated a significant improvement in performance from pre-test to post-test. A recent follow-up study by Hsu and Tsai (2013) similarly found null results for the effects of adding self-explanation prompting to an educational game.

Additional Evidence for Self-Explanation

In a study by Hausmann and Chi (2002), college students learned about the human circulatory system by reading a text-based lesson presented on a computer. Some students were prompted to "type comments to themselves"

(p. 5) as they read the lesson, whereas other students only read the text. The results indicated that the two groups did not significantly differ in terms of performance on a final comprehension test ($d = 0.11$). This study suggests that prompting students simply to comment to themselves does not guarantee that they will generate quality self-explanations.

Does learning from diagrams promote the self-explanation effect? Ainsworth and Loizou (2003) investigated this question by asking college students to learn from either a text-based or diagram-based lesson on the human circulatory system. The results indicated that the diagram group greatly outperformed the text group on subsequent retention and transfer tests. This finding suggests that presenting diagrams helps students generate better-quality explanations, thereby promoting deep learning.

In a related study, Butcher (2006) asked college students to learn about the human heart and circulatory system by self-explaining aloud while studying one of three lesson formats: text, text with simple diagrams, or text with detailed diagrams. The results indicated that students who studied a lesson that included diagrams (i.e., either simplified or detailed) generated significantly more inferences during learning than those who studied only text. However, there were no significant differences across groups on subsequent inference questions related to the text. Overall, there is some support for the idea that diagrams promote the self-explanation effect beyond learning from text alone. The studies by Ainsworth and Loizou (2003) and Butcher (2006) did not include control groups who did not self-explain the material; therefore, these studies are not included in Table 7.1.

In a study by Ainsworth and Burcham (2007), college students learned about the human circulatory system from a text that was either maximally coherent (such as by replacing pronouns with nouns, adding elaborations, and adding connectives to show the relations between sentences) or minimally coherent (such as by using pronouns, excluding elaborations, and excluding connectives). Students were also either asked to self-explain aloud after every sentence they read (the self-explaining group) or to read the passage twice (the control group). Results indicated that the self-explaining group outperformed the control group on subsequent implicit knowledge and knowledge inference questions (i.e., transfer), and that this benefit was strongest when students studied texts that were maximally coherent (average $d = 1.41$) compared to minimally coherent (average $d = 0.68$).

In a study by de Bruin, Rikers, and Schmidt (2007), college students were instructed to predict the next move of a computer-based chess opponent. Some students were asked to also self-explain why their prediction represented the best move, whereas other students did not self-explain. In a subsequent test phase, students who self-explained their predictions attained significantly more checkmates than those who only predicted them (d = 1.51).

Chamberland and colleagues (2011) tested whether asking students to generate self-explanations fosters medical students' ability to solve clinical cases. The results indicated that students who generated self-explanations during training were better able to diagnose unfamiliar cases on a subsequent transfer test (d = 0.75), whereas the groups did not differ in their diagnostic performance for familiar cases (d = −0.27). A recent study by Larsen, Butler, and Roediger (2013) also found positive support for self-explanation in medical education (d = 0.68).

Self-Explanation Training Programs

Self-explanation features have also been incorporated within broader training programs designed to teach students subjects such as computer programming, physics, geometry, and reading comprehension strategies. For example, Bielaczyc, Pirolli, and Brown (1995) tested the effects of explicitly training students how to use a set of self-explanation and self-regulation strategies to learn about computer programming. The training consisted of modeling and scaffolding techniques so that students could observe and apply the various strategies (e.g., identifying and elaborating main ideas from text, connecting concepts between texts and examples). A control group was provided with a similar set of strategies but did not receive explicit training in how to use them. The results indicated that students who received explicit training showed significantly larger problem-solving performance gains from pre-test to post-test than the control group. This study suggests that explicit training programs that incorporate self-explanation features can effectively enhance problem-solving performance.

Conati and VanLehn (2000) tested the effects of a computer-based training program designed to support students' self-explanations of physics worked examples. In their experiment, some students studied worked examples related to Newton's laws of motion using the training program, which including feedback and coaching, whereas other students studied the worked examples without receiving feedback or coaching. Results indicated that the self-explanation training program was particularly effective for students with relatively low prior knowledge.

Wong, Lawson, and Keeves (2002) tested the effects of training high school students to self-explain while learning about theorems in geometry.

The training consisted of students listening to a recording of a model answering a series of self-explanation questions and practice responding to questions on their own (e.g., "What parts of this page are new to me?"). A control group did not receive training and instead used their normal study strategies during learning. The results indicated that students who received self-explanation training significantly outperformed the control group on far transfer problems that required students to apply their knowledge of a new theorem to different problem types.

McNamara (2004) tested the effectiveness of a reading strategy program, called Self-Explanation Reading Training (SERT), on college students' comprehension of scientific texts. SERT consists of both reading strategy instruction and practice in generating self-explanations. In the training phase of the experiment, four scientific texts were provided to students; some students received SERT, whereas other students read the texts aloud. After training, both groups self-explained while reading an additional text. The results indicated that SERT was only effective in improving comprehension and self-explanation quality for students with low prior knowledge.

McNamara, Levinstein, and Boonthum (2004) then incorporated SERT within a web-based application called Interactive Strategy Training for Active Reading and Thinking (iSTART). iSTART involves interacting with animated characters (i.e., students and a teacher) within a simulated classroom. For example, trainees are first tasked with identifying the strategies used in the self-explanations of animated student characters. Then they receive practice generating their own self-explanations, with the guidance of the animated instructor character. McNamara and colleagues (2006) tested whether receiving iSTART would improve the reading comprehension of scientific texts in adolescents. Students receiving iSTART were compared to students who were given brief instruction in how to self-explain text. After training, both groups self-explained a text and completed a comprehension test on the material. The results indicated that iSTART improved reading comprehension performance over the control group for students with high and low prior knowledge. Further, students with low prior knowledge receiving iSTART benefited on text-based questions, whereas students with high prior knowledge receiving iSTART benefited on questions requiring inference making. A recent study by Kurby and colleagues (2012) reports similar benefits of training students using iSTART. Overall, incorporating self-explanation features within a reading strategy training program appears to benefit students' comprehension of scientific texts.

WHAT ARE THE BOUNDARY CONDITIONS
FOR SELF-EXPLAINING?

The research evidence presented in this chapter provides strong support for the self-explanation effect, demonstrating positive effects across subject areas and lesson formats. It also suggests important boundary conditions under which self-explaining is likely to be most effective. First, self-explaining may be most useful for conceptual learning materials (such as how a scientific system works) rather than more procedural learning materials. Second, self-explaining is particularly effective when instruction minimizes extraneous processing, such as through studying worked examples or adding cueing features to animations. Third, there is some evidence that the self-explanation effect is particularly strong for learners with lower prior knowledge. However, some learners may need explicit training in how to generate quality self-explanations.

Another possible boundary condition is the type of self-explanation prompting provided to students. One basic distinction between prompting types consists of classifying prompts as open, in which students openly think aloud or openly respond to questions; or focused, in which students complete a provided explanation or select explanations from a list. Although research comparing prompting types has been relatively mixed, there is some support for providing more focused prompting (e.g., selecting from a menu) compared to asking students to openly generate self-explanations. Similarly, if prompting is open, students may benefit from more specific wording (such as prompts to explain particular aspects of a diagram) rather than more general prompts (such as prompts to explain an entire diagram). Future research should aim to provide clearer guidelines regarding different prompting methods and to better specify what constitutes self-explanation.

HOW CAN WE APPLY SELF-EXPLAINING?

Students can use self-explaining as a study strategy when reading scientific texts or studying diagrams that represent complex scientific systems. They are also likely to benefit from self-explaining the solution steps of worked examples to themselves when learning to solve math problems. Within computer-based environments, adding self-explanation prompts that are more focused (rather than general) may help learners better identify discrepancies between the material and their prior knowledge. In some cases, it may even be appropriate to prompt learners to select explanations from a list. Although the research evidence suggests that more focused prompting may be most effective, further research is needed to establish more precise guidelines for how to best provide self-explanation prompting within different learning environments and for different learners. Similarly, future research should focus on striking a balance between the extent to which learners are forced to generate information on their own and the extent to which it is directly provided to them (such as in the form of instructional explanations).

Some students may need moderate amounts of explicit training in how to generate self-explanations effectively. The training should include short segments of modeling of how to self-explain by an effective learner, followed by practice with feedback (e.g., Renkl et al., 1998). Research suggests self-explaining is a learnable skill that can greatly improve learner understanding of a lesson, but learners may need considerable guidance in how to be an effective self-explainer. Further research is needed to determine the appropriate level of training in how to self-explain effectively and the appropriate level of guidance as to what constitutes a quality self-explanation.

CONCLUSION

Generating self-explanations requires students to assimilate to-be-learned information with their prior knowledge. This involves generating inferences from the material presented, which helps students better monitor their own learning and construct accurate mental models. The available research evidence provides strong support for the effects of generating self-explanations on measures of deep learning, yielding a median effect size of $d = 0.68$ across fifty-four experimental comparisons. This research indicates that generating self-explanations can be beneficial across several subject areas and within various learning environments. Self-explaining may be particularly effective when learning from diagrams and worked examples. Further, more focused self-explanation prompting may be most useful within computer-based learning environments such as educational games and simulations. Overall, there is strong support that self-explaining promotes generative processing required for deep learning.

REFERENCES

Ainsworth, S., & Burcham, S. (2007). The impact of text coherence on learning by self-explanation. *Learning and Instruction*, 17, 286–303.
Ainsworth, S., & Loizou, A. T. (2003). The effects of self-explaining when learning with text or diagrams. *Learning and Instruction*, 17, 286–303.

Aleven, V. A. W. M. M., & Koedinger, K. R. (2002). An effective metacognitive strategy: learning by doing and explaining with a computer-based cognitive tutor. *Cognitive Science*, 26(2), 147–79.

Atkinson, R. K., Renkl, A., & Merrill, M. M. (2003). Transitioning from studying examples to solving problems: effects of self-explanation prompts and fading worked-out steps. *Journal of Educational Psychology*, 95(4), 774–83.

Berthold, K., Eysink, T. H. S., & Renkl, A. (2009). Assisting self-explanation prompts are more effective than open prompts when learning with multiple representations. *Instructional Science*, 37, 345–63.

Berthold, K., & Renkl, A. (2009). Instructional aids to support a conceptual understanding of multiple representations. *Journal of Educational Psychology*, 101(1), 70–87.

Berthold, K., Roder, H., Knorzer, D., Kessler, W., & Renkl, A. (2011). The double-edged effects of explanation prompts. *Computers in Human Behavior*, 27, 69–75.

Bielaczyc, K., Pirolli, P. L., & Brown, A. L. (1995). Training in self-explanation and self-regulation strategies: investigating the effects of knowledge acquisition activities on problem solving. *Cognition and Instruction*, 13(2), 221–52.

Butcher, K. R. (2006). Learning from text with diagrams: promoting mental model development and inference generation. *Journal of Educational Psychology*, 98(1), 183–97.

Chamberland, M., St-Onge, C., Setrakian, J., Lanthier, L., Bergeron, L., Bourget, A. Rikers, R. (2011). The influence of medical students' self-explanations on diagnostic performance. *Medical Education*, 45, 688–95.

Chi, M. T. H. (2000). Self-explaining expository texts: the dual processes of generating inferences and repairing mental models. In R. Glaser (Ed.) *Advances in Instructional Psychology* (pp. 161–238). Mahwah, NJ: Lawrence Erlbaum Associates.

(2009). Active-constructive-interactive: a conceptual framework for differentiating learning activities. *Topics in Cognitive Science*, 1, 73–105.

Chi, M. T. H., Bassok, M., Lewis, M., Reimann, P., & Glaser, R. (1989). Self-explanations: how students study and use examples in learning to solve problems. *Cognitive Science*, 13, 145–82.

Chi, M. T. H., de Leeuw, N., Chiu, M., & LaVancher, C. (1994). Eliciting self-explanations improves understanding. *Cognitive Science*, 18, 439–77.

Cho, Y. H., & Lee, S. E. (2013). The role of co-explanation and self-explanation in learning from design examples of PowerPoint presentation slides. *Computers and Education*, 69, 400–7.

Conati, C., & VanLehn, K. (2000). Toward computer-based support of meta-cognitive skills: a computational framework to coach self-explanation. *International Journal of Artificial Intelligence in Education*, 11(4), 389–415.

de Bruin, A., Rikers, R., & Schmidt, H. (2007). The effect of self-explanation and prediction on the development of principled understanding of chess in novices. *Contemporary Educational Psychology*, 32(2), 188–205.

de Koning, B. B., Tabbers, H. K., Rikers, R. M. J. P., & Paas, F. (2011). Improved effectiveness of cueing by self-explanations when learning from a complex animation. *Applied Cognitive Psychology*, 25, 183–94.

Dunlosky, J., Rawson, K. A., Marsh, E. J., Nathan, M. J., & Willingham, D. T. (2013). Improving students' learning with effective learning techniques: promising directions from cognitive and educational psychology. *Psychological Science in the Public Interest*, 14, 4–58.

Ferguson-Hessler, M. G. M., & de Jong, T. (1990). Studying physics texts: differences in study processes between good and poor performers. *Cognition and Instruction*, 7(1), 41–54.

Fonseca, B. A., & Chi, M. T. H. (2011). Instruction based on self-explanation. In R. E. Mayer & P. A. Alexander (Eds.), *Handbook of Research in Learning and Instruction* (pp. 296–319). New York, NY: Routledge.

Gadgil, S., Nokes-Malach, T. J., & Chi, M. T. H. (2012). Effectiveness of holistic mental model confrontation in driving conceptual change. *Learning and Instruction*, 22(1), 47–61.

Gerjets, P., Scheiter, K., & Catrambone, R. (2006). Can learning from molar and modular worked examples be enhanced by providing instructional explanations and prompting self-explanations? *Learning and Instruction*, 16, 104–21.

Glogger, I., Schwonke, R., Holzapfel, L., Nuckles, M., & Renkl, A. (2012). Learning strategies assessed by journal writing: prediction of learning outcomes by quantity, quality, and combinations of learning strategies. *Journal of Educational Psychology*, 104(2), 452–68.

Grobe, C. S., & Renkl, A. (2006). Effects of multiple solution methods in mathematics learning. *Learning and Instruction*, 16, 122–38.

(2007). Finding and fixing errors in worked examples: can this foster learning outcomes? *Learning and Instruction*, 17, 612–34.

Hausmann, R. G. M., & Chi, M. T. H. (2002). Can a computer interface support self-explaining? *Cognitive Technology*, 7(1), 4–14.

Hilbert, T. S., & Renkl, A. (2009). Learning how to use a computer-based concept-mapping tool: self-explaining examples helps. *Computers in Human Behavior*, 25, 267–74.

Hilbert, T. S., Renkl, A., Kessler, S., & Reiss, K. (2008). Learning to prove in geometry: learning from heuristic examples and how it can be supported. *Learning and Instruction*, 18, 54–65.

Hsu, C.-Y., & Tsai, C.-C. (2011). Investigating the impact of integrating self-explanation into an educational game: a pilot study. *Edutainment Technologies* (pp. 250–4). Taipei, Taiwan: Springer Berlin Heidelberg.

(2013). Examining the effects of combining self-explanation principles with an educational game on learning science concepts. *Interactive Learning Environments*, 21(2), 104–15.

Johnson, C. I., & Mayer, R. E. (2010). Applying the self-explanation principle to multimedia learning in a computer-based game-like environment. *Computers in Human Behavior*, 26, 1246–52.

King, A. (1992). Comparison of self-questioning, summarizing, and notetaking-review as strategies for learning from lectures. *American Educational Research Journal*, 29(2), 303–23.

Kurby, C. A., Magliano, J. P., Dandotkar, S. Woehrle, J., Gilliam, S., & McNamara, D. S. (2012). Changing how students process and comprehend texts with computer-based self-explanation training. *Journal of Educational Computing Research*, 47(4), 429–59.

Kwon, K., Kumalasari, C. D., & Howland, J. L. (2011). Self-explanation prompts on problem-solving performance in an interactive learning environment. *Journal of Interactive Online Learning*, 10(2), 96–112.

Larsen, D. P., Butler, A. C., & Roediger, H. L., III. (2013). Comparative effects of test-enhanced learning and self-explanation on long-term retention. *Medical Education*, 47(7), 674–82.

Lin, L., & Atkinson, R. K. (2013). Enhancing learning from different visualizations by self-explanation prompts. *Journal of Educational Computing Research*, 49(1), 83–110.

Matthews, P., & Rittle-Johnson, B. (2009). In pursuit of knowledge: comparing self-explanations, concepts, and procedures as pedagogical tools. *Journal of Experimental Child Psychology*, 104, 1–21.

Mayer, R. E. (2014). Cognitive theory of multimedia learning. In R. E. Mayer (Ed.), *The Cambridge Handbook of Multimedia Learning* (2nd ed.). New York, NY: Cambridge University Press.

   (2009). *Multimedia Learning* (2nd ed.). New York, NY: Cambridge University Press.

Mayer, R. E., & Johnson, C. I. (2010). Adding instructional features that promote learning in a game-like environment. *Journal of Educational Computing Research*, 42(3), 241–65.

McEldoon, K. L., Durkin, K. L., & Rittle-Johnson, B. (2013). Is self-explanation worth the time? A comparison to additional practice. *British Journal of Educational Psychology*, 83(4), 615–32.

McNamara, D. S. (2004). SERT: self-explanation reading training. *Discourse Processes*, 38(1), 1–30.

McNamara, D. S., Levinstein, I. B., & Boonthum, C. (2004). iSTART: interactive strategy training for active reading and thinking. *Behavior Research Methods, Instruments & Computers*, 36(2), 222–33.

McNamara, D. S., O'Reilly, T. P., Best, R. M., & Ozuru, Y. (2006). Improving adolescent students' reading comprehension with iSTART. *Journal of Educational Computing Research*, 34(2), 147–71.

Mwangi, W., & Sweller, J. (1998). Learning to solve compare word problems: the effect of example format and generating self-explanations. *Cognition and Instruction*, 16(2), 173–99.

Nokes-Malach, T. J., VanLehn, K., Belenky, D. M., Lichtenstein, M., & Cox, G. (2013). Coordinating principles and examples through analogy and self-explanation. *European Journal of Psychology of Education*, 28(4), 1237–73.

O'Reilly, T., Symons, S., & MacLatchy-Gaudet, H. (1998). A comparison of self-explanation and elaborative interrogation. *Contemporary Educational Psychology*, 23, 434–45.

Pine, K. J., & Messer, D. J. (2000). The effect of explaining another's actions on children's implicit theories of balance. *Cognition and Instruction*, 18(1), 35–51.

Pirolli, P., & Recker, M. (1994). Learning strategies and transfer in the domain of programming. *Cognition and Instruction*, 12 (3), 235–75.

Pressley, M., McDaniel, M. A., Turnure, J. E., Wood, E., & Ahmad, M. (1987). Generation and precision of elaboration: effects on intentional and incidental learning. *Journal of Experimental Psychology: Learning, Memory, and Cognition*, 13, 291–300.

Renkl, A. (1997). Learning from worked-out examples: a study on individual differences. *Cognitive Science*, 21(1), 1–29.

(1999). Learning mathematics from worked-out examples: analyzing and fostering self-explanations. *European Journal of Psychology of Education*, 14(4), 477–88.

Renkl, A., Stark, R. Gruber, H., & Mandl, H. (1998). Learning from worked-out examples: the effects of examples variability and elicited self-explanations. *Contemporary Educational Psychology*, 23, 90–108.

Rittle-Johnson, B. (2006). Promoting transfer: effects of self-explanation and direct instruction. *Child Development*, 77(1), 1–15.

Schworm, S., & Renkl, A. (2006). Computer-supported example-based learning: when instructional explanations reduce self-explanations. *Computers & Education*, 46, 426–45.

(2007). Learning argumentation skills through the use of prompts for self-explaining examples. *Journal of Educational Psychology*, 99(2), 285–96.

Siegler, R. S., & Chen, Z. (2008). Differentiation and integration: guiding principles for analyzing cognitive change. *Developmental Science*, 11(4), 433–53.

Van der Meij, J., & De Jong, T. (2011). The effects of directive self-explanation prompts to support active processing of multiple representations in a simulation-based learning environment. *Journal of Computer Assisted Learning*, 27(5), 411–23.

Wong, R. M. F., Lawson, M. J., & Keeves, J. (2002). The effects of self-explanation training on students' problem solving in high school mathematics. *Learning and Instruction*, 12, 233–62.

Wylie, R., & Chi, M. T. H. (2014). The self-explanation principle in multimedia learning. In R. E. Mayer (Ed.), *The Cambridge Handbook of Multimedia Learning* (2nd ed.; pp. 413–32). New York, NY: Cambridge University Press.

8

Learning by Teaching

SUMMARY

Learning by teaching involves improving one's own understanding of previously studied material through the act of teaching it to others. For example, after reading a scientific text, a student might enhance his or her own understanding of the material by explaining the important concepts to another student. In seventeen out of nineteen experimental tests, students who studied and then taught the material to others performed better on a test of the material than those who did not teach, yielding a median effect size of $d = 0.77$. Concerning boundary conditions, teaching was most effective when students generated explanations that involved making sense of the material rather than simply restating it. Learning by teaching was also more effective when students originally studied with the expectation of later teaching and when teaching included meaningful interactions with another student (e.g., providing feedback and answering questions). Learning by teaching can be applied to learning from text, multimedia, and interaction with computer-based pedagogical agents, and to helping students understand scientific concepts. It also is a fundamental component of popular classroom activities, such as peer tutoring, cooperative learning, and small-group discussions. The available empirical research on learning by teaching is somewhat limited, but suggests that teaching is a promising learning strategy for promoting deep understanding.

BOX 1. *Overview of Learning by Teaching*	

Definition	Learners teach others about previously studied material.
Example	Learners are asked to study a multimedia lesson on a scientific process and then to explain to another student how the process works.
Theoretical rationale	Asking students to teach others encourages students to select the most relevant information from a lesson and organize it into a coherent explanation, and can involve integrating the material with existing knowledge. Although teaching is intended to foster generative processing, the benefits of learning by teaching may depend on whether students go beyond simply restating the material, and instead reflect and elaborate on the material.
Empirical rationale	The learning-by-teaching effect is upheld in seventeen of nineteen tests, yielding a median effect size of $d = 0.77$.
Boundary conditions	The learning-by-teaching effect may be strongest when learners study the material with the expectation of later teaching it, when they reflect upon their own understanding (i.e., reflective knowledge building) rather than merely restate the material from the lesson (i.e., knowledge telling), and when they are prompted with deep questions by their pupils.
Applications	Learning by teaching applies to learning about scientific concepts from text or multimedia, through interacting with other people, or by interacting with a computer-based pedagogical agent.

CHAPTER OUTLINE

1. Example of Teaching as a Learning Strategy
2. What Is Learning by Teaching?
3. How Does Learning by Teaching Foster Learning?
4. What Is the Evidence for Learning by Teaching?
5. What Are the Boundary Conditions of Learning by Teaching?
6. How Can We Apply Learning by Teaching?
7. Conclusion

EXAMPLE OF TEACHING AS A LEARNING STRATEGY

Please take a moment and read the short lesson below on the Doppler effect. After studying the lesson, we will ask you to orally explain how the Doppler effect works as if you were teaching a student who has little prior knowledge of the subject.

The Doppler Effect

The Doppler effect is very common, though many people do not know what causes it. For example, imagine a person is standing on a street corner as a fire truck approaches with its siren blaring: The perceived pitch of the siren will sound higher to the observer as it approaches; as it passes by, the observer will perceive the pitch as getting lower. In order to understand how this process works, it is important to first understand some of the basic characteristics of sound waves.

Sound waves have two primary characteristics: wavelength and frequency. Wavelength is the distance between adjacent waves. Frequency is the number of waves passing through a given point during a period of time. Longer sound waves require more time to travel a given distance, so they occur less frequently and have a lower pitch. Shorter sound waves require less time to travel a given distance, so they occur more frequently and have a higher pitch.

Motion influences the frequency and wavelength of waves. To illustrate, imagine a bug jiggling on the surface of a pond. If the bug is stationary, the waves on the surface of the water around it will be at the same frequency and length in all directions. When the bug moves to the right, the waves it produces become shorter and more frequent to the right of the bug and longer and less frequent to the left of the bug.

To relate the bug analogy to the Doppler effect, imagine that a fire truck is approaching an observer with its siren blaring. As the fire truck approaches, the observer receives the sound waves at a higher frequency. Specifically, the sound waves take less time to reach the observer because they are being compressed closer together between the fire truck and the observer. As a result, the observer experiences an increasing pitch. As the fire truck passes by, the observer receives the waves at a lower frequency. Specifically, the sound waves take longer to reach the observer because they are being stretched farther apart between the fire truck and the observer. As a result, the observer experiences a decreasing pitch.

Now, without referring back to the lesson, please take two minutes to explain aloud how the Doppler effect works, perhaps to friend or family member, or simply as if you were talking to a hypothetical student.

Does teaching others improve one's own learning? In a series of experiments by Fiorella and Mayer (2013a, 2014), students who studied a lesson on the Doppler effect and then presented a video-recorded lecture of the material as if they were teaching another student outperformed students who studied the lesson normally on a delayed comprehension test. This suggests that the act of teaching the contents of a lesson to someone else promotes a deeper understanding of the material that persists over time.

In this chapter, we explore the available research evidence on the benefits of learning by teaching. In particular, we are concerned with how explaining material to others can be used as an effective learning strategy to enhance meaningful learning outcomes such as comprehension and transfer.

WHAT IS LEARNING BY TEACHING?

Learning by teaching involves learning material more deeply through the process of teaching it to others. Teaching refers to explaining material to others for instructional purposes – for example, explaining to a peer how a scientific process works or how to solve a math problem. Yet the teaching process consists of more than the act of explaining to others. For example, merely preparing to teach – studying with the expectation of later teaching others – can influence learning beyond studying normally for a test (Bargh & Schul, 1980; Benware & Deci, 1984; Fiorella & Mayer, 2013a). Further, student-teacher interactions such as answering student questions may also play an important role in learning by teaching (Roscoe & Chi, 2007, 2008). Thus, one challenge of research on learning by teaching is to explain how different aspects of the teaching process uniquely and interdependently contribute to learning (Fiorella & Mayer, 2013a).

Much of the research on learning by teaching has focused on the benefits that peer tutoring offers for the tutor (e.g., Cohen, Kulik, & Kulik, 1982; Roscoe & Chi, 2007) – what is sometimes referred to as *tutor learning* (Roscoe & Chi, 2007). For example, in cross-age tutoring, older students often benefit from tutoring younger students (e.g., Cloward, 1967; Morgan & Toy, 1970; Galbraith & Winterbottom, 2011). In reciprocal teaching, students learn by taking turns teaching the contents of a lesson to each other (e.g., Fantuzzo et al., 1989; King, Staffieri, & Adelgais, 1998; Palincsar & Brown, 1984). According to a review by Roscoe and Chi (2007), tutors generally benefit from participating in peer-tutoring programs such as cross-age tutoring and reciprocal teaching; however, the effects of such programs can vary considerably. Further, studies following this program-based approach are often unable to pinpoint how different features influence learning. For example, in reciprocal teaching it is unclear whether learning gains are due to the act of teaching, the process of being taught by peers, or other factors unrelated to teaching, such as receiving guidance from the actual teacher. Similar challenges exist with other popular classroom activities related to learning by teaching, including cooperative learning (e.g., Slavin, 1983) and learning from small-group discussions (e.g., Cohen, 1994; Webb, 1982). Thus, this chapter focuses on research that aims to isolate the effects of teaching-specific activities (e.g., explaining to others) on student learning.

HOW DOES LEARNING BY TEACHING FOSTER LEARNING?

According to an early framework proposed by Bargh and Schul (1980), learning by teaching consists of three distinct stages, as shown in Figure 8.1. Each stage is thought to offer unique learning benefits. First, preparing to teach (without actually teaching) may promote learning beyond normal studying for a test because the mere expectation of teaching others motivates students to better select relevant information and organize it into a coherent representation during learning (e.g., Benware & Deci, 1984). Second, the act of explaining material to others may offer additional benefits because it requires learners to actively use the material in a meaningful way – that is, in a way that helps students ground the information in their existing knowledge (e.g., Fiorella & Mayer, 2013a). Finally, interacting with students, such as by answering questions, may offer metacognitive benefits – that is, it may encourage students to reflect on their understanding of the material while teaching (e.g., Roscoe & Chi, 2008). In short, understanding how learning by teaching works depends on determining the relative effects of preparing, explaining, and interacting.

In terms of the cognitive theory of multimedia learning, teaching primes the cognitive processes of selecting, organizing, and integrating, as shown in Box 2. Selecting involves including only the most relevant information from

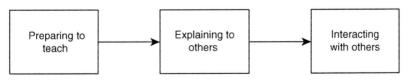

FIGURE 8.1. Three Stages of Learning by Teaching.

BOX 2. *Three Cognitive Processes Activated by Learning by Teaching*

Cognitive process	How learning by teaching primes the process
Selecting	Learners select the most relevant material to include in their explanation to others.
Organizing	Learners rearrange the selected information into a coherent explanation to provide to others.
Integrating	Learners explain the material to others by making connections between the material and their existing knowledge.

---

a lesson in one's explanation to others. Organizing involves rearranging the selected information into an explanation that can be used to help others understand the material. Integrating involves making sense out of the to-be-learned material by connecting it with relevant existing knowledge. Thus, the cognitive benefits of learning by teaching depend on the extent to which learners invest effort toward actively constructing a coherent representation of the material throughout the teaching process.

WHAT IS THE EVIDENCE FOR LEARNING BY TEACHING?

Table 8.1 presents the effect sizes of nineteen experimental comparisons investigating the effects of learning by teaching. Experiments included in the analysis compared the effects of studying a lesson (with or without the expectation of teaching) and then explaining the material to others (with or without interacting with others) to a control group that studied the material (with or without the expectation of teaching) but did not explain it to others. The teaching effect was upheld in seventeen of nineteen tests, yielding a median effect size of $d = 0.77$. Studies that did not include an appropriate control group or provided insufficient statistics are not included in this analysis. In the following sections, we discuss the core evidence for teaching as a generative learning strategy and then consider related evidence from research on learning by interacting with a computer-based teachable agent.

Core Evidence for Learning by Teaching

In a classic study, Bargh and Schul (1980) tested the effects of preparing to teach and actually teaching on learning outcomes. In Experiment 1, participants studied verbal material with instructions that they would

TABLE 8.1. *Effect sizes for learning by teaching*

Citation	Subject	Population	Comparison	Outcome	Effect size
Annis (1983), explain and interact	History	College	Prepare for test	Bloom's taxonomy	1.00
Annis (1983), explain and interact	History	College	Prepare to teach	Bloom's taxonomy	0.83
Coleman, Brown, & Rivkin (1997)	Natural selection	College	Summarize	Near transfer	0.77
Coleman, Brown, & Rivkin (1997)	Natural selection	College	Summarize	Far transfer	0.79
Coleman, Brown, & Rivkin (1997)	Natural selection	College	Self-explain	Near transfer	0.48
Coleman, Brown, & Rivkin (1997)	Natural selection	College	Self-explain	Far transfer	0.51
Roscoe & Chi (2008), explain	Human visual system	College	Self-explain	Comprehension	-1.63
Roscoe & Chi (2008), explain and interact	Human visual system	College	Self-explain	Comprehension	-1.12
Roscoe & Chi (2008), explain and interact	Human visual system	College	Explain to others	Comprehension	0.60
Gregory et al. (2011), explain and interact, immediate test	Cardiology	Medical	Prepare to teach	Comprehension	2.10
Gregory et al. (2011), explain and interact, delayed test	Cardiology	Medical	Prepare to teach	Comprehension	1.30
Fiorella & Mayer (2013a, Exp. 1) immediate test	Doppler effect	College	Prepare for test	Comprehension	0.82
Fiorella & Mayer (2013a, Exp. 1) immediate test	Doppler effect	College	Prepare to teach	Comprehension	0.31
Fiorella & Mayer (2013a, Exp. 2), delayed test	Doppler effect	College	Prepare for test	Comprehension	0.79
Fiorella & Mayer (2013a, Exp. 2), delayed test	Doppler effect	College	Prepare to teach	Comprehension	0.70
Fiorella & Mayer (2014a, Exp. 2), delayed test	Doppler effect	College	Prepare for test	Comprehension	0.56
Fiorella & Mayer (2014a, Exp. 2), delayed test	Doppler effect	College	Prepare for test	Comprehension	0.90
Fiorella & Mayer (2013b, Exp. 1), delayed test	Human ear	College	Prepare for test	Comprehension	0.77
Fiorella & Mayer (2013b, Exp. 1), delayed test	Human ear	College	Practice recall test	Comprehension	0.55
MEDIAN					0.77

take a test or with instructions that they would teach the information to a peer. Following the study period, both groups were tested on the material (without ever actually teaching it). Results indicated that those who prepared to teach another student outperformed those who prepared for a test on recognition and recall tests, yielding a teaching expectancy effect. In Experiment 2, students were given a verbal and a problem-solving task (i.e., the Tower of Hanoi) and were asked either to work alone silently, think aloud while solving the problems, or teach another person while solving the problems. Results indicated that asking students to teach another person while problem solving did not result in better learning. However, the authors concluded that this might have been due to short duration and relatively artificial nature of the teaching task. Unfortunately, this study did not include sufficient statistics to calculate effect size.

Annis (1983) attempted to isolate the effects of preparing to teach and actually teaching on learning within a peer-tutoring context. In the experiment, some students read a short history lesson and then taught the material to a peer. Other students read the lesson with the expectation of teaching (but did not actually teach), or they read the lesson normally with the expectation of being tested on the material. All students were then given a test one week later with questions targeting each of the six levels of Bloom's taxonomy (i.e., knowledge, comprehension, application, analysis, synthesis, and evaluation). First, results provided mixed support for a teaching expectancy effect – that is, students who prepared to teach performed somewhat better than those who read the lesson normally. Second, students who tutored a peer performed better than both those who read normally (average d = 1.00) and those who prepared to teach without actually teaching (average d = 0.83). This study suggests that there may be additive benefits associated with preparing to teach and actually teaching. However, it is important to note that students who taught in this study did so by interacting with their peer, which included answering questions. Thus, it is unclear the extent to which the added benefits of teaching were due to explaining to others or interacting with others.

In a study by Coleman, Brown, and Rivkin (1997), students studied a lesson on natural selection and then either summarized the material, explained the material to themselves, or explained the material to another student. All students then took near and far transfer tests on the material. Results indicated that students who explained to a peer significantly outperformed students who self-explained (near transfer: d = 0.48; far transfer: d = 0.51) and students who summarized on near and far transfer tests (near transfer: $d = 0.77$; far transfer: $d = 0.79$). In contrast to the study by Annis (1983), students who taught the material in the study by Coleman, Brown, and Rivkin did not interact with another student. Thus, this study suggests that explaining material to others offers learning benefits beyond summarizing or self-explaining. It is important to note, however, that students in this experiment studied with different expectations (i.e., to explain or summarize the material to oneself or to others); therefore, it is unclear to what extent the effects are due to preparing to teach or the act of explaining the material to others.

One potential challenge of learning by teaching is that students may not generate quality explanations while teaching. To investigate this issue, Roscoe and Chi (2008) analyzed the quality of tutor-tutee interactions during one-way (i.e., nonreciprocal) peer tutoring, including the quality of tutor explanations and tutors' responses to tutee questions. Students studied a lesson on the human visual system and then either provided a video-recorded lecture of the material (the explain-to-other group), explained to and interacted with a peer (the explain-and-interact group), or self-explained the material (the self-explain group). Results indicated that the explain-to-other group performed significantly worse than the self-explain group on a subsequent comprehension test ($d = -1.63$). The explain-and-interact group also performed significantly worse than the self-explain group on the comprehension test ($d = -1.12$). Analysis of process-based data of tutor-tutee interactions offers one possible explanation for this result – that is, tutors often showed a *knowledge-telling bias* in which they merely restated the to-be-learned material with minimal elaboration or integration. In contrast, tutors learned best when they displayed evidence of *reflective knowledge building* – that is, when they monitored their own understanding, generated inferences, and elaborated upon the material. There was also evidence that the knowledge-telling bias may be partially avoided through quality tutee questions that require the tutor to generate inferences. Overall, this study suggests that improving the quality of tutor-tutee interactions is critical to maximizing the benefits of learning by teaching. It also suggests that explaining to a hypothetical student (such as by making a videotaped explanation) may not capture some important aspects of the learning-by-teaching process.

A recent study by Roscoe (2014) further emphasized the importance of reflective knowledge-building behaviors in learning by teaching. Results indicated that factors such as the number of comprehension-monitoring statements made while teaching, the domain knowledge of the tutor, and the questions asked by the tutee all played an important role in promoting understanding.

Learning by teaching is also a popular instructional approach in medical education, but does it improve student learning? In a study by Gregory and colleagues (2011), third-year medical students prepared to teach second-year students about cardiac life support algorithms and how to interpret electrocardiogram (ECG) readings. Students then taught second-year students about algorithms or about ECG, or they did not teach. Results indicated the greatest learning gains on topics for which students both prepared to teach and actually taught (d = 2.10). These benefits also persisted over the course of a two-month delay (d = 1.30). This study provides support for the use of learning by teaching in medical education and suggests that preparing to teach and actually teaching may have unique contributions to learning outcomes.

In a series of experiments, Fiorella and Mayer (2013a, 2013b, 2014) took a closer look at the relative benefits of preparing to teach and explaining material to others. For example, in a study by Fiorella and Mayer (2013a), college students studied a short lesson on how the Doppler effect works with the expectation of later teaching the material or with the expectation of later being tested on the material (the study group). Of those expecting to teach, some students then actually taught the material by providing a video-recorded lecture (the teach group), whereas other students only prepared to teach (the prepare group). Results indicated that the teach group significantly outperformed the study group (d = 0.82), but not the prepare group (d = 0.31) on an immediate comprehension test (Experiment 1). However, the teach group significantly outperformed both the study group (d = 0.79) and the prepare group (d = 0.70) on a delayed comprehension test (Experiment 2). A follow-up study by Fiorella and Mayer (2014) found similar results when overall learning time was made equivalent across groups – in particular, the teach group significantly outperformed the study group (d = 0.56) and the prepare group (d = 0.90) on a delayed comprehension test. Finally, Fiorella and Mayer (2013b) found that preparing to teach and actually teaching led to better performance on a delayed comprehension test than a group receiving additional study time (d = 0.77) and a group that studied the material and then took a practice recall test on the material (d = 0.55). Overall, this research clarifies previous research by Annis (1983) and suggests that the act of teaching coupled with preparing to teach results in meaningful learning outcomes that are persistent over time.

Related Evidence for Learning by Teaching

Recent research suggests that students can also learn by teaching a computer-based pedagogical agent, or *teachable agent*. Learning from teachable agents typically involves students creating explanations or knowledge maps to help an on-screen agent understand a concept. Then students test the agent by asking it questions, and in the process receive feedback and guidance intended to help them improve the quality of their explanations. For example, in one experiment by Biswas and colleagues (2005), fifth grade students learned about how river ecosystems work either through being tutored by a computer-based agent or by interacting with a teachable agent called Betty's Brain. Students who learned by teaching did so by creating concept maps of the material; Betty then used the maps to answer questions and provide students with feedback. Some students taught a base version of the agent, whereas others taught an enhanced version that provided students with self-regulation strategies throughout the learning process. Results indicated that interacting with the enhanced version of Betty's Brain better prepared students for future learning than those who did not receive this support or those who learned by being tutored. This study did not include a control group that only studied material without being tutored or teaching the material; nonetheless, it suggests that monitoring one's own understanding is an important component of learning by teaching.

Follow-up studies (Chin et al., 2010; Leelawong and Biswas, 2008; Segedy, Kinnebrew, & Biswas, 2013) report similar benefits of interacting with Betty's Brain, including helping students better apply their knowledge of river ecosystems to solve novel problems. A study by Holmes (2007) also found that students generated deeper explanations when they interacted with Betty's Brain compared to when they explained without interacting with the agent. Further, a more recent study by Segedy, Kinnebrew, and Biswas (2013) reports evidence that students learn better when the agent provides a more enhanced form of contextualized conversational feedback (i.e., feedback that is presented in a conversational style and specifically grounded in students' task goals) compared to receiving more conventional dialogue. Overall, this research indicates that teachable agents can provide students with the types of metacognitive guidance and tutor-tutee interactions that support learning by teaching. However, these studies do not allow us to isolate the effects of engaging in teaching-specific activities (e.g., preparing, explaining, or interacting) on learning.

Do learners benefit from watching a teachable agent use the information it was taught? Research by Okita and colleagues (2013; Okita & Schwartz, 2013) investigated this question by providing some students with recursive feedback after interacting with a teachable agent. In one study (Okita et al., 2013), students taught a computer-based agent about human biology. Students who observed their teachable agent then use the material it learned by playing a game with another agent performed better on a subsequent transfer test than students who taught and received a more traditional form of feedback and performed better than students who only prepared to teach the material but did not actually teach. Another study by Okita and Schwartz (2013) found similar results when students taught and received recursive feedback from virtual agents in the online game Second Life. Overall, this research suggests that observing the consequences of teaching (i.e., receiving recursive feedback) may provide additive benefits beyond only teaching and receiving typical feedback.

Matsuda and colleagues (2013) investigated the effects of learning from an online, gamelike teachable agent called SimStudent. In three classroom experiments, students tutored SimStudent on skills such as solving linear equations by providing it with examples and feedback. Results indicated that learning by teaching SimStudent did not significantly enhance learning beyond learning from a cognitive tutor. However, analysis of process data suggested that learning by teaching was most effective when students engaged in more teaching-related activities (such as providing accurate feedback and hints) and when students generated high-quality explanations of target problems. This result further emphasizes the importance of providing students with direct guidance in how to teach (such as how to generate high-quality explanations and provide feedback) to maximize the benefits of learning by teaching.

WHAT ARE THE BOUNDARY CONDITIONS OF LEARNING BY TEACHING?

The benefits of learning by teaching appear to depend somewhat on the extent to which students reflect on their own understanding of the material and integrate it with their existing knowledge while teaching (Roscoe & Chi, 2007). Unfortunately, students may engage in a knowledge-telling bias in which they simply restate the to-be-learned material. Thus, students need to receive instructional support on how to generate high-quality explanations and how to engage in teaching-related activities effectively, such as providing a student with appropriate feedback or examples. Receiving deep questions from tutees during teaching may help avoid knowledge telling and instead foster more generative processing during learning by teaching. Interacting with a computer-based teachable agent and receiving recursive feedback may also help prompt students to reflect on their own understanding of the material, thereby promoting deep learning. In short, learning by teaching is most effective when it consists of high-quality explanations and productive interactions with students or pedagogical agents.

Studying with the expectation of teaching others may also play an important role in learning by teaching, particularly when it is paired with actually teaching (Fiorella & Mayer, 2014). Research on the teaching expectancy effect suggests that preparing to teach (without actually teaching) may improve learning outcomes under some conditions (such as on immediate learning tests). However, there may be instances in which stress or other social factors moderate the potential benefits associated with the prospect of teaching others (Ehly, Keith, & Bratton, 1987; Herberg & Levin, 2012; Renkl, 1995). One possibility is that preparing to teach requires more study time and that reducing time constraints during the preparation phase might help alleviate excessive stress or anxiety. This area of learning by teaching is in need of further research.

HOW CAN WE APPLY LEARNING BY TEACHING?

Learning by teaching can be applied as a study strategy to help students understand academic material such as how a scientific process works or how to solve complex problems. Its effectiveness may not depend on the presence of another person, but students may benefit from interacting with others – for example, by answering tutee questions that encourage them to reflect on their own understanding of the material or by observing their tutees use the material. Thus, successful peer tutoring may require that tutees receive training in how to ask meaningful questions. Further, studying material with the expectation of teaching may help promote better-quality explanations when students actually do teach, particularly if they receive guidance and support in how to prepare to teach effectively. Learning by teaching can also be applied with computer-based learning environments, such as by interacting with a teachable agent or within an educational game. Technology-based platforms for learning by teaching have the potential of providing feedback and metacognitive support to help students generate better-quality explanations.

Learning by teaching can also be applied as part of an instructional program within the classroom. For example, the idea that students learn by teaching others is prevalent among popular educational practices such as peer tutoring (e.g., King, Staffieri, & Adelgais, 1998), cooperative learning environments (e.g., Slavin, 1983), and learning from small-group discussions (e.g., Cohen, 1994; Webb, 1982). Effective implementation of learning by teaching into such programs is likely to depend on the extent to which the program is structured to foster high-quality explanations and productive interactions between students, such as by offering students challenging questions to prime deeper forms of teaching (Roscoe & Chi, 2007).

CONCLUSION

The idea that students learn by teaching others is popular in education, yet empirical research on learning-by-teaching effects is somewhat limited. Although there is considerable research on the benefits that peer tutoring provides for the tutor (i.e., "tutor learning"), further research is needed to better understand how each stage of learning by teaching (i.e., preparing, explaining, and interacting) uniquely and interdependently contributes to learning. For example, research should take a closer look at how preparing to teach influences the way that students study material or how the quality of students' explanations or interactions between students are influenced by different learning conditions. Nonetheless, the available research evidence provides promise for the benefits of learning by teaching. In particular, students understand academic material better when they explain it to others in a way that encourages them to reflect on their understanding and connect the material with their existing knowledge. Further, some students may need explicit guidance in how to generate high-quality explanations, either in the form of meaningful interactions with another student or by receiving metacognitive support from a computer-based agent. Overall, research suggests that teaching others can be an effective learning strategy for promoting one's own deep understanding of the material.

REFERENCES

Annis (1983). The processes and effects of peer tutoring. *Human Learning*, 2, 39–47.

Bargh, J. A., & Schul, Y. (1980). On the benefits of teaching. *Journal of Educational Psychology*, 72(5), 593–604.

Benware, C. A., & Deci, E. L. (1984). Quality of learning with an active versus passive motivational set. *American Educational Research Journal*, 21, 755–65.

Biswas, G., Leelawong, K., Schwartz, D., & Vye, N. (2005). Learning by teaching: a new agent paradigm for educational software. *Applied Artificial Intelligence*, 19(3–4), 363–92.

Chin, D. B., Dohmen, I. M., Cheng, B. H., Oppezzo, M. A., Chase, C. C., & Schwartz, D. L. (2010). Preparing students for future learning with teachable agents. *Educational Technology Research and Development*, 58(6), 649–69.

Cloward, R. D. (1967). Studies in tutoring. *Journal of Experimental Education*, 36(1), 14–25.

Cohen, E. G. (1994). Restructuring the classroom: conditions for productive small groups. *Review of Educational Research*, 64, 1–35.

Cohen, P. A., Kulik, J. A., & Kulik, C-L. (1982). Education outcomes of tutoring: a meta-analysis of findings. *American Educational Research Journal*, 19, 237–48.

Coleman, E. B., Brown, A. L., & Rivkin, I. D. (1997). The effect of instructional explanations on learning from scientific texts. *Journal of the Learning Sciences*, 6(4), 347–65.

Ehly, S., Keith, T. Z., Bratton, B. (1987). The benefits of tutoring: an exploration of expectancy and outcomes. *Contemporary Educational Psychology*, 12, 131–4.

Fantuzzo, J. W., Riggio, R. E., Connelly, S., & Dimeff, L. A. (1989). Effects of reciprocal peer tutoring on academic achievement and psychological adjustment: a component analysis. *Journal of Educational Psychology*, 81, 173–7.

Fiorella, L., & Mayer, R. E. (2013a). The relative benefits of learning by teaching and teaching expectancy. *Contemporary Educational Psychology*, 38(4), 281–8.

(2013b). *Teaching as a Generative Learning Strategy*. Poster presented at the Psychonomics Society Annual Meeting, Toronto, ON.

(2014). Role of expectations and explanations in learning by teaching. *Contemporary Educational Psychology*, 39(2), 75–85.

Galbraith, J., & Winterbottom, M. (2011). Peer-tutoring: what's in it for the tutor? *Educational Studies*, 37(3), 321–32.

Gregory, A., Walker, I., McLaughlin, K., & Peets, A. D. (2011). Both preparing to teach and teaching positively impact learning outcomes for peer teachers. *Medical Teacher*, 33(8), e417-e422.

Herberg, J. S., Levin, D. T., & Saylor, M. M. (2012). Social audiences can disrupt learning by teaching. *Journal of Experimental Social Psychology*, 48(1), 213–19.

Holmes, J. (2007). Designing agents to support learning by explaining. *Computers & Education*, 48(4), 523–47.

King, A., Staffieri, A., & Adelgais, A. (1998). Mutual peer tutoring: effects of structuring tutorial interaction to scaffold peer learning. *Journal of Educational Psychology*, 90(1), 134–52.

Leelawong, K., & Biswas, G. (2008). Designing learning by teaching agents: the Betty's Brain system. *International Journal of Artificial Intelligence in Education*, 18(3), 181–208.

Matsuda, N., Yarzebinski, E., Keiser, V., Raizada, R., Cohen, W. W., Stylianides, G. J., & Koedinger, K. R. (2013). Cognitive anatomy of tutor learning: lessons learned with SimStudent. *Journal of Educational Psychology*, 105(4), 1152–63.

Morgan, R. F., & Toy, T. B. (1970). Learning by teaching: a student-to-student compensatory tutoring program in a rural school system and its relevance to the educational cooperative. *Psychological Record*, 20(2), 159–69.

Okita, S. Y., & Schwartz, D. L. (2013). Learning by teaching human pupils and teachable agents: the importance of recursive feedback. *Journal of the Learning Sciences*, 22(3), 375–412.

Okita, S. Y., Turkay, S., Kim, M., & Murai, Y. (2013). Learning by teaching with virtual peers and the effects of technological design choices on learning. *Computers & Education*, 63, 176–96.

Palincsar, A. S., & Brown, A. L. (1984). Reciprocal teaching of comprehension-fostering and comprehension-monitoring activities. *Cognition and Instruction*, 1(2), 117–75.

Renkl, A. (1995). Learning for later teaching: an exploration of meditational links between teaching expectancy and learning results. *Learning and Instruction*, 5, 21–36.

Roscoe, R. D. (2014). Self-monitoring and knowledge-building in learning by teaching. *Instructional Science*, 42, 327–51.

Roscoe, R. D., & Chi, M. T. H. (2007). Understanding tutor learning: knowledge-building and knowledge-telling in peer tutors' explanations and questions. *Review of Educational Research*, 77(4), 534–74.

(2008). Tutor learning: the role of explaining and responding to questions. *Instructional Science*, 36(4), 321–50.

Segedy, J. R., Kinnebrew, J. S., & Biswas, G. (2013). The effect of contextualized conversational feedback in a complex open-ended learning environment. *Educational Technology Research and Development*, 61, 71–89.

Slavin, R. E. (1983). *Cooperative Learning*. New York, NY: Longman.

Webb, N. M. (1982). Peer interaction and learning in cooperative small groups. *Journal of Educational Psychology*, 74(5), 642–55.

9

Learning by Enacting

SUMMARY

Learning by enacting involves engaging in task-relevant movements during learning. For example, students may perform relevant gestures while learning to use a math operation, or they may manipulate physical or virtual objects to comprehend a text passage or to understand abstract math or science concepts. Evidence for learning by enacting is somewhat mixed, with support found in thirty-six of forty-nine experimental tests, yielding a median effect size of $d = 0.51$. Concerning boundary conditions, the effects of learning by enacting appear to be strongest when learners possess relatively high prior knowledge and when they are provided with sufficient guidance and practice on mapping academic content to task-relevant movements. In other words, learners must possess the skills or receive the guidance necessary to recognize how objects and movements relate to underlying abstract principles. Further research is needed to determine how learning by enacting applies beyond the elementary grades and how concrete manipulatives can be designed to promote transfer. Overall, the research evidence on learning by enacting is relatively limited and fragmented, but suggests that learners can benefit from grounding academic content in meaningful action.

	BOX 1. *Overview of Learning by Enacting*
Definition	Learners engage in task-relevant movements during learning.
Example	Learners are asked to physically manipulate concrete objects corresponding to characters and events described in a text.
Theoretical rationale	Learning by enacting helps learners map to-be-learned information onto meaningful real-world objects and actions. It involves selecting which components of the to-be-learned material to enact, organizing this information into a coherent action-based representation, and integrating it with relevant prior knowledge and experiences.
Empirical rationale	The learning by enacting effect is upheld in thirty-six of forty-nine tests, yielding median effect size of $d = 0.51$.
Boundary conditions	The learning by enacting effect may be strongest for students who possess relatively high prior knowledge, and when learners are provided with sufficient guidance and practice in recognizing how movements are linked to underlying concepts.
Applications	Learning by enacting applies primarily to younger children, to listening and reading comprehension, to learning abstract math concepts, and to learning from manipulating physical or virtual objects.

CHAPTER OUTLINE

1. Example of Enacting as a Learning Strategy
2. What Is Learning by Enacting?
3. How Does Learning by Enacting Foster Learning?
4. What Is the Evidence for Learning by Enacting?
5. What Are the Boundary Conditions of Learning by Enacting?
6. How Can We Apply Learning by Enacting?
7. Conclusion

EXAMPLE OF ENACTING AS A LEARNING STRATEGY

Suppose you asked a group of second graders to read and recall the following story:

> *Ben needs to feed the animals.*
> *He pushes the hay down the hole.*
> *The goat eats the hay.*
> *Ben gets eggs from the chicken.*

He puts the eggs in the cart.
He gives the pumpkins to the pig.
All of the animals are happy now.

You ask some of the children to simply read and reread the story. Others you ask to use a set of toy farm animals and objects to represent critical sentences in the story as they read. For example, a child may choose to place hay near a toy goat to enact the third sentence in the story.

Does manipulating toys during reading improve recall of critical events from a story? Research by Glenberg and colleagues (2004; Glenberg, Goldberg, & Zhu, 2011) indicates that when children act out events in a story (such as the preceding one) using physical objects (such as toys), they are often better able to recall major events from stories than if they only read and reread the story. This and other related research on learning by enacting suggests that children benefit by engaging in task-relevant movements that encourage them to map events described in a text onto meaningful objects and actions.

In this chapter, we explore the research evidence for learning by enacting. In particular, we are concerned with how enacting (such as by gesturing or manipulating objects) influences learning of educationally relevant materials (such as learning from text and learning to solve math problems).

WHAT IS LEARNING BY ENACTING?

In learning by enacting, students engage in task-relevant movements during learning, such as gesturing or manipulating objects. For example, enacting occurs when a student performs gestures to represent strategies for solving math problems (e.g., Cook, Mitchell, & Goldin-Meadow, 2008). Enacting also occurs when a student manipulates physical objects – sometimes referred to as *concrete manipulatives* – to help act out events described in a text (e.g., Glenberg et al., 2004) or to better represent abstract math concepts and procedures (e.g., Fujimura, 2001). Importantly, in learning by enacting it is the learner (rather than the teacher) who is doing the enacting. Enacting serves to ground academic content in students' prior knowledge and experiences interacting with the physical world. Thus, the primary aim of learning by enacting is for students to recognize how their own actions are linked to the underlying meaning of the material.

Much of the research related to learning by enacting has focused on the use of concrete manipulatives to teach math concepts to young children (Carbonneau, Marley, & Selig, 2013; Sowell, 1989). Concrete manipulatives are physical objects such as blocks or toys that can be manipulated by the learner or instructor to help represent abstract concepts. A recent meta-analysis by Carbonneau, Marley, and Selig (2013) included fifty-five experimental tests, yielding small-to-medium effects favoring instruction using concrete manipulatives compared to instruction involving only abstract symbols. Yet much of this research is not directly relevant to this chapter because it involves teacher-led instruction with manipulatives, rather than isolating the effects of learner enactment with concrete manipulatives. There is also a large research base on the effects of self-performed tasks on learning (e.g., Bender & Levin, 1976; Noice & Noice, 2001; Saltz & Donnenwerth-Nolan, 1981); however, this research has focused primarily on basic memory tasks rather than authentic academic learning situations. In short, the focus of this chapter is on whether students learn academic content more effectively by manipulating physical objects themselves (or engaging in other task-relevant movements such as gestures) compared to students who are presented with the same material but do not engage in movements.

HOW DOES LEARNING BY ENACTING FOSTER LEARNING?

Research on learning by enacting is grounded in early stage-based theories of cognitive development (e.g., Bruner, 1964; Piaget, 1962). For example, according to Bruner (1964), children progress through different modes of representing information, beginning with an enactive mode – in which children use actions to represent information – and later developing iconic and symbolic modes of representation.

More recently, learning by enacting has often been discussed in terms of embodied theories of cognition (Paas & Sweller, 2012; Pouw, van Gog, & Paas, 2014), which hold that cognitive processes are deeply grounded in the body's interactions with the external world (Barsalou, 2008; Wilson, 2002). As such, cognitive representations are viewed as sensorimotor simulations grounded in perception and action, rather than merely the manipulation of abstract symbols (Barsalou, 1999, 2008). One educational implication of this view is that the positioning of one's body may influence how knowledge is represented and acquired (de Koning & Tabbers, 2011; Paas & Sweller, 2012). For example, research suggests that gesturing may serve as *simulated action* used to help represent language (Goldin-Meadow & Alibali, 2013). Similarly, manipulating physical objects may help children index information presented in a text onto meaningful perceptual symbols (Glenberg, 2008). Using concrete objects may also help learners to extract meaning from abstract math concepts (e.g., Fujimura, 2001). Recently researchers have focused on ways to optimize the use of instructional manipulatives for

BOX 2. *Three Cognitive Processes Activated by Learning by Enacting*

Cognitive process	How learning by enacting primes the process
Selecting	Learners determine which components of the to-be-learned material to enact.
Organizing	Learners construct a coherent action-based representation of the selected information.
Integrating	Learners make connections between the performed action and relevant prior knowledge and experiences.

different learning situations, such as by considering the level of concreteness or perceptual fidelity of the objects (Belenky & Schalk, 2014; Fyfe et al., 2014). Overall, both gesturing and object manipulation are intended to help students map to-be-learned information onto relevant sensorimotor processes, thereby aiding in understanding.

According to the cognitive theory of multimedia learning, enacting primes the cognitive processes of selecting, organizing, and integrating, as shown in Box 2. Selecting involves determining which aspects of the to-be-learned information to enact. Organizing involves constructing a coherent action-based representation of the material that can be used to execute the movement. Integrating involves making connections between the movement performed and relevant prior knowledge and experiences. Thus, the cognitive benefits of enactment depend on the extent to which learners are able to successfully form a coherent action-based representation of the to-be-learned material that fits with their existing knowledge.

WHAT IS THE EVIDENCE FOR LEARNING BY ENACTING?

Table 9.1 presents the effect sizes of forty-nine experimental comparisons investigating the effects of learning by enacting, along with information about the citation, type of action, instructional materials, population, and outcome measure. Experiments included in the analysis compared the test performance of students who performed task-relevant movements during learning (e.g., gestures, object manipulation, hand movements) compared to a control group that learned the same material but did not perform the movements. Studies that did not include an appropriate control group, did not isolate the effects of enacting, or provided insufficient statistics to calculate effect size are not included in this analysis. Similarly, the analysis does not include studies in which students observed teachers or peers engage

TABLE 9.1. *Effect sizes for learning by enacting*

Citation	Enactment	Material	Population	Outcome	Effect size
Broaders et al. (2007, Exp. 2)	Gestures	Math equivalence	Elementary	Comprehension	0.51
Rubman & Waters (2000), skilled third graders	Magnets	Reading	Elementary	Comprehension	0.61
Rubman & Waters (2000), unskilled third graders	Magnets	Reading	Elementary	Comprehension	0.17
Rubman & Waters (2000), skilled sixth graders	Magnets	Reading	Middle school	Comprehension	0.49
Rubman & Waters (2000), unskilled sixth graders	Magnets	Reading	Middle school	Comprehension	0.51
Glenberg et al. (2004, Exp. 1), physical manipulation	Toys	Reading	Elementary	Recall	1.37
Glenberg et al. (2004, Exp. 1), physical manipulation, new text without manipulation	Toys	Reading	Elementary	Recall	−0.47
Glenberg et al. (2004, Expt. 2), physical manipulation	Toys	Reading	Elementary	Recall	1.27
Glenberg et al. (2004, Expt. 2), physical manipulation, toys absent	Toys	Reading	Elementary	Recall	−0.37
Glenberg et al. (2004, Exp. 3), physical and imagined manipulation, toys absent	Toys	Reading	Elementary	Recall	1.16
Glenberg, Goldberg, & Zhu (2011), physical manipulation	Toys	Reading	Elementary	Comprehension	0.38
Glenberg, Goldberg, & Zhu (2011), virtual manipulation	Toys	Reading	Elementary	Comprehension	1.09
Glenberg, Goldberg, & Zhu (2011), physical and imagined manipulation, familiar story	Toys	Reading	Elementary	Comprehension	−0.15
Glenberg, Goldberg, & Zhu (2011), physical and imagined manipulation, unfamiliar story	Toys	Reading	Elementary	Comprehension	0.00
Glenberg, Goldberg, & Zhu (2011), virtual and imagined manipulation, familiar story	Toys	Reading	Elementary	Comprehension	0.57
Glenberg, Goldberg, & Zhu (2011), virtual and imagined manipulation, unfamiliar story	Toys	Reading	Elementary	Comprehension	0.26

Study	Material	Domain	Level	Measure	Effect
Marley, Levin, & Glenberg (2010, Exp. 1), physical manipulation	Toys	Reading	Elementary	Recall	1.45
Marley, Levin, & Glenberg (2010, Exp. 1), physical and imagined manipulation, toys present	Toys	Reading	Elementary	Recall	1.47
Marley, Levin, & Glenberg (2010, Exp. 1), physical and imagined manipulation, toys absent	Toys	Reading	Elementary	Recall	1.09
Marley, Levin, & Glenberg (2010, Exp. 2), physical manipulation	Toys	Reading	Elementary	Recall	0.86
Marley, Levin, & Glenberg (2010, Exp. 2), physical and imagined manipulation, toys present	Toys	Reading	Elementary	Recall	0.84
Biazek, Marley, & Levin (2010), physical manipulation	Toys	Listening	Preschool	Recall	0.91
Marley et al. (2011), 1st graders, physical manipulation	Toys	Listening	Elementary	Recall	1.33
Marley et al. (2011), 3rd graders, physical manipulation	Toys	Listening	Elementary	Recall	2.02
Marley et al. (2011), 1st graders, physical and imagined manipulation	Toys	Listening	Elementary	Recall	0.00
Marley et al. (2011), 3rd graders, physical and imagined manipulation	Toys	Listening	Elementary	Recall	0.48
Marley & Szabo (2010), physical manipulation, toys present	Toys	Listening	Preschool	Recall	0.73
Marley & Szabo (2010), physical and imagery, toys present	Toys	Listening	Preschool	Recall	0.89
Marley & Szabo (2010), physical and imagery, toys absent	Toys	Listening	Preschool	Recall	0.33
Marley, Levin, & Glenberg (2007), physical manipulation, toys present	Toys	Listening	Elementary	Recall	1.33
Lucow (1964)	Cuisenaire rods	Arithmetic	Elementary	Retention	0.78
Moody, Abell, & Bausell (1971)	Candies	Arithmetic	Elementary	Retention	-0.07
Moody, Abell, & Bausell (1971)	Candies	Arithmetic	Elementary	Transfer	-0.04

(continued)

TABLE 9.1. (continued)

Citation	Enactment	Material	Population	Outcome	Effect size
Fennema (1972)	Cuisenaire rods	Arithmetic	Elementary	Recall	−0.56
Fennema (1972)	Cuisenaire rods	Arithmetic	Elementary	Transfer	−0.78
Threadgill-Sowder & Juilfs (1980)	Blocks and cards	Logic	Middle school	Retention	−0.11
Threadgill-Sowder & Juilfs (1980)	Blocks and cards	Logic	Middle school	Transfer	−0.25
Moreno & Mayer (1999, Expt. 1)	Virtual bunny	Arithmetic	Middle school	Transfer	0.55
Fujimura (2001, Expt. 1)	Magnets	Proportional reasoning	Elementary	Retention	0.73
Butler et al. (2003)	Shapes and beans	Fractions	Middle school	Retention	0.39
Olkun (2003), concrete manipulatives	Tangram pieces	Geometry	Elementary	Retention	0.44
Olkun (2003), virtual manipulatives	Tangram pieces	Geometry	Elementary	Retention	0.30
Martin & Schwartz (2005, Expt. 1), manipulatives present	Tiles and pie wedges	Fractions	Elementary	Retention	2.21
Sherman & Bisanz (2009), manipulatives present	Trays of objects	Math equivalence	Elementary	Retention	1.99
McNeil et al. (2009, Expt. 1), perceptually rich manipulatives	Bills and coins	Money word problems	Elementary	Retention	−0.20
McNeil et al. (2009, Expt. 2), perceptually rich manipulatives	Bills and coins	Money word problems	Elementary	Retention	−0.57
McNeil et al. (2009, Expt.2), bland manipulatives	Bills and coins	Money word problems	Elementary	Retention	0.05
Stull et al. (2012, Expt. 2), manipulatives present	Concrete models	Organic chemistry	College	Retention	1.52
Stull et al. (2012, Expt. 3), manipulatives present	Concrete models	Organic chemistry	College	Retention	0.84
MEDIAN					0.51

in enacting rather than having students do the enacting. The learning by enacting effect was upheld in thirty-six of forty-nine tests, yielding a median effect size of $d = 0.51$. In the following sections, we discuss the evidence for enacting, derived primarily from research on gesturing and object manipulation with young children.

Learning by Gesturing

One reason that performing gestures may promote learning is that it activates implicit knowledge that is not directly expressed in speech. In a study by Broaders and colleagues (2007), third and fourth graders were asked to gesture while explaining their solutions to math equivalence problems, or they were told not to gesture or given no gesture instructions. Experiment 1 found that children told to gesture added significantly more correct problem-solving strategies compared to the baseline (when all groups were given no gesture instructions) than the other two groups. Experiment 2 sought to test whether gesturing made children more receptive to new instruction, thereby resulting in better learning outcomes. In support of this hypothesis, the results indicated that children who were told to gesture while explaining their solutions achieved higher post-test scores on solving new math equivalence problems ($d = 0.51$) than children who were told not to gesture. Overall, this study extends prior correlational research showing a link between gesture and learning (e.g., Church & Goldin-Meadow, 1986; Cook & Goldin-Meadow, 2006; Pine, Lufkin, & Messer, 2004) and suggests that gesturing while explaining may help children access implicit knowledge of problem-solving strategies, which in turn makes students more prepared to benefit from further instruction.

In a study by Cook, Mitchell, and Goldin-Meadow (2008), children were given pre-instruction on how to solve math equivalence problems. The pre-instruction was presented via speech (e.g., "I want to make one side equal to the other side"), gesture (e.g., by the instructor moving her hands under each side of the equation), or gesture and speech. Children then mimicked the instructor by repeating the speech, performing the gestures, or both. Following pre-instruction, all children received instruction in how to solve a new set of equivalence problems, during which the instructor demonstrated a strategy in both speech and gesture. Next, children were given a problem to solve on their own and were asked to mimic the same behavior they performed during pre-instruction. Finally, all children completed immediate and delayed (four weeks) post-tests that were similar to the pretests. Results indicated students who were instructed to gesture outperformed those not instructed to gesture on the delayed retention test; however, insufficient statistics were provided to calculate effect size. Overall, this study suggests that engaging in gesturing may help learners represent problem solving strategies, resulting in more persistent learning outcomes.

Goldin-Meadow, Cook, and Mitchell (2009) investigated whether instructing children to gesture during instruction improves learning of math concepts. In the experiment, children were given instruction on how to solve math equivalence problems. During the pre-instruction phase, children in the no-gesture condition were given a sample problem and taught the words, "I want to make one side equal to the other side." Other children were taught the same words plus either a correct gesture or a partially correct gesture. Students instructed on the correct gesture were taught how to use a grouping gesture that involved summing two values on one side of the equation to find the value of the blank on the other side of the equation. Students instructed on the partially correct gesture were taught the same grouping strategy, but it involved grouping the wrong two numbers. After pre-instruction, all children were given verbal instruction on a new problem, followed by practice repeating the words or words and gestures they learned during pre-instruction. Results indicated that children who were given instruction on the correct grouping gesture performed better than the partially correct gesture group, which performed better than the no-gesture group, on a final post-test containing new equivalence problems. Further, this effect of gesture was mediated by whether children incorporated the grouping gesture into their speech when explaining their solutions to problems on the post-test. Unfortunately, this study did not provide sufficient statistics to calculate effect size. Nonetheless, the results suggest that students may be able to extract information from their gestures to support their learning.

In addition to academic learning, gesture may also facilitate spatial problem solving (e.g., Chu & Kita, 2008, 2011; Hegarty et al., 2005; Schwartz & Black, 1996). For example, in a study by Chu and Kita (2011), participants were encouraged to gesture, prohibited to gesture, or given no specific gesture instructions when solving mental rotation problems. Results indicated that the gesture-encouraged group showed significantly lower error rates during problem solving than the other two groups; importantly, this advantage extended to problem solving when none of the groups were allowed to gesture. A subsequent experiment found that this effect even transferred more generally to performance on a paper-folding task. This finding suggests that gesturing may help people make better internal spatial transformations.

In summary, engaging in task-relevant gestures appears to promote learning, presumably by lessening cognitive demands and allowing learners to use relevant body movements to help represent problem-solving strategies. It is important to note that the studies by Goldin-Meadow and colleagues (Church & Goldin-Meadow, 1986; Cook & Goldin-Meadow, 2006; Cook, Mitchell, & Goldin-Meadow, 2008; Goldin-Meadow, Cook, & Mitchell, 2009) provided learners with instructions not only to gesture, but *how* to gesture. Thus, learners may need to be shown how to represent problem-solving strategies effectively in gesture.

Object Manipulation and Text Comprehension

Much of the research on learning by enacting involves the manipulation of objects such as blocks or toys, or what are often called concrete manipulatives. One benefit of manipulating objects during learning from text (e.g., reading a story) is that it may help young readers monitor their own understanding. For example, in a study by Rubman and Waters (2000), third and sixth graders read expository passages on various topics, such as fish, that contained either implicit or explicit inconsistencies. After reading a story once, some students reread the story, whereas other constructed a storyboard out of magnetic cutouts representing different objects and characters while they reread the story. After the second reading of the story, all students were asked whether there was anything unusual about the story (e.g., "Did everything in the story make sense?"). Finally, all students were asked to retell the story in their own words. Results indicated that students who constructed a storyboard were much more likely to detect inconsistencies within the story, and this effect was particularly large for less-skilled readers. Further, storyboard construction generally resulted in greater recall of critical propositions from the story than rereading the story, for skilled third graders (skilled: $d = 0.61$, unskilled: $d = 0.17$) and for both skilled and unskilled sixth graders (skilled: $d = 0.49$, unskilled: $d = 0.51$). Taken together, these results suggest that acting out a story using physical objects may help students better abstract important ideas from the text, thereby resulting in improved comprehension monitoring.

In a study by Glenberg and colleagues (2004), elementary school students read stories describing different scenarios (e.g., animals on a farm). Over the course of six training sessions, some children read the stories and practiced manipulating toys to represent the characters and events from the story, whereas other children only read the stories without access to toy characters. In Experiments 1 and 2, manipulating toys while reading stories led to greater recall of those stories (Experiment 1 average $d = 1.37$; Experiment 2 average $d = 1.27$) compared to a read-only control, but generally led to worse performance when students were asked to read and freely recall a new passage without the ability to physically manipulate the toys (Experiment 1: $d = -0.47$; Experiment 2: $d = -0.37$). In Experiment 3, children first learned how to manipulate toys physically and then were instructed on how to imagine manipulating toys while reading. This time participants who received physical and imagined manipulation instruction outperformed the reread condition when asked to read and recall a new passage without being able to engage in physical manipulation ($d = 1.16$). This research suggests that children may have difficulty internalizing manipulation strategies on their own, thereby detracting from their ability to apply them to new situations where they are not able to manipulate objects physically. Thus, they may need explicit instruction and practice imagining they are manipulating objects during reading. Imagining as a learning strategy is explored in Chapter 5.

In a study by Glenberg, Goldberg, and Zhu (2011), first and second graders either read and reread stories or they manipulated toys while reading. Of those manipulating toys, some students manipulated physical toys, whereas other students manipulated virtual toys. Results indicated that both physical and virtual manipulation resulted in better comprehension than rereading (physical $d = 0.38$; virtual $d = 1.09$). One week later, students in both manipulation groups were given imagined manipulation instruction, whereas the control group reread the same texts. Then all students read and were tested on a familiar and an unfamiliar passage. Students in the virtual manipulation group significantly outperformed the reread group for the familiar passage ($d = 0.57$), but not for the unfamiliar passage ($d = 0.26$). Students in the physical manipulation group did not outperform the control group on either passage (familiar $d = -0.15$; unfamiliar $d = 0.00$). Overall, these findings suggest that virtual manipulation may help students focus on the relations between familiar texts and their meaning.

In two experiments by Marley, Levin, and Glenberg (2010), second and third grade Native American students read and reread stories or they read and manipulated physical toys while reading. In both experiments, students who physically manipulated toys while reading recalled more from the stories than students who reread the stories (Experiment 1: $d = 1.45$; Experiment 2: $d = 0.86$). The students also generally benefited from receiving subsequent imagined manipulation instruction. Thus, this study provides further support for the idea that asking students to physically manipulate toys helps them map events from stories onto meaningful movements. Providing subsequent imagined manipulation instruction then helps students internalize this strategy so they can use it when physical objects are no longer present.

Other research by Marley and colleagues (Biazak, Marley, & Levin, 2010; Marley & Szabo, 2010; Marley, Levin, & Glenberg, 2007, Marley et al., 2011) has found that the benefits of physical and imagined manipulation extend to enhancing the listening comprehension of even younger learners. For example, in a study Biazak, Marley, and Levin (2010), preschoolers either listened to a story and were asked to think about what was happening in the story after each action sentence or they were asked to manipulate toys after each action sentence was read. Results indicated that children in the activity group recalled significantly more action propositions from the story than children in the listen-only group ($d = 0.91$). This effect was also particularly strong for children who scored highly on an initial pretest of listening comprehension. Similarly, Marley and colleagues (2011) found that benefits of enacting were generally stronger for third graders than for first graders. Apparently, enacting may be most effective for relatively high-skilled learners.

In summary, children are more likely to understand text or spoken passages when they are able to make connections between the words and meaningful objects. These connections can be made either by manipulating physical objects (e.g., toys) or by manipulating virtual objects on a computer. However, learners may need explicit instruction in how to internalize learning by enacting so that it can be applied to new situations.

Concrete Manipulatives in Math and Science Learning

In mathematics education, *concrete manipulatives* are physical objects (such as sticks, blocks, or beads) that students manipulate to learn about abstract math concepts (such as fractions, multiplication, or geometry). Concrete manipulatives have long been prevalent within early math instruction (Kieren, 1971; Sowell, 1989); however, controlled experimental research testing the effects of using manipulatives as a learning strategy is somewhat limited (Carbonneau, Marley, & Selig, 2013). For example, many studies focus on teacher-led use of manipulatives or the use of manipulatives within a broader instructional program, or they do not include an appropriate control group that does not use manipulatives (e.g., Cramer, Post, & delMas, 2002; Hiebert, Wearne, & Taber, 1991; Miller, 1964; Reimer & Moyer, 2005; Smith & Montani, 2008; Yuan et al., 2010). In this section, we focus on experimental studies that attempt to isolate the effects of students using manipulatives to learn math and science concepts.

In a classic study by Brownell and Moser (1949), third graders learned how to solve two-column subtraction problems by either manipulating bundles of sticks or by receiving standard symbolic instruction. Students who learned with the manipulatives showed greater transfer to new types of subtraction problems than students who learned from standard instruction. This study provides early evidence that concrete manipulatives can provide students with a more meaningful representation of math concepts that they can then apply to solving new types of problems. In another early study by Lucow (1964), third graders learned about multiplication and division either by solving problems using Cuisenaire rods (the manipulatives group) or by solving problems with conventional instruction (the control group). Results indicated that the manipulatives group outperformed the control group on a subsequent retention test (average $d = 0.78$). Overall, these early studies suggest that manipulating physical objects can be an effective way to teach students about basic math concepts.

Other studies provide less promising evidence for the use of concrete manipulatives in math. In a study by Moody, Abell, and Bausell (1971), third grade students learned about multiplication by placing candies in the apertures of an egg carton (the manipulatives group) or through more conventional textbook instruction (the control group). Results indicated that the manipulatives group did not differ from the control group on subsequent retention (average $d = -0.07$) and transfer (average $d = -0.04$) tests. Similarly, in a study by Fennema (1972), second graders learned about multiplication either by using concrete models or through traditional symbolic instruction. Students assigned to the concrete condition used Cuisenaire rods to represent basic multiplication problems (the concrete group), whereas other students received practice solving the same problems with numbers and symbols (the symbolic group). Results indicated that the symbolic group significantly outperformed the concrete group on subsequent recall ($d = -0.56$) and transfer tests ($d = -0.78$). Finally, in a study by Threadgill-Sowder and Juilfs (1980), seventh graders learned about logical connectives either by manipulating colored blocks and cards (the manipulatives group) or by completing equivalent workbook exercises presented in symbolic form (the control group). Results indicated that the manipulatives group did not significantly differ from the control group on measures of retention ($d = -0.11$) or transfer ($d = -0.25$). These studies suggest that using concrete manipulatives may actually hinder learning in some situations.

Does enacting help students learn about computer programming? In a study by Mayer (1976), college students learned about how to use a computer programming language by acting out programming commands using a concrete model of the computer, which included a memory scoreboard, input window, list of programs, and output pad. Students who learned by manipulating the model performed better on subsequent far transfer problems than students who learned by viewing an experimenter-controlled concrete model; however, insufficient statistics were provided to calculate effect sizes.

In a study by Moreno and Mayer (1999), sixth graders solved addition and subtraction problems involving signed numbers (e.g., 4 − 5 = ___). Some students solved the problems by moving a bunny along a number line within virtual environment (the enacting group), whereas others solved the same problems presented symbolically (the control group). Results indicated that the enacting group showed significantly larger pre- to post-test gains on higher-difficulty problems than the control group (d = 0.55).

In a study by Fujimura (2001), Japanese fourth graders learned how to solve concentration-comparison problems such as the following:

> Yukio and Masachi each make orange juice by mixing water and concentrate. Yukio has 2 deciliters of water and 8 cups of concentrate. Masashi has 3 deciliters of water and 9 cups of concentrate. Which juice is more concentrated, Yukio's or Masashi's, or is the concentration the same? Why do you think so?

Some students were given brief training with concrete manipulatives, including a magnetic board, blue strips to represent deciliters of water, and orange dots to represent cups of concentrate. Results of Experiment 1 indicated that students who received training using the manipulatives performed significantly better on a post-test consisting of new problems than a control group that did not receive the training (d = 0.73). Importantly, follow-up studies indicated that the concrete manipulatives were more beneficial for high-skilled students than for low-skilled students. This is consistent with other research on the use of manipulatives for teaching math (e.g., Boulton-Lewis et al., 1997; Uttal, Liu, & DeLoache, 1999). Apparently, learning to use concrete manipulatives may create extraneous cognitive load for students who have not automated the component skills necessary for successful problem solving.

In a study by Butler and colleagues (2003), middle school students with mathematics disabilities learned about fractions by receiving instruction following a representational-abstract sequence (the control group) or a concrete-representational-abstract sequence over the course of ten lessons (the concrete group). Concrete instruction involved using fraction circles, beans, and squares to solve fraction problems; representational instruction involved using representational drawings of fraction concepts; and abstract instruction involved solving problems with numbers and symbols. Results indicated that the concrete group generally outperformed the control group on a subsequent retention test of the material (average d = 0.39). Similarly, in a study by Olkun (2003), fourth and fifth grade students learned about geometry by solving puzzles using concrete Tangram pieces or equivalent computer-based manipulatives. A control group of students did not use manipulatives but instead continued with normal classroom activities. Results indicated that students solving the puzzles with either type of manipulatives outperformed the control group on a subsequent retention test (concrete: d = 0.44; computer: d = 0.30).

In a series of experiments by Martin and Schwartz (2005), fourth graders solved fraction problems by physically manipulating tiles and pie wedges or by drawing on a picture of the pieces. Experiment 1 indicated that physical manipulation of the pieces led to better interpretations of fraction concepts than using a pictorial representation (d = 2.21). Further, there was evidence that high-knowledge learners were able to manipulate the pieces more effectively than low-knowledge learners. Finally, using concrete manipulatives led to better transfer performance on new fraction problems when the manipulatives were relatively unstructured rather than structured. In particular, students performed better on the transfer test when they learned by manipulating squares (i.e., unstructured manipulatives) compared to pies (i.e., structured manipulatives). Overall, this study further highlights the importance of prior knowledge in learning by enacting and also suggests that the design of concrete manipulatives can influence whether students are able to abstract general principles during learning and apply them to new situations.

Sherman and Bisanz (2009) provided second grade children with either symbolic or nonsymbolic instruction on how to solve math equivalence problems. The symbolic instruction consisted of numbers and math symbols (e.g., 5 + 2 = 4 + ___), whereas the nonsymbolic instruction consisted of physical trays of objects separated by a divider (i.e., to represent the equal sign). Results indicated that children in the nonsymbolic group solved more than twice as many problems correctly as children in the symbolic group (d = 1.99). A follow-up study indicated that experience with nonsymbolic instruction transferred to better performance on symbolic problems. Overall, this study indicates that concrete manipulatives can be used to help children understand the underlying concepts involved in math equivalence problems.

A study by McNeil and colleagues (2009) demonstrates an additional consideration for the design of concrete manipulatives. In Experiment 1, fourth and sixth graders solved word problems that involved money;

some students were given bills and coins to help them solve problems, whereas other students were not given the manipulatives. Results indicated that the manipulatives group performed slightly, but significantly, worse than the control group ($d = -0.20$). In Experiment 2, the authors tested whether this negative effect was due to the perceptually rich nature of the manipulatives. Students were given perceptually rich bills and coins, relatively bland bills and coins, or no bills and coins. Results again indicated that the perceptually rich manipulatives hurt performance ($d = -0.57$); however, students who used the bland manipulatives did not differ significantly from the control group ($d = 0.05$). Overall, these findings provide evidence of the potential limitations associated with using concrete manipulatives.

The study by McNeil and colleagues (2009) is related to a popular debate among researchers regarding the merits of providing more concrete or more abstract forms of instruction (e.g., Brown, McNeil, & Glenberg, 2009; McNeil & Fyfe, 2012; Sloutsky, Kaminski, & Heckler, 2005; Uttal et al. 2009). In particular, concrete forms of instruction (such as learning by enacting with perceptually rich concrete manipulatives) may improve learning on specific tasks, but it may not help learners apply their knowledge to new situations. One possible solution is to use *concreteness fading* (e.g., Fyfe et al., 2014; Goldstone & Son, 2005; McNeil & Fyfe, 2012) – that is, to begin instruction by using concrete methods to help learners ground the material in prior knowledge and experiences, then gradually incorporate more abstract forms of instruction to help learners learn general principles that they can use to solve novel problems. For example, when teaching students about math concepts, instruction may begin by providing students with experience physically manipulating bundles of sticks and then gradually move toward representing problems using math symbols. In short, concreteness fading offers a compromise that is generally supported in the research literature (Fyfe et al., 2014; McNeil & Fyfe, 2012). It relates to learning by enacting because asking learners to manipulate physical (or virtual) objects can be considered a way of concretizing to-be-learned material. Thus, enacting must also enable learners to recognize the material's underlying conceptual principles.

Finally, can manipulating concrete models help college students translate between different representations in organic chemistry? In a study by Stull and colleagues (2012), students completed trials in which they were given one two-dimensional representation of a molecule and were asked to draw the molecule in a different format. Some students were given concrete models that they could manipulate to help them translate between representations, whereas other students were not given concrete models. Results indicated that students who were given models to use generally drew more accurate diagrams than students who did not use the models. However, not all students who were given concrete models made use of them. When comparing only those students who used the models to assist in translation to students who did not receive models, large effects were found on drawing accuracy (Experiment 2: $d = 1.52$; Experiment 3: $d = 0.84$). This suggests concrete models can help students translate between different representations, but some students may need direct instruction in how to take advantage of the models.

Physical versus Virtual Manipulatives in Science Learning

Although this chapter has focused primarily on the effects of physical enactment on learning, research has also investigated the effects of manipulating computer-based virtual objects. However, much of this research compares physical and virtual manipulation to each other rather than to a no-enactment control condition (e.g., Flannagan, 2013; Manches, O'Malley, & Benford, 2010; Stull, Barrett, & Hegarty, 2013; Suh & Moyer, 2007). For example, studies by Klahr and colleagues (Klahr et al., 2007; Triona & Klahr, 2003) have shown that physical and virtual manipulation offer similar learning benefits for teaching students about scientific reasoning.

Several recent studies by Zacharia and colleagues (de Jong, Linn, & Zacharia, 2013; Olympiou & Zacharia, 2012; Olympiou, Zacharia & de Jong, 2013; Zacharia & Olympiou, 2011; Zacharia, Loizou, & Papaevripidou, 2012) have investigated the use of physical, virtual, and blended (i.e., physical and blended) activity-based "laboratories" to teach scientific concepts such as light and color. This research generally suggests that both virtual and physical activities can offer learning benefits, but that each may also offer unique instructional affordances. For example, virtual activity may be most useful when students are learning about unobservable phenomena, whereas physical activity may be most appropriate when the task involves direct measurement. In a recent review, de Jong, Linn, and Zacharia (2013) propose that blended instruction that incorporates both virtual and physical activity may be optimal.

WHAT ARE THE BOUNDARY CONDITIONS FOR LEARNING BY ENACTING?

The research evidence for learning by enacting is somewhat inconsistent (Ball, 1992; McNeil & Jarvin, 2007) and suggests that an enacting learning strategy may be effective only under certain conditions. For example, research on object manipulation in text comprehension and learning math concepts suggests that students that are higher skilled or possess relatively high levels of prior knowledge may be more likely to benefit from enacting than less-skilled or low-knowledge learners. In other words, possessing relevant component skills may be a prerequisite for learning with concrete manipulatives. Lacking such skills risks learners engaging in extraneous processing, thereby failing to see the connections between their movements and the academic content. In this way, inexperienced learners may benefit less from learning by enacting than learners with more experience. One potential remedy is to ensure that students receive considerable practice and guidance in how to use manipulatives productively. In contrast, students are unlikely to benefit from enacting when they expected to discover underlying principles for themselves without instructional support (Alfieri et al., 2011). In the case of text comprehension, students may benefit from receiving instruction in how to internalize the manipulation strategy so that they can use it when they no longer have access to physical objects. In the case of concrete manipulatives in math, students may benefit from concreteness fading instruction, such that students begin by manipulating concrete objects and gradually receive more abstract forms of instruction. In short, only when learners are able to recognize how objects and movements relate to abstract principles are they prepared to apply this knowledge to solve novel problems

In the case of learning by gesturing, the primary limiting factor is the lack of available research evidence. Although there has been considerable research on the role of gesturing in language and learning (Goldin-Meadow & Alibali, 2013), only a small subset of that work has focused on whether instructing students to gesture improves learning. Further research is needed to determine whether the benefits of gesturing during learning extend to other academic domains and student populations. Research on learning by enacting has primarily focused on children in the elementary grades; further work is needed that explores the effects of enacting on learning in older students.

HOW CAN WE APPLY LEARNING BY ENACTING?

Based on the current research base, learning by enacting applies primarily to helping younger children in the elementary grades comprehend sentences and understand math concepts when they are provided with sufficient instructional guidance and practice. Research suggests two broad methods for applying enacting: learning by gesturing and learning by manipulating physical objects. In the case of gesturing, children appear to benefit when they are instructed to engage in specific hand gestures related to solving problems in math. In other words, gesturing instruction can be used as a complementary method for learners to represent problem-solving strategies. However, further research on learning by gesturing is needed before specific guidelines for implementation can be made.

In the case of object manipulation, concrete objects can be used to represent characters and events described in a text or they can be used to represent abstract math concepts. In applying learning from concrete manipulatives, it is important that the students first possess basic component skills (e.g., addition, subtraction) before using concrete objects to represent more advanced math concepts (e.g., proportions). This may require that students receive some form of pretraining on relevant components skills (e.g., basic arithmetic). Students should then be provided with direct guidance and practice in how to map the to-be-learned material successfully to actions involving the objects. Educators should be sensitive to how perceptual features of the objects (e.g., excessive detail or colors) may distract students from the instructional goal. Finally, gradually fading instruction from the use of concrete manipulatives to more abstract (e.g., symbolic) forms of instruction may also help promote transfer (Fyfe et al., 2014; McNeil & Fyfe, 2012). In short, skilled students provided with guided practice are most likely to successfully recognize how their actions relate to underlying principles, thereby enhancing their ability to apply this knowledge to new situations.

CONCLUSION

The available research evidence on learning by enacting is somewhat limited but suggests that, under some conditions, engaging in task movements can promote student learning. One drawback of learning by enacting is that it may require considerably more training and guided practice than other generative learning strategies, although, this may be due to its use primarily with younger children. Learning by enacting is unique among generative learning strategies in that it focuses on how the positioning of learners' bodies influences cognitive processing and learning. Consistent with other generative learning strategies, the value of learning by enacting depends on how well learners are able to apply the strategy to help construct a meaningful representation of the to-be-learned material that fits with their existing knowledge. Learning by enacting is an emerging area of interest among educational researchers (e.g., Marley & Carbonneau, 2014), and more work is needed to better understand the cognitive processes involved during enactment and how this translates to specific practical guidelines for educators. Overall, learning by enacting offers a promising learning strategy for priming constructive cognitive processes by grounding to-be-learned material in meaningful action.

REFERENCES

Alfieri, L., Brooks, P. J., Aldrich, N. J., & Tenenbaum, H. R. (2011). Does discovery-based instruction enhance learning? *Journal of Educational Psychology*, 103(1), 1–38.

Ball, D. L. (1992). Magical hopes: manipulatives and reform of math education. *American Educator*, 16(2), 14–18.

Barsalou, L. W. (1999). Perceptual symbol systems. *Behavioral and Brain Sciences*, 22, 577–660.

(2008). Grounded cognition. *Annual Review of Psychology*, 59, 617–45.

Belenky, D. M., & Schalk, L. (2014). The effects of idealized and grounded materials on learning, transfer, and interest: an organizing framework for categorizing external knowledge representations. *Educational Psychology Review*, 26, 27–50.

Bender, B. G., & Levin, J. R. (1976). Motor activity, anticipated motor activity, and young children's associative learning. *Child Development*, 47(2), 560–2.

Biazak, J. E., Marley, S. C., & Levin, J. R. (2010). Does an activity-based learning strategy improve preschool children's memory for narrative passages? *Early Childhood Research Quarterly*, 25, 515–26.

Boulton-Lewis, G., Cooper, T., Atweh, B., Pillay, H., Wilss, L., & Mutch, S. (1997). Processing load and the use of concrete representations and strategies for solving linear equations. *Journal of Mathematical Behavior*, 16, 379–97.

Broaders, S. C., Cook, S. W., Mitchell, Z., & Goldin-Meadow, S. (2007). Making children gesture brings out implicit knowledge and leads to learning. *Journal of Experimental Psychology: General*, 136(4), 539–50.

Brown, M. C., McNeil, N. M., & Glenberg, A. M. (2009). Using concreteness in education: real problems, potential solutions. *Child Development Perspectives*, 3(3), 160–4.

Brownell, W. A., & Moser, H. E. (1949). Meaningful vs. mechanical learning: a study on grade 3 subtraction. *Duke University Research Studies in Education*, 8 (1), 1–15.

Bruner, J. S. (1964). The course of cognitive growth. *American Psychologist*, 19(1), 1–15.

Butler, F. M., Miller, S. P., Crehan, K., Babbitt, B., & Pierce, T. (2003). Fraction instruction for students with mathematics disabilities: comparing two teaching sequences. *Learning Disabilities Research & Practice*, 18(2), 99–111.

Carbonneau, K. J., Marley, S. C., & Selig, J. P. (2013). A meta-analysis of the efficacy of teaching mathematics with concrete manipulatives. *Journal of Educational Psychology*, 105(2), 380–400.

Chu, M., & Kita, S. (2008). Spontaneous gestures during mental rotation tasks: insights into the microdevelopment of the motor strategy. *Journal of Experimental Psychology: General*, 137, 706–23.

(2011). The nature of gestures' beneficial role in spatial problem solving. *Journal of Experimental Psychology: General*, 140(1), 102–16.

Church, R. B., & Goldin-Meadow, S. (1986). The mismatch between gesture and speech as an index of transitional knowledge. *Cognition*, 23, 43–71.

Cook, S. W., & Goldin-Meadow, S. (2006). The role of gesture in learning: do children use their hands to change their minds? *Journal of Cognition and Development*, 7(2), 211–32.

Cook, S. W., Mitchell, Z., & Goldin-Meadow, S. (2008). Gesturing makes learning last. *Cognition*, 106, 1047–58.

Cramer, K. A., Post, T. R., & delMas, R. C. (2002) Initial fraction learning by fourth- and fifth-grade students: A comparison of the effects of using the Rational Number Project Curriculum. *Journal for Research in Mathematics Education*, 33(2), 111–44.

De Jong, T., Linn, M. C., & Zacharia, Z. C. (2013). Physical and virtual laboratories in science and engineering education. *Science*, 340(6130), 305–8.

De Koning, B. B., & Tabbers, H. K. (2011). Facilitating understanding of movements in dynamic visualizations: an embodied perspective. *Educational Psychology Review*, 23, 501–21.

Fennema, E. H. (1972). The relative effectiveness of a symbolic and a concrete model in learning a selected mathematical principle. *Journal for Research in Mathematics Education*, 3(4), 233–8.

Flannagan, R. (2013). Effects of learning from interaction with physical or mediated devices. *Cognitive Processing*, 14, 213–15.

Fujimura, N. (2001). Facilitating children's proportional reasoning: a model of reasoning processes and effects of intervention on strategy change. *Journal of Educational Psychology*, 93(3), 589–603.

Fyfe, E. R., McNeil, N. M., Son, J. Y., & Goldstone, R. L. (2014). Concreteness fading in mathematics and science instruction: a systematic review. *Educational Psychology Review*, 1–17.

Glenberg, A. M. (2008). Embodiment for education. In P. Calvo & T. Gomila, *Handbook of Cognitive Science: An Embodied Approach* (pp. 355–72). Amersterdam, the Netherlands: Elsevier.

Glenberg, A. M., Goldberg, A. B., & Zhu, X. (2011). Improving early reading comprehension using embodied CAI. *Instructional Science*, 39, 27–39.

Glenberg, A. M., Gutierrez, T., Levin, J. R., Japuntich, S., & Kaschak, M. P. (2004). Activity and imagined activity can enhance young children's reading comprehension. *Journal of Educational Psychology*, 96(3), 424–36.

Goldin-Meadow, S., & Alibali, M. W. (2013). Gesture's role in speaking, learning, and creating language. *Annual Review of Psychology*, 64, 257–83.

Goldin-Meadow, S., Cook, S. W., & Mitchell, Z. A. (2009). Gesturing gives children new ideas about math. *Psychological Science*, 20(3), 267–72.

Goldstone, R. L., & Son, J. Y. (2005). The transfer of scientific principles using concrete and idealized simulations. *Journal of the Learning Sciences*, 14(1), 69–110.

Hegarty, M., Mayer, S., Kriz, S., & Keehner, M. (2005). The role of gestures in mental animation. *Spatial Cognition and Computation*, 5, 330–56.

Hiebert, J., Wearne, D., & Taber, S. (1991). Fourth graders' gradual construction of decimal fractions during instruction using different physical representations. *Elementary School Journal*, 91(4), 321–41.

Kieren, T. E. (1971). Manipulative activity in mathematics learning. *Journal for Research in Mathematics Education*, 2, 228–34.

Klahr, D., Triona, L., Lara, M., & Williams, C. (2007). Hands on what? The relative effectiveness of physical versus virtual materials in an engineering design project by middle school children. *Journal of Research in Science Teaching*, 44(1), 183–203.

Lucow, W. H. (1964). An experiment with the Cuisenaire method in grade three. *American Educational Research Journal*, 1(3), 159–67.

Manches, A., O'Malley, C., & Benford, S. (2010). The role of physical representations in solving number problems: a comparison of young children's use of physical and virtual materials. *Computers and Education*, 54(3), 622–40.

Marley, S. C., & Carbonneau, K. J. (2014). Future directions for theory and research with instructional manipulatives: commentary on the special issue papers. *Educational Psychology Review*, 26(1), 91–100.

Marley, S. C., Levin, J. R., & Glenberg, A. M. (2007). Improving Native American children's listening comprehension through concrete representations. *Contemporary Educational Psychology*, 32, 537–50.

(2010). What cognitive benefits does an activity-based reading strategy afford young Native American readers? *Journal of Experimental Education*, 78(3), 395–417.

Marley, S. C., & Szabo, Z. (2010). Improving children's listening comprehension with a manipulation strategy. *Journal of Educational Research*, 103(4), 227–38.

Marley, S. C., Szabo, Z., Leven, J. R., & Glenberg, A. M. (2011). Investigation of an activity-based text-processing strategy in mixed-age child dyads. *Journal of Experimental Education*, 79(3), 340–60.

Martin, T., & Schwartz, D. L. (2005). Physically distributed learning: adapting and reinterpreting physical environments in the development of fraction concepts. *Cognitive Science*, 29, 587–625.

Mayer, R. E. (1976). Some conditions of meaningful learning for computer programming: advance organizers and subject control of frame sequencing. *Journal of Educational Psychology*, 68, 143–50.

McNeil, N. M., & Fyfe, E. R. (2012). "Concreteness fading" promotes transfer of mathematical knowledge. *Learning and Instruction*, 22, 440–8.

McNeil, N. M., & Jarvin, L. (2007). When theories don't add up: disentangling the manipulatives debate. *Theory into Practice*, 46(4), 309–16.

McNeil, N. M., Uttal, D. H., Jarvin, L., & Sternberg, R. J. (2009). Should you show me the money? Concrete objects both hurt and help performance on mathematics problems. *Learning and Instruction*, 19, 171–84.

Miller, J. W. (1964). An experimental comparison of two approaches to teaching multiplication of fractions. *Journal of Educational Research*, 57(9), 468–71.

Moody, W. B., Abell, R., & Bausell, R. B. (1971). The effect of activity-oriented instruction upon original learning, transfer, and retention. *Journal for Research in Mathematics Education*, 2(3), 207–12.

Moreno, R. & Mayer, R. E. (1999). Multimedia-supported metaphors for meaning making in mathematics. *Cognition and Instruction*, 17, 215–48.

Noice, H., & Noice, T. (2001). Learning dialogue with and without movement. *Memory & Cognition*, 29(6), 820–7.

Olkun, S. (2003). Comparing computer versus concrete manipulatives in learning 2D geometry. *Journal of Computers in Mathematics and Science Teaching*, 22(1), 43–56.

Olympiou, G., & Zacharia, Z. C. (2012). Blending physical and virtual manipulatives: an effort to improve students' conceptual understanding through science laboratory experimentation. *Science Education*, 96(1), 21–47.

Olympiou, G., Zacharia, Z. C., & de Jong, T. (2013). Making the invisible visible: enhancing students' conceptual understanding by introducing representations of abstract objects in a simulation. *Instructional Science*, 41, 575–87.

Paas, F., & Sweller, J. (2012). An evolutionary upgrade of cognitive load theory: using the human motor system and collaboration to support the learning of complex cognitive tasks. *Educational Psychology Review*, 24, 27–45.

Piaget, J. (1962). *Play, Dreams, and Imitation in Childhood*. New York, NY: Norton.

Pine, K. J., Lufkin, N., & Messer, D. (2004). More gestures than answers: children learning about balance. *Developmental Psychology*, 40, 1059–67.

Pouw, W. T. J. L., van Gog, T., & Paas, F. (2014). An embedded and embodied cognition review of instructional manipulatives. *Educational Psychology Review*, 26(1), 51–72.

Reimer, K., & Moyer, P. S. (2005). Third-graders learn about fractions using virtual manipulatives: a classroom study. *Journal of Computers in Mathematics and Science Teaching*, 24(1), 5–25.

Rubman, C. N., & Waters, H. S. (2000). A, B seeing: the role of constructive processes in children's comprehension monitoring. *Journal of Educational Psychology*, 92(3), 503–14.

Saltz, E., & Donnenwerth-Nolan, S. (1981). Does motoric imagery facilitate memory for sentences? A selective interference test. *Journal of Verbal Learning & Verbal Behavior*, 20(3), 322–32.

Schwartz, D. L., & Black, J. B. (1996). Shuttling between depictive models and abstract rules: induction and fallback. *Cognitive Science*, 20, 457–97.

Sherman, J., & Bisanz, J. (2009). Equivalence in symbolic and nonsymbolic contexts: benefits of solving problems with manipulatives. *Journal of Educational Psychology*, 101(1), 88–100.

Sloutsky, V. M., Kaminski, J. A., & Heckler, A. F. (2005). The advantage of simple symbols for learning and transfer. *Psychonomic Bulletin & Review*, 12(3), 508–13.

Smith, L. F., & Montani, T. O. (2008). The effects of instructional consistency: using manipulatives and teaching strategies to support resource room mathematics instructions. *Learning Disabilities*, 15(2), 71–6.

Sowell, E. J. (1989). Effects of manipulative materials in mathematics instruction. *Journal for Research in Mathematics Education*, 20(5), 498–505.

Stull, A. T., Barrett, T., & Hegarty, M. (2013). Usability of concrete and virtual models in chemistry instruction. *Computers in Human Behavior*, 29(6), 2546–56.

Stull, A. T., Hegarty, M., Dixon, B., & Stieff, M. (2012). Representational translation with concrete models in organic chemistry. *Cognition & Instruction*, 30(4), 404–34.

Suh, J., & Moyer, P. (2007). Developing students' representational fluency using virtual and physical algebra balances. *Journal of Computers in Mathematics and Science Teaching*, 26(2), 155–73.

Threadgill-Sowder, J. A., & Juilfs, P. A. (1980). Manipulative versus symbolic approaches to teaching logical connectives in junior high school: an aptitude X treatment interaction study. *Journal for Research in Mathematics Education*, 11(5), 367–74.

Triona, L. M., & Klahr, D. (2003). Point and click or grab and heft: comparing the influence of physical and virtual instructional materials on elementary school students' ability to design experiments. *Cognition and Instruction*, 21(2), 149–73.

Uttal, D. H., Liu, L. L., DeLoache, J. S. (1999). Taking a hard look at concreteness: Do concrete objects help young children learn symbolic relations? In L. Balter & C. S. Tamis-LeMonde (Eds.), *Child psychology: A handbook of contemporary issues* (pp. 177–192). New York: Psychology Press.

Uttal, D. H., O'Doherty, K., Newland, R. Hand, L. L., & DeLoache, J. (2009). Dual representation and the linking of concrete and symbolic representations. *Child Development Perspectives*, 3(3), 156–9.

Wilson, M. (2002). Six views of embodied cognition. *Psychonomic Bulletin & Review*, 9(4), 625–36.

Yuan, Y., Lee, C.-Y., Wang, C.-H. et al. (2010). A comparison study of polyominoes explorations in a physical and virtual manipulative environment. *Journal of Computer Assisted Learning*, 26(4), 307–16.

Zacharia, Z. C., Loizou, E., & Papaevripidou, M. (2012). Is physicality an important aspect of learning through science experimentation among kindergarten students? *Early Childhood Research Quarterly*, 27(3), 447–57.

Zacharia, Z. C., & Olympiou, G. (2011). Physical versus virtual manipulative experimentation in physics learning. *Learning and Instruction*, 21(3), 317–31.

10

Learning Strategies That Foster
Generative Learning

SUMMARY

A generative learning strategy is an activity initiated by a learner during learning with the goal of making sense of the material. Based on a review of research, we have identified eight strategies intended to prime generative learning processes that produce median effect sizes of at least $d = 0.40$: summarizing ($d = 0.50$ based on thirty comparisons), mapping ($d = 0.62$ based on twenty-five comparisons involving concept maps; $d = 0.43$ based on six comparisons involving knowledge maps; and $d = 1.07$ based on eight comparisons involving matrix graphic organizers), drawing ($d = 0.40$ based on twenty-eight comparisons), imagining ($d = 0.65$ based on twenty-two comparisons), self-testing ($d = 0.57$ based on seventy-six comparisons), self-explaining ($d = 0.61$ based on fifty-four comparisons), teaching ($d = 0.77$ based on nineteen comparisons), and enacting ($d = 0.51$ based on forty-nine comparisons). Compared to other reviews of learning strategies, this review finds two relatively new additions to the collection of effective learning strategies: drawing and enacting. Our list does not include low-level strategies aimed mainly at attending to individual pieces of information (such as highlighting, keyword mnemonic, and rereading); management strategies (such as time management, test anxiety reduction, goal setting, help seeking, and test preparation); and practice strategies (such as distributed practice and interleaved practice). This chapter addresses the theoretical and practical implications of research on learning strategies, and offers a research agenda aimed at methodological, empirical, theoretical, and practical advances. Overall, learning to learn is part of the hidden curriculum in that we expect students to be effective learners but rarely teach them the strategies they need. With today's focus on twenty-first-century skills, helping students develop the generative learning strategies they need to become self-regulated learners is more crucial than ever.

EMPIRICAL CONTRIBUTIONS: EIGHT LEARNING STRATEGIES THAT FOSTER GENERATIVE LEARNING

As we noted in the introduction to this book (in Chapter 1), there are two approaches to improving student learning: (a) the *instructional design approach*, in which we change the instruction so the presented material is more likely to prime appropriate cognitive processing during learning; and (b) the *learning strategies approach*, in which we change the learner by teaching how to engage in activities for interacting deeply with the presented material. In this book, we take the learning strategies approach by asking what students can do during learning to improve their learning (Weinstein & Mayer, 1985). In particular, we focus on generative learning strategies – activities initiated by the learner during learning that are intended to help make sense of the material (Mayer, 1988, 1994, 1996; Weinstein & Mayer, 1985). Overall, we systematically examine the research evidence to identify learning strategies that work – which we define as learning strategies that improve test performance by at least 0.4 standard deviations across a substantial number of rigorous experimental comparisons.

Table 10.1 summarizes the fruits of our investigations – the identification of eight learning strategies shown to be effective in promoting student learning, at least under certain conditions. The first four learning strategies involve activities aimed at helping learners translate the presented text into another form of representation – a spoken or written summary, a spatial representation of the words consisting of nodes and links or a matrix, a drawing that depicts the text, or a mental image that depicts the text. The act of translating from one form of representation into another is intended

TABLE 10.1. *Eight learning strategies that foster generative learning*

Learning strategy	Description	Comparisons	Effect size	Strongest when
Summarizing	Create a written or oral summary of the material	26 of 30	0.50	Learners are trained; lessons are short texts
Mapping	Create a concept map	23 of 25	0.62	Learners are inexperienced; learners receive guidance
	Create a knowledge map	5 of 6	0.43	
	Create a matrix organizer	8 of 8	1.07	
Drawing	Create a drawing that depicts the text	26 of 28	0.40	Learners are trained; learners receive scaffolding and support
Imagining	Imagine a drawing that depicts the text	16 of 22	0.65	Learners are experienced; materials are well designed
Self-testing	Give yourself a practice test on the material	70 of 76	0.57	Learners receive feedback; practice test matches final test
Self-explaining	Create a written or oral explanation of confusing parts of the material	44 of 54	0.61	Learners are inexperienced; prompting is focused
Teaching	Explain the material to others	17 of 19	0.77	Learners expect to teach
Enacting	Move objects to act out the material	36 of 49	0.51	Learners are experienced; learners are trained

to encourage the learner to select the relevant pieces of information for inclusion in the new representation, organize it so the pieces of information fit together, and integrate it with relevant prior knowledge by fitting it within an existing structure.

As you can see in the top four rows of Table 10.1, summarizing yields a median effect size of $d = 0.50$ based on thirty comparisons; mapping yields a median effect size of $d = 0.62$ based on twenty-five comparisons for concept maps, $d = 0.43$ based on six comparisons for knowledge maps, and $d = 1.07$ based on eight comparisons for matrix organizers; drawing yields a median effect size of $d = 0.40$ based on twenty-eight comparisons; and imagining yields a median effect size of $d = 0.65$ based on twenty-two comparisons. Some important boundary conditions are that students may need training or guidance in how to apply the learning strategies, and the learning strategies may work best for short, well-designed texts. In the case of imagining, the learning strategy is more effective for high-knowledge learners, perhaps because it imposes heavy cognitive load; and in the case of mapping, the learning strategy is more effective for low-knowledge learners, perhaps because high-knowledge learners are more likely to engage spontaneously in useful learning strategies.

The final four learning strategies require somewhat more elaborating or generating on the part of the learner – giving oneself a practice test on the material, explaining difficult portions of the material to oneself, teaching the material to others, and acting out the material with concrete objects. These kinds of elaborative activities are primarily intended to prime deep cognitive processes such as organizing the material into a coherent structure and integrating the material with relevant prior knowledge.

As you can see in the bottom four rows of Table 10.1, self-testing yields a median effect size of $d = 0.57$ based on seventy-six comparisons, self-explaining yields a median effect size of $d = 0.68$ based on forty-five comparisons, teaching yields a median effect size of $d = 0.77$ based on nineteen comparisons, and enacting yields a median effect size of $d = 0.51$ based on forty-nine comparisons. Some important boundary conditions in which learning strategies are most effective are that the practice test matches the final test (for self-testing), learners do not naturally self-explain (for self-explaining), learners expect to subsequently teach the presented material (for teaching), and learners are trained (for enacting). In the case of enacting, the learning strategy is more effective for high-knowledge learners, perhaps because the task is not well defined; and in the case of self-explaining, the learning strategy is more effective for low-knowledge learners, perhaps because high-knowledge learners spontaneously self-explain without being told to do so.

SYSTEMATIZATION CONTRIBUTIONS: RELATION TO OTHER REVIEWS OF LEARNING STRATEGIES

Our goal in this book is to identify the most effective learning strategies for promoting generative learning, as summarized in Table 10.1, but you might be wondering about how this list is related to other learning strategies. Table 10.2 lists some learning strategies examined in reviews published over the past twenty years that explicitly rate the strategies' effectiveness based on research evidence. These reviews are as follows:

1. An article examining the research evidence for ten learning techniques published by the Association for Psychological Science in *Psychological Science in the Public Interest* (Dunlosky et al., 2013)

TABLE 10.2. *Learning strategies proposed in other reviews*

	Dunlosky et al. (2013)	Dembo & Junge (2005)	Nist & Holschuh (2000)	Pressley et al. (1995)
Generative strategies				
Summarizing	✓	✓	✓	✓
Mapping		✓	✓	✓
Drawing				
Imagining	✓			✓
Self-explaining	✓			
Self-testing	✓		✓	
Teaching		✓	✓	
Enacting				
Lows-level strategies				
Highlighting	✓		✓	
Keyword mnemonic	✓			✓
Rereading	✓			
Practice methods				
Distributed practice	✓			
Interleaved practice	✓			
Management strategies				
Time management		✓		
Test anxiety reduction		✓		
Goal setting		✓		
Help seeking		✓		
Test preparation		✓		

2. A chapter on twelve learning strategies in O'Neil's (2005) *What Works in Distance Education* (Dembo & Junge, 2005)
3. A chapter on seven learning strategies for comprehension at the college level in Flippo and Caverly's (2000) *Handbook of College Reading and Study Strategy Research* (Nist & Holschuh, 2000)
4. A classic chapter on reading comprehension strategies in Pressley and Woloshyn's (1995) *Cognitive Strategy Instruction That Really Improves Children's Academic Performance* (Pressley et al., 1995)

As can be seen in Table 10.2, our list of eight effective learning strategies contains two learning strategies not found on other lists – drawing and enacting – which represent relatively new additions to the collection of effective learning strategies. What is missing from our list of eight generative learning strategies are low-level strategies, management strategies, and practice strategies, which we describe in the following paragraphs.

First, our list does not include three low-level strategies listed by Dunlosky and colleagues (2013) and others aimed mainly at helping learners attend to individual pieces of information: *highlighting* – which involves underlining, marking, or copying key words from a printed or on-screen text; *rereading* – which involves repeating a portion of the text; and *keyword mnemonic* – which is an imagery-based strategy for memorizing word pairs (such as foreign language vocabulary). These strategies are not mainly intended to foster generative learning processes aimed at making sense of the material.

We have not included highlighting in this book because it appears to be aimed mainly at lower-level cognitive processing – selecting relevant words – which is not enough to constitute generative learning. Furthermore, Dunlosky and colleagues (2013) concluded: "We rate highlighting and underlining as having low utility. In most situations that have been examined and with most participants, highlighting does little to boost performance. It may help when students have the knowledge needed to highlight more effectively, or when texts are difficult, but it may actually hurt performance on higher-level tasks that require inference making" (p. 21). However, research is needed to determine how to use highlighting in ways that support generative learning, such as teaching students how to recognize important to-be-highlighted material based on a mental outline of the material; or asking students to annotate highlighted material with structural cues such as "1, 2, 3" (to promote the cognitive process of organizing) or external cues such as names of related ideas (to promote the cognitive process of integrating).

We have not included rereading in this book because it also appears to involve low-level processing – repeating printed or on-screen words – and it has not been studied sufficiently. Dunlosky and colleagues (2013, p. 29) concluded: "Given that rereading is the study technique that students most commonly report using, it is perhaps ironic that no experimental research has assessed its impact on learning in educational settings." They concluded that rereading is of low utility because it is less effective than other techniques. However, students who use metacognitive strategies such as comprehension monitoring – that is, evaluating how well they understand each portion of a text – may be inclined to reread confusing portions of the text. Research is needed to determine how the learning strategy of rereading can be linked to metacognitive strategies that are used to make sense of the material.

Although the keyword method has been shown to be effective in some academic tasks such as memorizing foreign language vocabulary (Levin, 1981; Mayer, 2008), it may not be appropriate for fostering deeper understanding of complex academic lessons. While acknowledging that the keyword mnemonic has promise for "keyword-friendly materials" (p. 24), Dunlosky and colleagues (2013) rate the keyword mnemonic as low utility and recommend against wide adoption. Future research is needed to determine whether teaching of well-supported mnemonic strategies for memorizing paired associates (such as the keyword technique) or word lists (such as the method of loci or the pegword method) can help students automate their factual knowledge so they subsequently can allocate more cognitive resources to deeper processing. For example, Levin and Levin (1990) have shown that mnemonic techniques can be used to facilitate high-order thinking in a science lesson.

Second, our list does not include practice strategies such as distributed practice (spreading practice over time rather than massing practice at one time) and interleaved practice (mixing practice on different problems or materials rather than blocking practice on one type of problem or material at a time), because they tend to represent practice-scheduling strategies rather than learning strategies. In other words, these strategies are more concerned with how to schedule practice rather than with asking learners to engage in tasks to help them actively make sense of the material. Furthermore, in many studies, the instructor determines the timing and composition of the practice rather than learner. Consistent with a long history in classic psychological research on memorizing word lists, Dunlosky and colleagues (2013) rate distributed practice as having high utility and interleaving practice as having moderate utility in educational settings. Similarly, other recent research-based recommendations for improving studying have touted distributed practice and interleaved practice (Bourne & Healy, 2014; Pashler et al., 2007). Research is needed to determine the effectiveness of practice strategies when they are taught as learning strategies that the learner is allowed to choose rather than when they are imposed by the instructor.

Third, our list does not contain a collection of management strategies listed by Dembo and Junge (2005): time management, test anxiety reduction, goal setting, help seeking, and test preparation. Management strategies are beyond the scope of this book because they are not aimed primarily at fostering generative processing, but rather at preparing the learner to learn. Dembo and Junge (2005) conclude that there is medium-to-high support for each of these five strategies. Further research is needed to determine how management strategies can be coordinated with generative learning strategies.

Finally, in some cases the reviews listed in Table 10.2 use broader terms than our eight generative learning strategies. "Note-taking" (cited by Dembo & Junge, 2005) can be broken down into more specific forms of note-taking that are addressed in our reviews of summarizing and mapping. Similarly, "annotating" (cited by Dembo & Junge, 2005, and Nist & Holschuh, 2000) can be broken down into more specific forms of annotating that are addressed in our reviews of summarizing, mapping, drawing, and self-explaining. In other cases, the reviews listed in Table 10.2 use different wording than ours and so can be renamed. All of the reviews use terms such as "elaborative interrogation" (and "self-questioning"), which are addressed in our review of self-explanation. Similarly, Dembo and Junge (2005) and Nist and Holschuh (2000) use the term "elaborative verbal rehearsal" to refer to the same kind of learning strategy that we call teaching.

Only three of our effective learning strategies were discussed in Weinstein and Mayer's (1986) classic taxonomy of learning strategies – summarizing and self-explanation, which fit within their category of "complex elaboration strategies," and mapping, which fits within their category of "complex organizational strategies." Thus, over the thirty years since the publication of Weinstein and Mayer's taxonomy of learning strategies, there has been solid growth in research on generative learning strategies – which fall mainly within Weinstein and Mayer's categories of "complex elaboration strategies" and "complex organizational strategies." Weinstein and Mayer also described basic rehearsal strategies (such as rereading), complex rehearsal strategies (such as highlighting), basic elaboration strategies (such as keyword mnemonic), and basic organizational strategies (such as clustering in recall of word lists), which we view as low-level strategies in Table 10.2. Finally, Weinstein and Mayer include categories for metacognitive strategies (such as comprehension monitoring) and affective/motivational strategies (such as anxiety reduction), which we hope to see more fully included as research on learning strategies progresses in the future.

Overall, our list of eight generative learning strategies helps systematize the learning strategies identified in other reviews. In particular, our criteria for inclusion are that the learning strategy is clearly defined and distinct, focuses on encouraging generative processing during learning, and has a supporting research base. No other review contains all of the learning strategies in this book, and two learning strategies are not included in any other reviews (i.e., drawing and enacting). Learning strategies that do not focus on generative learning are not included in this book (i.e., low-level strategies, practice-scheduling strategies, and management strategies), although they can have useful roles to play in promoting learning. Finally, broad categories (such as note-taking or annotating) are broken down into more clearly focused strategies (such as summarizing, mapping, drawing, or self-explaining), so their effectiveness can be assessed more clearly.

THEORETICAL CONTRIBUTIONS: IMPLICATIONS OF LEARNING STRATEGIES FOR LEARNING THEORY

The research reviewed in this book provides evidence for a generative theory of learning in which meaningful learning depends on engaging in appropriate cognitive processing during learning. In particular, the research provides ample support the *learning strategies hypothesis*: interventions aimed at fostering generative processing during learning (i.e., selecting, organizing, and integrating) will result in better learning outcomes as reflected in transfer performance and long-term retention.

For more than a century, the psychology of learning has been grappling with an appropriate metaphor of learning. During its early period, the field was dominated by a view of learning as strengthening or weakening of associations (which can be called the *response strengthening* metaphor) and subsequently was dominated by a view of learning as adding information to memory (which can be called the *information acquisition* metaphor). These views share a focus on the quantity of learning – that is, how much is learned (or how strongly something is encoded) – and regard what is learned as pieces of information or as associations between a stimulus and a response. Learning is generally measured by retention tests, aimed at determining how much is remembered.

The generative theory of learning offers an alternative conception of learning as *knowledge construction*, in which the learner actively builds a mental representation based on what is presented, what the learner already knows, and which cognitive processes are performed during learning. In contrast to the focus on the quantity of learning, the generative theory of learning focuses on the quality of learning (such as the construction of a mental model or schema). In contrast to the focus on pieces of information or stimulus-response associations, the generative theory of learning focuses on the how the learning outcome is organized and integrated with other knowledge. Learning is generally measured by transfer tests and long-term retention tests, aimed at determining how well the material is understood.

The current state of research on generative learning strategies, as summarized in this book, provides support for generative learning theory by showing that students can build qualitatively better learning outcomes when they are encouraged to engage in generative processing during learning. However, more work is needed to better specify the nature of meaningful learning outcomes and the conditions under which generative learning strategies are most effective in helping students build them. Given the focus on short-term studies reported in this book, a particular challenge is to determine whether there is evidence of long-term application of learning strategies.

PRACTICAL CONTRIBUTIONS: IMPLICATIONS OF LEARNING STRATEGIES FOR EDUCATIONAL PRACTICE

We expect students to be effective learners, but we rarely help them learn how to learn. Thus, the development of generative learning strategies is part of what can be called the *hidden curriculum* – something we expect students to learn but actually do not teach. Successful students may pick up some learning strategies on their own – though perhaps not to their maximum effectiveness – whereas less successful students may not. Overall, students rarely use generative learning strategies spontaneously (Kiewra, 2005). An important practical contribution of this book is to provide a more explicit description of eight generative learning strategies that have been shown to be effective under certain conditions, and therefore can be considered in efforts to incorporate learning strategies more prominently into the curriculum.

There is widespread consensus that today's education should prepare students with the twenty-first-century skills they will need for life and work (Pellegrino & Hilton, 2012). High on the list of twenty-first-century skills called for by business leaders and educators are high-level cognitive competencies such as creativity, innovation, problem solving, decision making, analysis, argumentation, interpretation, evaluation, and the like. Furthermore, skills such as being able to come up with creative solutions, evaluate information, or offer a compelling argument depend on what can be called *transferable knowledge* (Pellegrino & Hilton, 2012) – that is, knowledge that can be used in new ways and in new situations. These calls for twenty-first-century skills based on transferable knowledge are in sync with the focus of this book – helping students become self-regulated learners who possess effective learning strategies for meaningful learning and know when to use them. An important challenge is to determine whether students can learn to use appropriate learning strategies across their life rather than solely within the context of a research study.

This book lists eight useful candidates to consider for helping students become more effective learners, but care is needed to select strategies that are appropriate and feasible for particular learners and learning tasks. We note that different students may need different amounts and kinds of training on learning strategies before they learn and different levels of guidance as they learn. For example, different approaches may be warranted for students with high versus low proficiency, in which low-proficiency students may need more training, guidance, and direct cueing to use learning strategies, whereas high-proficiency students may be able to use appropriate learning strategies without external aids.

Finally, the transition from research to practice requires careful adjustments and assessments throughout implementation. It is unlikely that instructors will find it useful to implement all of these strategies at the same time, as this approach might be overwhelming. It is also important that students see the value in using the learning strategies, so it might be useful to provide exercises that demonstrate better learning when using appropriate learning strategies. It may be necessary to assess each learner's current learning strategies in order to determine which ones may need more direct instruction. However, the development of useful assessments of learning strategies can be a particular practical challenge.

FUTURE DIRECTIONS: AN AGENDA FOR RESEARCH ON LEARNING STRATEGIES

The research summarized in this book contributes to a growing consensus for the benefits of applying the science of learning to education (Ambrose et al., 2010; Bourne & Healy, 2014; Brown, Roediger, & McDaniel, 2014; Dunlosky et al., 2013; Mayer, 2011). For more than a century, psychologists have been studying how learning works, but within the past few decades a fruitful collaboration has developed between psychology and education, or more specifically between cognition and instruction (Mayer, 1992). The result is a growing research base that has promise for achieving the century-old dream of evidence-based practice in education (Mayer, 2008). In particular, this book constitutes the latest progress report in the exciting efforts to understand how learning strategies can improve student learning.

Although much progress has been made in establishing the effectiveness of the eight generative learning strategies described in this book, we take the liberty in this section of suggesting a research agenda for the future. In particular, we call for methodological advances, empirical advances, theoretical advances, and practical advances.

Methodological Advances

Concerning methodological advances, it would be useful to sharpen the eight learning strategies reviewed in this book in order to determine more precisely which aspects are most important in improving learning. In short, we want to know, what is the "active ingredient" in each learning strategy that produces improvements in student understanding? We also call for expanding the scope of what is manipulated (i.e., independent variables) beyond the eight learning strategies examined in this book, with a particular focus on teaching metacognitive and motivational strategies.

Similarly, it would be useful to expand the scope of what is measured (i.e., dependent measures) to include more direct measures of cognitive processing during learning (such as selecting, organizing, and integrating), as well as effort during learning. We also call for the development of embedded tests that assess what is learned within the context of the learning task itself rather than as an add-on. Future research continues to need transfer tests that can help gauge the depth of learning, and delayed tests that gauge the duration of learning.

Empirical Advances

Concerning empirical contributions, it would be useful to specify further the boundary conditions for the effectiveness of various learning strategies. The research reviewed in this book mainly establishes the effectiveness of some learning strategies, so an important next step is to determine whether the learning strategies work better for certain learners (e.g., students with low knowledge versus students with high knowledge), certain kinds of learning tasks (e.g., learning conceptual knowledge versus learning procedural knowledge), and certain learning contexts (e.g., formal classroom environments versus online courses). Another important issue concerns how much training to give before learning and how much guidance to give during learning. Finally, research is needed to determine how to help students select appropriate learning strategies, that is, to know the conditions under which one learning strategy might be more effective than another.

Theoretical Advances

Concerning theoretical advances, it would be useful to better incorporate motivation and metacognition in cognitive theories of learning such as the selecting-organizing-integrating (SOI) model of generative learning summarized previously. The version of generative learning theory presented in this book focuses on orchestrating three cognitive processes: selecting relevant information, organizing it into a coherent representation, and integrating it with relevant knowledge from long-term memory. As the theory develops, it is worthwhile to consider the metacognitive issue of how the cognitive processes are orchestrated and the motivational issue of what causes learners to exert the needed effort to engage in generative learning processes. For example, concerning metacognition, Kiewra (2005) has added *regulating* as a fourth cognitive process, which includes monitoring and adjusting the other cognitive processes during learning. As an intriguing first step, Jairam and colleagues (2014) have shown the benefits of a training program that incorporates metacognitive strategies in addition to the cognitive strategies of selecting, organizing, and integrating. Concerning motivation, Moreno (2007; Moreno & Mayer, 2007) has proposed the cognitive affective theory of learning with media, which includes motivational processes that initiate and maintain active cognitive processing during learning. Mayer (2014) has shown the value of adding motivation to the SOI model, as a way to improve learning from multimedia messages. Overall, more work is needed to specify the role of metacognitive and motivational processes in generative learning.

Practical Advances

Concerning practical advances, it would be useful to examine the robustness of learning strategies in authentic academic learning tasks, such as over an entire course or program of study. Most of the evidence on effective learning strategies reviewed in this book comes from short-term, laboratory experiments, with immediate tests, so an important next step is to determine how the well the learning works in practical contexts – such as classrooms, online courses, professional training, and informal learning environments – over the long term. Further, it would be useful to determine how the various learning strategies can be used in tandem, such as in Kiewra's (2005; Jairam et al., 2014) SOAR program.

Overall, given today's focus on preparing students for the twenty-first century (Pellegrino & Hilton, 2012), the search for effective learning strategies that promote understanding is once again a central topic in education. We will consider this book a success to the degree it encourages progress in understanding how, when, and for whom generative learning strategies improve meaningful learning.

REFERENCES

Ambrose, S. A., Bridges, M. W., DiPietro, M., & Lovett, M. C. (2010). *How Learning Works: Seven Research-Based Principles for Smart Teaching*. San Francisco, CA: Jossey-Bass.

Bourne, L. E., & Healy, A. F. (2014). *Train Your Mind for Peak Performance*. Washington, DC: American Psychological Association.

Brown, P. C., Roediger, H. L., & McDaniel, M. A. (2014). *Make It Stick: The Science of Successful Learning*. Cambridge, MA: Harvard University Press.

Dembo, M. H., & Junge, L. G. (2005). Learning strategies. In H. F. O'Neil (Ed.), *What Works in Distance Learning: Guidelines* (pp. 25–40). Greenwich, CT: Information Age Publishing.

Dunlosky, J., Rawson, K. A., Marsh, E. J., Nathan, M. J., & Willingham, D. T. (2013). Improving students' learning with effective learning strategies: promising directions from cognitive and educational psychology. *Psychological Science in the Public Interest*, 14(1), 4–58.

Flippo, R. F. & Caverly, D. C. (Eds.). *Handbook of College Reading and Study Strategy Research*. Mahwah, NJ: Erlbaum.

Jairam, D., Kiewra, K. A., Rogers-Kasson, S., Patterson-Hazley, M., & Marxhausen, K. (2014). SOAR versus SQ3R: a test of two study systems. *Instructional Science*, 42, 409–20.

Kiewra, K. A. (2005). *Learn How to Study and SOAR to Success*. Upper Saddle River, NJ: Pearson Prentice Hall.

Levin, J. R. (1981). The mnemonic 80s: keywords in the classroom. *Educational Psychologist*, 16, 65–82.

Levin, M. E., & Levin, J. R. (1990). Scientific mnemonomies: methods for maximizing more than memory. *American Educational Research Journal*, 27, 301–21.

Mayer, R. E. (1988). Learning strategies: an overview. In C. Weinstein, E. Goetz, & P. Alexander (Eds.), *Learning and Study Strategies* (pp. 11–22). Orlando, FL: Academic Press.

(1992). Cognition and instruction: on their historic meeting within educational psychology. *Journal of Educational Psychology*, 84, 405–12.

(1994). Study habits and strategies. In T. Husen & T. N. Postlethwaite (Eds.), *International Encyclopedia of Education* (2nd ed; pp. 5829–31). Oxford, England: Pergamon Press.

(1996). Learning strategies for making sense out of expository text: the SOI model for guiding three cognitive processes in knowledge construction. *Educational Psychology Review*, 8, 357–71.

(2008). *Learning and Instruction* (2nd ed). Upper Saddle River, NJ: Pearson Merrill Prentice Hall.

(2011). *Applying the Science of Learning*. Upper Saddle River, NJ: Pearson.

(2014). Incorporating motivation into multimedia learning. *Learning and Instruction*, 29, 171–3.

Moreno, R. (2007). Optimising learning from animations by minimizing cognitive load: Cognitive and affective consequences of signaling and segmentation methods. *Applied Cognitive Psychology*, 21, 765–81.

Moreno, R., & Mayer, R. E. (2007). Interactive multimodal learning environments. *Educational Psychology Review*, 19, 309–26.

Nist, S. L., & Holschuh, J. L. (2000). Comprehension strategies at the college level. in R. F. Flippo & D. C. Caverly (Eds.), *Handbook of College Reading and Study Strategy Research* (pp. 75–104). Mahwah, NJ: Erlbaum.

O'Neil, H. F. (Ed.). (2005). *What Works in Distance Learning: Guidelines*. Greenwich, CT: Information Age Publishing.

Pashler, H., Bain, P., Bottage, B., Graesser, A. Koedinger, K., McDaniel, M., & Metcalfe, J. (2007). *Organizing Instruction and Study to Improve Student Learning*. Washington, DC: Institute of Educational Sciences, U. S. Department of Education.

Pellegrino, J. W., & Hilton, M. L. (2012). *Education for Life and Work: Developing Transferable Knowledge and Skills in the 21st Century*. Washington, DC: National Academies Press.

Pressley, M., Symons, S., McGoldrick, J. A., & Snyder, B. L. (1995). Reading comprehension strategies. In M. Pressley & V. Woloshyn (Eds.), *Cognitive Strategy Instruction That Really Improves Children's Academic Performance* (pp. 57–100). Cambridge, MA: Brookline.

Pressley, M. & Woloshyn, V. (Eds.). (1995). *Cognitive Strategy Instruction That Really Improves Children's Academic Performance*. Cambridge, MA: Brookline.

Weinstein, C. E., & Mayer, R. E. (1985). The teaching of learning strategies. In M. C. Wittrock (Ed.), *Handbook of Research on Teaching* (3rd ed; pp. 315–27). New York, NY: Macmillan.

AUTHOR INDEX

Hall, R. H., 48
Hall, V. C., 68–71
Hare, V. C., 30
Harris, K., xi
Hattie, J., xi, 15
Haugwitz, M., 54
Hausmann, R. G. M., 141
Healy, A. F., 199
Heckler, A. F., 183
Hegarty, M., 176, 184
Heinze-Fry, J. A., 52
Herberg, J. S., 163
Hiebert, J., 179
Hilton, M. L., 6, 16, 201–2, 205
Holley, C. D., 47, 55, 59, 74
Holmes, J., 161
Holschuh, J. L., 197, 199
Hooper, S., 29
Horton, P. B., 48
Howard, C. D., 118
Hsu, C.-Y., 141

Jairam, D., 47, 56, 204–5
Jarvin, L., 182, 184–5
Jawitz, P. B., 86
Johnson, C. I., 101, 112, 137–8
Jones, M. L., 85
Juilfs, P. A., 180
Junge, L. G., 197, 199

Kahle, J. B., 52
Kaminski, J. A., 183
Kang, S. H. K., 100–1, 110
Kao, L. S., 117
Karpicke, J. D., 100–1, 110, 116–18
Katona, G., 15
Kauffman, D. F., 47, 56, 74
Keeves, J., 143
Kehoe, E. J., 30
Keith, T. Z., 163
Kelly, J. W., 115–16
Kieren, T. E., 179
Kiewra, K. A., 7–8, 47, 56, 74, 201, 204–5
King, A., 31, 32, 133, 154, 163–4
Kinnebrew, J. S., 161
Kintsch, E., 24
Kintsch, W., 24
Kirby, J. R., 34
Kita, S., 176
Klahr, D., 184
Koedinger, K. R., 137

Kornell, N., 117
Kourilsky, M., 15–16
Kulhavy, R. W., 28, 85
Kwon, K., 138

Lambiotte, J. G., 48
Larsen, D. P., 143
LaVancher, C., 126–7
Lawson, M. J., 143
Lawton, S. Q. C., 23–4
Leahy, W., 90–1
Lee, S. E., 139
Leelawong, K., 161
Leeming, F. C., 115
Lehman, J. D., 52
Leopold, C., 30, 72–4, 82, 91–2, 94
Leutner, D., 30, 72–4, 76, 91–2, 94
Levin, D. T., 163
Levin, J. R., 66, 85, 92, 170, 178–9, 198
Levin, M. E., 85, 198
Levinstein, I. B., 144
Lin, L., 139
Linden, M., 15–16
Linn, M. C., 184
Lipsky, S., 31
Liu, L. L., 181
Liu, P., 53–4
Loizou, A. T., 142, 184
Lopez, M. J., 58
Lucow, W. H., 180
Lufkin, N., 175
Lyle, K. B., 115

MacLatchy-Gaudet, H., 134
Manches, A. L., 184
Mandl, H., 135
Marks, C., 15–16, 22, 25
Marley, S. C., 169–70, 178–9, 186–7
Marsh, E. J., 119, 196
Martin, T., 182
Marxhausen, K., 204
Mathews, P., 141
Matsuda, N., 162
Mayer, R. E., 6, 7–8, 10, 12, 14–17, 24, 45, 47, 56–8, 66, 73–4, 76, 82, 84, 92, 94, 101, 112, 120, 129, 137–8, 154–5, 160, 163, 180–1, 193, 198–200, 202–4
McDaniel, M. A., 113–14, 117–18
McDermott, K. B., 110, 112
McEldoon, K. L., 141
McGoldrick, J. A., 197

SUBJECT INDEX

Lightning Source UK Ltd.
Milton Keynes UK
UKOW01n0621100416

271932UK00002B/32/P